# THE RISE OF THE AFRICAN NOVEL

D1551748

**AFRICAN PERSPECTIVES**
*Kelly Askew and Anne Pitcher*
*Series Editors*

*Unsettled History: Making South African Public Pasts,*
by Leslie Witz, Gary Minkley, and Ciraj Rassool

*African Print Cultures: Newspapers and
Their Publics in the Twentieth Century,*
edited by Derek R. Peterson, Emma Hunter,
and Stephanie Newell

*Seven Plays of Koffi Kwahulé: In and Out of Africa,*
translated by Chantal Bilodeau and Judith G. Miller
edited with Introductions by Judith G. Miller

*The Rise of the African Novel:
Politics of Language, Identity, and Ownership,*
by Mukoma Wa Ngugi

# The Rise of the African Novel

*Politics of Language, Identity,
and Ownership*

Mukoma Wa Ngugi

University of Michigan Press
Ann Arbor

Published in the United States of America by the
University of Michigan Press
Manufactured in the United States of America
⊗ Printed on acid-free paper

2021   2020   2019   2018      4   3   2   1

A CIP catalog record for this book is available from the British Library.

Library of Congress Cataloging-in-Publication Data

Names: Mũkoma wa Ngũgĩ, author.
Title: The rise of the African novel : politics of language, identity, and ownership / Mukoma
    Wa Ngugi.
Description: Ann Arbor : University of Michigan Press, 2018. | Series: African perspectives |
Identifiers: LCCN 2017052925 (print) | LCCN 2017053328 (ebook) | ISBN 9780472123360
    (e-book) | ISBN 9780472053681 (pbk. : alk. paper) | ISBN 9780472073689 (hardcover :
    alk. paper)
Subjects: LCSH: African fiction—19th century—History and criticism. | African
    fiction—20th century—History and criticism.
Classification: LCC PL8010.6 (ebook) | LCC PL8010.6 .M85   2018 (print) |
    DDC 809.39896—dc23
LC record available at https://lccn.loc.gov/2017052925

*For Tejumola Olaniyan and the late Daniel Kunene*
*with the hope this is the beginning of my paying forward*
*into the African literary tradition*

**Titi la Mama**
Shaban Robert

Titi la mama litamu, hata likiwa la mbwa,
Kiswahili naazimu, sifayo iliyofumbwa,
Kwa wasiokufahamu, niimbe ilivyo kubwa,
Toka kama mlizamu, funika palipozibwa,

Titile mama litamu, Jingine halishi hamu.

Lugha yangu ya utoto, hata sasa nimekua,
Tangu ulimi mzito, sasa kusema najua,
Ni sawa na manukato, moyoni mwangu na pua,
Pori bahari na mto, napita nikitumia,

Titile mama litamu, jingine halishi hamu.


**My Mother Tongue**
Translated from Kiswahili by Mukoma Wa Ngugi

My mother—tongue I declare I will sing your brightness
to the blind and those who have long lost memories of you
a mother's breast is sweet to her young, even a swine's
Mother, feed, flow, salve our wounds and clotted veins.

*A mother's breast is sweet, another simply will not fulfill*

Mother, as a child my tongue was weighed down. Now
that I can speak I see you were all around me, a perfume
to my heart and senses. Whether through the wilderness
the river Nile or the Indian ocean—Mother, you carry me across.

*My mother's breast is sweet, another won't satisfy my longing.*

## ACKNOWLEDGMENTS

Simply put, without my colleagues, friends, and family who are part of my literary community, this book would have been poorer if not altogether impossible: Vinay Dhawadker, Sara Guyer, Susan Friedman, Carole Boyce Davies, Dagmawi Woubshet, Satya Mohanty, Margo Crawford, Dean Makulini, Wangui Wa Goro, Carmen McCain, Ngugi Wa Thiong'o, Maureen Burke, Tee Ngugi, Wanjiku Wa Ngugi, Nducu Wa Ngugi, Okey Ndibe, Ndirangu Wachanga, Daniel Magaziner, Ishion Hutchinson, Valzhyna Mort, Naaborko Sackeyfio-Lenoch, Tim Lenoch, Carina Ray, and Lyrae Van Clief-Stefanon. Also with deep gratitude to George Olakunle, Evan Mwangi, and Sheri Englund for reading and commenting on the earlier drafts as well as to series editors Kelly Askew and Anne Pitcher and to Ellen Bauerle and Kevin M. Rennells at the University of Michigan Press for their collective critical eye and firm but gentle handling of the book. And finally to my literary agent, Julia Masnik at Watkins/Loomis for helping the manuscript find a happy home.

# CONTENTS

# *Manufacturing the African Novel*

## The Makerere Writers and Questions of Language, Identity, and Ownership

If I write in English in a country in which English may still be called a foreign language, or in any case is spoken only by a minority, what use is my writing?
— Chinua Achebe[1]

Nothing looks to fit him well.
— James Baldwin, describing the painting *Yoruba Man with a Bicycle*[2]

Chinua Achebe's *Things Fall Apart* has been translated into over 50 languages,[3] making it the most translated African novel. But almost 60 years after it was first published, there is no authoritative translation into Igbo, Achebe's mother tongue.[4] An equivalent instance would be if Conrad's *Heart of Darkness* had not been translated into Polish. But even then, the comparison would not work. As the late Obi Wali noted,[5] "Conrad's works, as we know, are considered part of English literature, not Polish literature, and the sole criterion for this is that his works are in English, not in Polish" (47). Achebe, on the other hand, understood himself as, and is read as, part of the African literary tradition. Indeed, *Things Fall Apart* has been translated into Polish at least two times while there are three competing translations in German.[6] To be sure, it has been translated into 10 or so African languages, but considering there are over 2,000 languages in Africa that is still an infinitesimal number. And more generally, other novels considered seminal in the African literary tradition, such as Ngugi Wa Thiong'o's *A Grain of Wheat*, Bessie Head's *A Question of Power*, and Wole Soyinka's *The Interpreters*, fare much worse on this criteria of translation into the author's mother tongue and wider African languages. Translating African novels into African languages is the exception, rather than the norm.

To answer the question of why there is no authoritative Igbo translation of what is known and accepted as Africa's most famous novel, one has to go back to the 1962 "African Writers of English Expression" conference convened at Makerere University, Uganda. In 1962, Africa was in the throes of decolonization and for the group of young writers attending the conference anything was possible. Their goal was to define, or at least agree upon, the parameters of an African literary aesthetic that would also be in the service of political and cultural decolonization. In reading their postconference write-ups in the journal *Transition*, the excitement with which they greeted their role as the instigators and vanguards of an emerging literary tradition is palpable. The writers in attendance, Chinua Achebe (age 32), Christopher Okigbo (age 32), Wole Soyinka (age 28), James Ngugi[7] (age 28), Bloke Modisane (age 39), and Ezekiel Mphahlele[8] (age 43), set in motion a literary tradition that would engulf subsequent generations in debates around the definition and category of African literature. They helped shape future debates about the languages of African literature, the role of writers in political change, the writer in continental Africa versus the diaspora, and the relationship of African aesthetics to European aesthetics. That only two women writers, Grace Ogot and Rebecca Njau, were present at the 1962 conference pointed to the question of gender in terms of literary production and representation. This question would later be addressed through the theoretical and literary works of writers such as Ama Ata Aidoo, Micere Mugo, Bessie Head, Buchi Emecheta, Mariama Ba, Tsitsi Dangarembga, and others; they demonstrated, as Carole Boyce Davies puts it, "the interconnectedness of race, class and sex oppression" (564).

The literary vanguard would in just a few short years run up against the repression and violence of postindependence African states. Disillusioned with the promises of decolonization, they turned their pens against their neocolonial governments and paid the price of death, detention, and exile. Chinua Achebe became a spokesperson for Biafran independence from Nigeria, doing ambassadorial work in both Africa and the West. Christopher Okigbo was shot dead fighting for Biafra's independence in 1967, five years after the conference. The Nigerian military government of General Yakubu Gowon detained Wole Soyinka for his peace activism in 1966. In 1977, the Kenyan government of Jomo Kenyatta detained Ngugi for his political writing and theater work in Gikuyu, his mother tongue. Both Ezekiel Mphahlele and

Bloke Modisane, coming from apartheid South Africa, were already living in exile at the time of the Makerere Conference, Mphahlele in France and Modisane in Britain. Achebe, Soyinka, and Ngugi each wound up in political exile, ultimately joined by writers like Micere Mugo from Kenya and Nawal El Saadawi from Egypt. The Makerere generation of African writers would suffer death, exile, and detention for not separating their literary aesthetics from the material work of politics, for not separating the author from the citizen.

Ugandan writer Rajat Neogy started *Transition* magazine a year before the conference. By the time it folded in 1976, it had become the most influential African literary journal.[9] Neogy was also not spared the fate of the writers he was publishing and was detained by Milton Obote's government in 1968. But in 1962, his journal was well on its way to becoming the single most important intellectual meeting ground for African intellectuals and writers and it provided a natural home for the Makerere Conference proceedings.

The Makerere Conference was not the first literary event to involve the African continent and diaspora. The First Congress of Black Writers and Artists was held in Paris in 1956, organized by *Presence Africaine*, a Paris-based literary journal, with a second conference in 1959, featuring writers such as Aimé Césaire, Léopold Sédar Senghor, Richard Wright, James Baldwin, George Lamming, Frantz Fanon, Édouard Glissant, Josephine Baker, and Jean-Paul Sartre (who had declared solidarity with third world revolutionary causes). After attending the 1956 conference, Ulli Beier, a German literary scholar and editor, and German literary critic Janheinz Jahn started the journal *Black Orpheus* with the goal of showcasing "African writers from French, Portuguese, and Spanish territories in English translation" and "works by West Indian and American Negro writers." (Lindfors, "A Decade of Black Orpheus," 509). A year before the Makerere Conference, Nigerian writers and artists including Achebe and Soyinka were brought together by Beier, then teaching at a university in Nigeria, to form the first Mbari Club, with the mandate "to support the arts: to organize drama and musical festivals, to publish literature, to mount art exhibitions, and to hold art classes."[10]

In a reminder that literature and politics in Africa have never been separate, it turned out that the CIA cultural front, the Congress for Cultural Freedom (CFF), had also in part financed both the Mbari Club and *Black Orpheus*. In fact, the CFF had also sponsored the Makerere Conference, but back then it was not known that the CIA was behind the CFF. *Transition* almost buckled under the weight of the revelation in 1967 that it was in part being funded by the CIA front.[11] But the journal survived; what mattered was the urgent task at hand—how to account for, define, and grow an African literary tradition.

In the foreword to his 1963 anthology of African poetry, *Poems from Black Africa*, Langston Hughes captured the literary mood by writing that the African "emotional climate" was "one of hope and of faith in a future that is coming more and more into the control of the peoples of Africa themselves" (13). The young and optimistic Ngugi also captured this excitement when he enthusiastically concluded in his postconference write-up, "With the death of colonialism, a new society is being born. And with it a new literature" ("A Kenyan at the Conference," 7).

Yet, even as the participants were heralding the new society,[12] the conference had declared boldly in its title that this was a gathering of "African Writers of English Expression." As Nigerian literary scholar Obi Wali asked in an essay published the same year as the Makerere Conference, "The Dead End of African Literature?," why was it so important to signal to the attendees that African writers using African languages were not welcome? One cannot conceive of English writers today writing English national literature in French, or the Chinese writing in Japanese, or the French in German. But for African writers writing in an imperially enforced foreign language was taken as the starting point. The question for the Makerere writers was not how to write, translate, and market books written in African languages. Rather, it was how best to make English work for the African literary imagination.

It was not for the lack of example. In the early 1900s, South African writers were writing in Xhosa, Zulu, Sesotho, and other African languages, with translations into English: Thomas Mofolo's *Moeti oa Bochabela* (published in 1907, later translated into English as *Traveller to the East* in 1934) and *Chaka*, written in 1909 but published in 1931;[13] R. R. R. Dhlomo's *An African Tragedy* (1928) and *UNomalanga kaNdengezi* (1934); Samuel Mqhayi's *Ityala Lamawele* (*The Lawsuit of the Twins*) (1912); and A. C Jordan's *Ingqumbo yeminyanya* (1940), translated as *The Wrath of the Ancestors* in 1964. Sol Plaatje's novel, *Mhudi* (1930) was the first full-length novel in English by a black South African writer (Couzens and Gray, 198). James Currey, a founding editor of Heinemann's African Writers Series, was well aware of this writing in African languages.[14] In *Africa Writes Back* he noted:

> the historic contribution by the mission presses in the early part of the twentieth century was later to be reflected in two novels. Lovedale had published Thomas Mofolo's *Chaka* in Sotho in 1925 and the quaint translations pub-

lished in English and French had an international impact, especially on the writers of negritude. Heinemann commissioned an unexpurgated translation from the academic and poet Dan Kunene. (187)

It was not the "quaint" early writing that interested Currey; it was more the political writing and contemporary literature produced by the politically conscious Makerere writers. When Currey worked on Heinemann Books' African Writers Series, he noted that what they wanted were books that "reflected first and foremost the realities of life suffered by the people oppressed by the laws of colour" (189).

Missionary presses like Lovedale were central to establishing early South African writing. Lovedale was founded by the Glasgow Missionary Society in 1823 with a mission to "promote Christian knowledge in southern Africa and to propagate "civilised" norms of conduct and moral behavior" (White, 69). Even though it specialized in educational and Christian books, starting in 1932 it branched out to publishing general literature books under the directorship of R. H. W. Shepherd. Shepherd believed that a "mission press needed to exercise a more creative responsibility and that it should provide more general reading matter for the African public" (White, 70). Shepherd himself did not believe that blacks and whites were equals; he saw himself as gently guiding Africans from heathenism to civilization. Some of the books they published bore the Christianizing fingerprints—for example, in Mofolo's *Traveller to the East*, the main character is on a Bunyan-like quest for enlightenment, starting from an African cultural darkness and moving toward Christianized virtue. Others, like Plaatje's *Mhudi* or Jordan's *Wrath of Ancestors*, did speak to the political and cultural tensions between African cultures and their European counterparts.

The larger point here is that just like the Makerere generation, these South Africans were writers and intellectuals that belonged to their times, and as apartheid became entrenched so did their resistance. For example, "Nkosi Sikelel' iAfrika," the national anthem of the African National Congress (formed in 1912), was a song of mourning to which Mqhayi added seven nationalist verses. Sol Plaatje, a nationalist and one of the founding members of the ANC, "arranged for the recording of 'Nkosi' in London,"[15] In his essay, "Retracing Nelson Mandela through the Lineage of Black Political Thought from Walter Rubusana to Steve Biko," Xolela Mangcu talks about how, as a young student, Nelson Mandela was influenced by Mqhayi's "cultural nationalism" (112–13).[16] Ntongela Masilela, who has done major work on these early South African writers, sees them as a movement not only conscious of each other and immersed in their political and cultural contexts, but aware of, influenced by, and influencing black Americans and the black diaspora in general.[17]

Jean Comaroff and John L. Comaroff write that[18] "like its European counterpart, modernity in Africa entailed a regenesis, a consciousness of new possibilities, and a rupture with the past—a past that, in the upshot, was flattened out, detemporalized, and congealed into 'tradition,' itself a thoroughly modern construct" (9). And the modernity of these early twentieth-century nationalist writers was not just locked within South Africa. As the Comaroffs point out, their ideas were to "suffuse anticolonial movements and post-independence nationalisms" (8). They were the precursors to decolonization. At the same time, they had an international Pan-African or black diaspora dimension to their political activism and vision. Laura Chrisman, in *Postcolonial Contraventions: Cultural Readings of Race, Imperialism and Transnationalism*, writes:

> That there was an intense transnational traffic between Plaatje and Du Bois, which had intellectual, financial, and professional dynamics, is clear. . . . Du Bois was responsible for the American publication of Plaatje's book *Native Life in South Africa*, and arranged for Plaatje to participate in the 1921 annual National Association to Advancement of Colored People convention. These were more than personal connections: there were significant parallels between the official political practices and values of the organisations the two men were active in. The early ANC, the Niagara movement and the NAACP overlapped in their constitutionalist, integrationist version of black nationalism: the formal emphasis fell on the franchise as the means to social justice and opportunity, and the legal protest against racial justice. (95)

*Native Life in South Africa* was an indictment of the increasingly oppressive and exploitative structures in what was soon to be full-blown apartheid. Understanding William Shakespeare's centrality to the English canon, Sol Plaatje also translated some of his plays, including *The Comedy of Errors*, into Setswana as *Diphosho–phosho* while translating Setswana proverbs into English.[19] Given how influential the South African modernists' influence is in South Africa, Africa in general, and the diaspora, the question of why we do not read them alongside literary figures in the decolonization movement in Africa is glaring.

The Makerere writers, like a literary tsunami, came and buried early South African writing underneath a torrent of realist novels written in English. They derailed the African literary tradition from one of writing in African languages and subsequently getting translated into other languages, and started us on the path of the realist African novel in English. They were so thorough that African literary criticism has failed to recover the missing literary epoch, as literary criticism followed the same tracks they laid down.

For example, in the authoritative and groundbreaking anthology of literary criticism, the 2009 *Cambridge Companion to the African Novel*, there is no sustained discussion of the early South African writing in African languages or English. In the *Cambridge Companion*, the chronology of literary events starts with the *Egyptian Book of the Dead* (c. 1500 BC) and ends with Achebe winning the Man Booker International Prize in 2007. In that chronology, the only mentions of the early South African writing are Mofolo's *Chaka* and Sol T. Plaatje's *Mhudi*. Mofolo's name is misspelled, rendered as Mfomo, and his two earlier titles are not featured. Instead of giving the 1925 original publication of *Chaka* in Sesotho, it gives the English translation publication date of 1930. Dhlomo and A. C. Jordan and others are nowhere to be found.

Peter J. Kalliney's *Commonwealth of Letters: British Literary Culture and the Emergence of Postcolonial Aesthetics* (2013) starts African literary conversations with European figures such as T. S. Eliot in dialogue with Amos Tutuola in the 1950s, as opposed to say DuBois and Plaatje. He follows the same orature—literary interface accounting of African literature. Tutuola is seen as stuck between the inferior aesthetics of orature and the superior and aesthetics of literary writing. To put it another way, imagine English literature missing a major literary epoch like modernism, for example. W. B. Yeats, Ezra Pound, D. H. Lawrence, T. S Eliot, or James Joyce would be absent—the English literary tradition would be unrecognizable.

I do not mean that absolutely no studies have been done. What I mean is that early African writing has not yet become part of the African literary and critical imagination. What I am asking is why we have not followed the few literary critics who for years have been calling our attention to early African writing and who have read early African writing within the African literary tradition. For example, Albert Gérard in *African Language Literatures: An Introduction to the Literary History of Sub-Saharan Africa* (1981) looks at early South African and Ethiopian literature. In *The Languages and Literatures of Africa*, Alain Ricard looks at how books across different African languages and European languages speak to each other. Janheinz Jahn, in *Neo-African*

*Literature: A History of Black Writing* (1969), surveys pioneer writing across Africa and the diaspora, starting with writing dating as far back as Afro pre-Islamic and Islamic literature in the AD 500s and ending with Negritude in the 1940s. Following this practice of rendering a truer African literary tradition, Simon Gikandi and Abiola Irele, in their coedited *The Cambridge History of African and Caribbean Literature* (2004), include essays on early writing from Ethiopia and South Africa, and literatures in Arabic and Kiswahili, to mention a few. And there are South African literary critics and historians, such as Ntongela Masilela, Daniel Kunene, Tim Couzens, and many others, who have written extensively on early South African writing. What I am doing in this book, at least in part, is trying to find answers as to why we haven't heeded their call and followed their examples.

Unlike Ian Watt's *The Rise of the Novel*, in which he looks at the literary history behind the English novel starting with Daniel Defoe's *Robinson Crusoe* and ending with *Tom Jones* by Henry Fielding, I am not writing the literary history of the African novel in English, or in African languages. Watt is asking and answering questions about where the novel came from, the novel's relationship to philosophical realism and individualism, why the novel came to prominence when it did, and who comprised the reading public.[20] In other words, I am not trying to do for African literature what Ian Watt did for the English novel. Or, more precisely, I am not following Firdous Azim who, in *The Colonial Rise of the Novel*, looks at the history of the novel through a feminist lens. Azim takes Ian Watt's blind spots and contradictions and fleshes them out to show that, while his work acknowledges the "position of women under the new bourgeois and the capitalist order," he nevertheless "overlooked [that] women were appearing not just as novel-readers, but as writers" (25). What I do in this book, while different, is, I think, something no less fundamental—I am trying to find out why early African writing, and the literary criticism that pays attention to it, remains on the margins as opposed to being part of the African literary tradition. I am asking, how is it that we have for generations, as scholars, writers and readers, and publishers—as the collective that makes African literature—how could we ignore a whole literary period that immediately precedes the one we celebrate?

In the authoritative *African Literature: An Anthology of Criticism and Theory* (2007), the editors Tejumola Olaniyan and Ato Quayson in their introduction to a section dealing with African languages and writing ask, "How is it that most of what is known as 'African Literature,' both within Africa itself and outside, is originally written in European languages?" (4). And Alain Ricard in his contributing essay, "Africa and Writing," argues that if we take early African writing and inscriptions into account, "the obsession with orality . . . is more an ideological and political posture than a well informed theoretical stand" (14). In *The Rise of the African Novel* I am exploring the question of why African literature means writing in European languages. That it is writing in African languages is not the default linguistic medium for African writing. In fact one can say that as presently constituted there is African Literature, and African literature in African languages. I am interested in the material conditions of publishing African literature, and the superstructures, ideological, political and literary that have pushed forward the idea of before the Makerere generation there was orature.

There is much to be gained by reading the early South African literature in relation to the literature of decolonization and to the transnational literature being produced by younger African writers like NoViolet Bulawayo and Chimamanda Adichie. In reading *The Wrath of Ancestors* in relation to Achebe's *No Longer at Ease* and NoViolet Bulawayo's *We Need New Names* it became clear to me that early South African writers were producing a literature of synthesis—that is, a literature that saw the possibility of European and African cultures not only coexisting but also learning from each other and being equal partners in cultural production.

By the time we get to Achebe's *No Longer at Ease*, the contradiction contained in the hope for synthesis has been laid bare, the idea that somehow an exploitative colonialism can be in a symbiotic relationship with the peoples and cultures that feeds its machinery. The decolonizing Nigerians want the British out but not the colonial structures. This a contradiction best captured by Simon Gikandi in *Maps of Englishness*. For those Africans who "detested colonial rule, which they fought tooth and nail, often ending up in prison" (xix), it was not a contradiction to at the same time believe in the "efficacy and authority of colonial culture," because "they wanted access to the privileges of colonial culture to be spread more equitably, without regard to race and creed" (xx). Or as Frantz Fanon puts it in *The Wretched of the Earth*, "The colonist's world is a hostile world, a world which excludes but also incites envy. We have seen how the colonized always dream of taking the colonist's place. Not of becoming a colonist, but of replacing him. This hostile, oppressive and aggressive world, bulldozing the colonized masses, represents not only the hell they would like to escape as quickly as possible but a paradise within arm's reach guarded by ferocious watchdogs" (16). Instead of decolonization the nationalist leaders replaced the colonists and occupied the seats of political, economic and cultural power.

In *We Need New Names* the contradictions of the impossible synthesis and the fallacious decolonization have come to full bloom. For the poor Zimbabweans, emigrating to South Africa, Europe, or the United States is the only option they have. And one can of course, as I do, follow other threads, language, and culture or race and blackness, or gender and patriarchy, in the form of the novel through the three literary epochs of early South African writing, literature of decolonization, and contemporary rooted transnational literature. African literary criticism has failed the African literary tradition by failing to take into account early South African writing and writing in other African languages such as Amharic and Hausa.

Thinking through the Makerere Conference and the writers in relation to the African literary tradition, a series of questions emerge: Why did they, from the very outset, work with a consensus of African literature in English despite the early South African example? What are the costs of starting Africa's literary tradition in the wrong literary and historical period? What does it mean for my generation of writers and scholars of African literature not to have an inclusive imaginative consciousness of our literary past? That our imagination and scholarship draw from a distorted literary tradition? That the kind of intertexuality that drives our writing begins with the Achebe generation and not with early South African writing? And what does African literary history and criticism look like when stood up on the foundations laid down by the early South African writers? In short, what would the African literary tradition look like if we read NoViolet Bulawayo or Chimamanda Adichie in relation to the Makerere and early South African writers?

## WHAT IS AFRICAN LITERATURE? THEN AND NOW

The questions around the identity of African literature are also central to my argument. And once again, the Makerere Conference of 1962 provides a good entry point, for there the question of what is African literature was discussed at great length.[21] According to Chinua Achebe's account in his 1965 essay, "English and the African Writer," the participants spent considerable time debating and eventually failing at a definition of African literature. Was African literature to be limited by being "produced in Africa or about Africa? Could African literature be on any subject, or must it have an African theme? Should it embrace the whole continent or South of the Sahara, or just Black Africa? And then the question of language. Should it be in indigenous African languages or should it include Arabic, English, French, Portuguese, Afrikaans, etc.?" (18). The conference failed to answer the question, but one year later a conference held at the Faculte des Lettres of Dakar University in Senegal succeeded in "tentatively" coming up with a definition. Ezekiel Mphahlele in a conference report for *Transition* recorded the definition

> as creative writing in which an African setting is authentically handled or to which experiences originating in Africa are integral. This therefore includes among others, writing by white Africans like Nadine Gordimer, Dan Jacobson, Doris Lessing, Elspeth Huxley, Alan Paton and so on, and that by non-Africans like William Plomer (a man of many fascinating worlds), Joyce Cary and Joseph Conrad (specifically, *The Heart of Darkness*). Graham Greene's *The Heart of the Matter* could have been given any setting outside Africa, and so it does not qualify. (16)

This definition raises many questions—who defines what is an authentic African setting? And these experiences originating from Africa—what is the appropriate length of time for a character to experience something African? Chinua Achebe pointed out the difficulty of limiting African literature. In the same 1965 essay, he wrote:

> I could not help being amused by the curious circumstances in which Conrad, a Pole, writing in English produced African literature! On the other hand if Peter Abrahams were to write a good novel based on his experiences in the West Indies it would not be accepted as African literature. (18)

Is the African novel an extension of the African writer so it qualifies no matter the setting and content? Or is it the setting alone that matters? This definition of African literature, that could allow for the inclusion of Conrad's *Heart of Darkness* as an African text, while a novel by an African writer set outside the continent could not, led Achebe to conclude that "you cannot cram African literature into a small, neat definition. I do not see African literature as one unit but as a group of associated units—in fact the sum total of all the national and ethnic literatures of Africa" (18). National literature for Achebe was "literature written in English; and the ethnic literatures are in Hausa, Ibo, Yoruba, Effik, Edo, Ijaw, etc" (27). By raising writing in English to national and major literature, and relegating African languages to producing ethnic literature, Achebe contributed to a language hierarchy that still undergirds and informs African literature today. But language hierarchy notwithstanding, for Achebe the term African literature could carry within it an immediately assumed diversity;[22] in the same way when one says European literature, a diverse history and array of writers is assumed.[23]

More than 50 years after the Makerere Conference the debate continues. But, whereas in 1965 the argument was for the recognition of African literature as diverse, the debate today is around whether the category of African literature has any meaning at all. Taiye Selasi, a contemporary African writer and the author of *Ghana Must Go*, delivered a keynote speech at the 2013 Berlin Book Fair entitled, "African Literature Doesn't Exist."[24] Selasi knew she was being deliberately provocative, stating, "I'm sure I'll regret having given this talk once the scholars swoop in, but for now, I'm young and idealistic enough to relish the risk of defeat," and terming her own paper an act of "blasphemy" (1). Her main argument, that in the West the category of African literature has come to mean one kind of writer and one kind of writing, has resonated with the younger generation of African writers. For her, ignoring Africa's diversity, where there are "over two thousand languages spoken," or "dismiss[ing] this linguistic complexity as a symptom of primitive clannishness, as if these two thousand languages were spoken by one hundred people apiece," (6) can only see a singular Africa. In addition, she argued, there is a tendency to see African writers as "sociologists in creative writers' clothing" which "betrays a fundamental disrespect for those writers' artistry" (8). She used Achebe's 1965 essay to make her point that the category, African literature, itself was the problem:

> Achebe, writing in 1965, concludes, "Any attempt to define African literature in terms which overlook the complexities of the African scene at the material time is doomed to failure." Fifty years later I would argue that the only way to define African literature is to overlook these complexities. (4)

For her the term is simply too opaque to allow for a diverse catalogue of literature and writers to shine through. But whereas for Achebe the point was to have the term "African literature" carry the complexity that came with it, Selasi argued for the bankruptcy of the term itself—the category could not help but carry within it a simplified sociological/anthropological reading of African literature.

When the very categories of African literature, African writing, and African writer are invoked, they have to be justified. For example, Kwame Dawes, the founding director of the African Poetry Book Fund, anticipated the debate over categorization during a 2015 interview with the National Book Foundation and preemptively stated:

> The term "Africa" is a complicated convenience of history. This makes it, despite what totalizing practices we fall into, as absurd to characterize African poetry as anything specific as it would be to characterize European poetry as anything specific. So, for our purposes, the only thing that allows us to call our series and our organization African is the historical convenience of geography. . . . There may be lines of connection between a poet from Nigeria and a poet from Botswana, but these may well be the same connections that these poets find with Croatian poets and Canadian poets.[25]

Unlike Selasi, who wants to abolish the term, Dawes tried to show the growing complexity of the term, how writing coming from the diaspora is part of the African literary tradition, where being amorphous and spilling outside categories is a strength, not a weakness that has to be beaten into a monolithic stability. In a press release announcing the 2015 Sillerman Prize, which the African Poetry Book Fund sponsors, Dawes said of the entries:

> The submissions we've received beautifully illustrate this reality. The lines of connection between African poets truly span the globe. This year we received work from poets working in the following countries: Sweden, Kenya, United States, Nigeria, United Kingdom, Dominica, France, Zimbabwe, Malawi, South Africa, Italy, Cameroon, Tanzania, Ghana, Netherlands, India, China, Germany, Uganda, Canada, Togo, Botswana, Taiwan, Egypt, and Ireland. These poets, hailing from four continents, have roots throughout the African continent.

There is little argument that African literature across multiple generations has suffered a kind of Africa-Is-a-Country[26] literary criticism that, in place of diverse aesthetics, reads it as anthropology—as representative of a single country, culture, and language—coming from a singular body politic.[27] The Africa-is-a-country literary criticism does not know what to do with writers outside the Makerere literary tradition.

What will African literary criticism, so narrowly constituted around the

Makerere writers, do with contemporary writers like Aminatta Forna whose parents are Scottish and Sierra Leonean? Forna's childhood was in Sierra Leone but she grew up in Britain, wrote a memoir and novel fueled by the Sierra Leonean war, and then published a novel, *The Hired Man* (2013), set in Croatia whose characters are trying to outlive or outrun the early 1990s Serbia-Croatia war. It is not by any plot-stretch an African novel, but it also clearly gets it "vital force," as Linda Gregg, the former US poet laureate, calls the fundamental experiences from which a shape shifting writer's imagination draws, from the Sierra Leonean war. In her essay on writing, "The Art of Finding," Gregg suggests these experiences (which need not be tragic) become "resonant sources deep inside that empower those subjects and ideas" into writing.[28] So eager were popular literary critics and readers to categorize Forna's *The Hired Man* into something familiar that she penned an essay for the *Guardian* titled "Do Not Judge a Book by the Author" in which makes she makes a plea to be read on the basis of the book and not her biography and origin.[29]

Simon Gikandi and Abiola Irele see their 2004 *Cambridge Companion* as "provid[ing] an account of the entire body of productions that can be considered to comprise this broad field as defined both by imaginative expression in African itself, and aspects of the continuum as represented by literature in the Caribbean and to some extent in North America" (xiv). They go a step further and call for an opening of African literature to writing produced by colonial settlers, explorers and adventurers:

> The term "African literature" has also been taken to refer, albeit in what may be considered a secondary sense, to the "colonial literature" produced by metropolitan European writers for whom Africa has served as the setting either for a complete cycle of works (Pierre Loti, Rider Haggard, Joyce Cary) or for single/specific works (as in the case of Joseph Conrad, Graham Greene, and Castro Soromenho). (xv)

Why not? Literary criticism, as I argue in chapter 4, deals with literature as it exists, as politically unpalatable as it may be. What we need is a mainstreaming of a borderless African literature. But, largely, we are dealing with a literary criticism that has largely ignored time and space—time because of the ahistorical nature of the criticism, and space because the literary criticism has been confined to continental African writers of the decolonization era.

The question about what constitutes African literature cannot be answered outside the question of how and why African writers and critics from former British colonies and their Western publishers created an African literary aesthetic that centered on the realist novel in English, and excluded the example set by early South African writers. And to these questions we must add why these same African writers and critics, after finding themselves in the peculiar position of producing national and Pan-African literatures and criticism in English, became the biggest defenders of English while condescending to African languages. And how, in turn, the post-Makerere African writers have responded to a literary tradition that privileged the English language over African languages. To put it differently, the discussions around the identity of African literature are not asking why the South African literary epoch is missing from our understanding of a contested African literary tradition. Questions around reception are masking the very serious fundamental and structural flaws in our construction of the African literary canon.

## THE ENGLISH METAPHYSICAL EMPIRE, PUBLISHING, AND THE STANDARD-ENGLISH-ONLY CONSENSUS

In a personal interview, my father, Ngugi Wa Thiong'o, who would later advocate writing in African languages, tried to capture the complete absence of the early South African writers and writing in African languages in general in the consciousness of the Makerere writers. It was not that they were ignoring the language question, the question simply did not exist; it was inconceivable to them that they could write in their mother tongues. Speaking about the 1962 Makerere Conference, "African Writers of English Expression," he said:

> The title of the conference precluded the question. No writer in an African language was invited. And no writing in an African language, even in translation, was ever discussed. You can look at it in a different way. Nearly all the writers present were products of the English Department. We had been socialized into taking English as the linguistic norm, our literary starting point. We never questioned that linguistic premise.[30]

In order to begin answering the question of why English became the "linguistic norm," we must look as far back as the growth of English in relation to the philological debates around its standardization in England in the 1700s. We must also consider the growth of English in Africa through colonial education before arriving at the debates around African writing in African and European languages and how they mirror yet remain different across different generations of African writers. To put it differently, questions around a diverse or singular African literary identity, language, politics and aesthetics cannot be answered outside what Michael Beach called an English "metaphysical empire" (119). In his essay, "The Creation of a Classical Language in the Eighteenth Century: Standardizing English, Cultural Imperialism, and the Future of the Literary Canon," Beach looked at the ways in which standardization of English was a successful attempt at making English a world language and carrier of Englishness—a well from which other cultures could draw the best of what English culture had to offer. Writing of standardizers like Samuel Johnson who in 1755 created an authoritative dictionary of Standard English, Beach argued that their hope was that English culture

> would become the building block of . . . a metaphysical empire, an empire of language and literature that would outlive the actual British Empire. . . . While sometimes openly disavowing the martial nature of Rome, theorists could still wax eloquent about its metaphysical empire and the continued transmission and reproduction of Latin and of Roman letters. These epic metaphysical empires were a source of great inspiration to those thinkers who fantasized that British texts would eventually become "classics" to formerly colonized peoples. (119)

This movement was not just about Standard English serving as nationalist armor by protecting English identity from outside forces while keeping Britain a solidified whole. "Standardizers" like Johnson were going after future history itself.

Today, the fact that the Commonwealth Prize is given for writing from Britain and former British colonies, and that the few major African literary prizes such as the Caine and Etisalat prizes are awarded for African writing in English, can be seen, for better and worse, as a celebration and perpetuation of the metaphysical empire. Indeed, in 2001 the Bengali Indian writer Amitav Ghosh withdrew his novel, *The Glass Palace*, from being considered for the Commonwealth Prize. He argued the term "can only be a misnomer so long as it excludes the many languages that sustain the cultural and literary lives of these countries" and the term "commonwealth literature" indeed "anchors an area of contemporary writing not within the realities of the present day, nor within the possibilities of the future, but rather within a disputed aspect of the past." In order to capture the absurdity of celebrating commonwealth literature, he went on to ask, "Would it not surprise us, for instance, if that familiar category 'English literature' were to be renamed 'the literature of the Norman Conquest'"?

It was the British publishers Heinemann's African Writers Series (AWS) and its canonization of the Makerere writers that made it possible for the Standard English–only consensus to become the norm. The AWS was founded by Alan Hill, a director at its educational books division. After witnessing the success of Achebe's *Things Fall Apart*, he felt there was a need for literary works written by Africans to be available not only in the Western market but in African countries. The Western market could bear the costs of hardback novels, but for the African market cheap paperbacks would be published (Currey, *Africa Writes Back*, 2). As Hill narrated in his autobiography, *In Pursuit of Publishing*, he also wanted to change the way books were published in Africa by big Western publishers whose sole interest he saw as profit, while "putting nothing back in the way of investment in local publishing and encouragement of local authors" (122–23). Seeing these companies driven by profit and nothing else "outraged" his "radical, nonconformist, missionary ethos" and he felt AWS could provide a "publishing service for African authors" (123).

It was not as altruistic as Alan Hill made it sound. Caroline Davis, in writing about the Oxford University–owned Three Crown Series, which just like Heinemann Educational Books in 1962 had started publishing African writers, connected the rise of British publishing of African authors with the fall of the British Empire. For her, the "end of formal colonization in Africa gave British publishing companies the opportunity to become more, not less, deeply entrenched in the cultural life of the continent" (*Creating Postcolonial Literature*, 227). Even though she did not use the term, she was in essence talking about the metaphysical empire when she analyzed the language used by a May 1976 committee convened to "examine the function, organization, and operations of the [Oxford University] Press and its relationship with the University." She concluded:

> The language of economic and cultural imperialism resonates in the report. OUP is described as "a leader among United Kingdom publishers and an instrument of learning, education, and culture of national and international importance." The committee resolved that the press's world expansion should continue, "not simply because of the financial rewards but because of the benefit to the spread of British culture and influence." (230–31)

The committee recognized that Oxford University Press was opening a new and largely untapped English-speaking market while bringing new fiction to Britain. They also acknowledged the same goal that Samuel Johnson had in the 18th century, the propagation of Englishness.

In this regard, Hill viewed Achebe's *Things Fall Apart* in relation and in contrast to an earlier English-language African novel, Amos Tutuola's *Palm Wine Drinkard*. Tutuola's novel, published in 1952, was written in "broken" English. Hill was aware that Africans viewed Tutuola's *Palm Wine Drinkard*, written in Standard Six (sixth grade English) and to much acclaim in the West, as doing a disservice to African literature and the image of Africa. He was also aware of its paternalistic reception by Western critics. In his autobiography, he recounted how the arrival of *Things Fall Apart* "came as a revelation to many of my colleagues in Britain whose opinion of Africans as writers had been influenced by the works of Amos Tutuola—particularly his quaintly-told allegorical fantasies" while for Africans Tutuola's book was "anathema to many educated Nigerians—to whom his linguistic virtuosity seemed plain illiteracy" (121). *Things Fall Apart*, in contrast, "affirmed permanent human and social values in the context of a traditional tribal society in crisis, and which expressed those values in terms which the Western educated reader could understand" (121).

*Things Fall Apart*, first published in 1958 by Heinemann and then republished in 1962 under AWS, was met with an almost palpable literary relief. It was not in the style of Tutuola; here English was standardized, and the content, rather than being bizarre, showed a dynamic Igbo culture clashing with British colonial culture. *Things Fall Apart* was the first of many AWS novels that in the words of Hill dealt with "the confrontation of two civilisations, European and African, and the shock this caused individuals and society" (124). Thus, Achebe was applauded for his learned handling of the English language and showcasing a dynamic precolonial African culture on the precipice of colonial domination. Norman MacKenzie, in his 1959 essay in support of English as the language of education in British colonies, compared Tutuola to Achebe:

> In English literature people like Chinua Achebe, the Nigerian novelist, have emerged from University Colleges in British territories and have begun to write of African themes in an English manner. But the British public has shown more interest in the work of Amos Tutuola whose highly imaginative books . . . are couched in the pidgin English of Nigeria. . . . It is true that the

unaccustomed themes drawn from the teeming folk-lore of West Africa are excitingly fresh to British readers, and that the strange style, with its child-like repetitions and incessant ambiguities, lulls them into the suspension of disbelief. . . . We can only hope that African writers will not adopt some debased form of English in an effort to titillate the British palate. (220)

The "English manner" MacKenzie refers to could also be a matter of form, the realist fiction tradition as opposed to the folkloric superstition-riddled tradition of Tutuola, and he was unhappy that English readers had not been more critical.

But it was the language use, which he called "debased," that he found most offensive. He praised Achebe for writing in the tradition of Standard English and derided Tutuola for writing in what he calls "Nigerian Pidgin English." In 1958[31] Mackay wrote:

Amos Tutuola has given us specialized and extremely interesting fantasy, and Cyprian Ekwensi excellent realism and the modern Lagos scene; but now at last a Nigerian writer has appeared who can give as a straightforward, penetrating and absolutely honest picture of African village life before the advent of the first missionaries. In powerfully realistic prose the writer set out to write a fictional but almost documentary account of the day to day happenings in a small Nigerian village without evasion, sophistry or apology. . . . Many books and anthropological treatises have told about the power of religious superstition, but here is one which forcefully but impartially gives us reasons for both. (243)

All in all, Tutuola's style and English usage were seen not as setting or contributing to a literary tradition, but rather as a one-off style that had no future. If it was true that Tutuola's style was a "fascinating cul-de-sac,"[32] Achebe's opened up a literary superhighway for African writing. So powerful has been the counternarrative to Tutuola's aesthetics and reception that Achebe was popularly credited with being the "father of modern African literature" (a term he himself did not accept[33]) even though Tutuola had published three novels before the arrival of *Things Fall Apart*. With Achebe joining AWS as editorial advisor in 1962, the series would go on to set the African literary tradition on the path of realist novels that, whether first in English or translated into English from French, were political and in Standard English even as they tried to "Africanize" that English.

The question of what kind of aesthetic those trapped within the metaphysical empire produced is central to the African literary tradition. What does practicing anticolonial and decolonization politics within the growing metaphysical empire mean in terms of literary production? Or, to put it differently, is it possible for an ideological superstructure in a Marxian sense to outgrow and exist outside its material base? How and why did the ideological superstructure of English continue to thrive beyond colonialism and the British Empire? When the questions are put this way, it becomes possible to circumvent literary cultural nationalism, and allows us to look at the African and British contradictions propelling the production of African literature. All in all, if I were to sum this whole book in one sentence, it would be to say that it is about how the early South African, Makerere, and post-Makerere writers and their literary critics have responded, for better and worse, to the English metaphysical empire.

## POST-MAKERERE WRITERS AND THE ENGLISH METAPHYSICAL EMPIRE

In a 2015 interview with *Jalada Africa* journal, Chika Unigwe described how, while going to school in Abuja, Nigeria, she was taught more French than Yoruba or Igbo:

> [I]n Igbo, Hausa and Yoruba we had to learn to count from one to ten, we had to learn to say the alphabet, we didn't even have written exams, we had oral exams where they would ask you to dance or to sing or to clap or to whatever just to see if you understood the phrases. . . . But by the time you'd done your third year of French in Secondary school, you were supposed to know enough French to write an entire essay, but nobody demanded that of the local languages.[34]

Growing up in Kenya, my generation was immersed in English in our schools and homes, part of a culture that accepted English as the language of progress and aesthetics, as the superior language. Kiswahili, the national language, was taught as a subject while our mother tongues were not taught at all. Unlike in Unigwe's case, we were expected to pass Kiswahili grammar and essay exams. But there were no real consequences for failing, unlike English, where failing meant not advancing from primary to high school, or from high school to the university. That is, excelling in Kiswahili but failing English meant the end of one's academic career. There was no incentive for 11–16 year olds to immerse themselves in Kiswahili. Ours was a movement from colonial to neocolonial education.

As a result, working within the English metaphysical empire has become so much the norm that some prominent post-Makerere writers cannot see the extent to which it distorts and contradicts their worldview. Nigerian novelist Helon Habila, in a blog post about judging the 2014 Caine Prize entitled "Tradition and the African Writer," was dismissive of African writing in African languages:

> Looking at this diversity and profusion of style and theme it feels strange to remember that there was a time, and not too long ago, when some theorists tried to limit what can or cannot be called African literature; some said a work can never be African literature unless it is in an African language—and actually, people like Ngugi wa Thiong'o still believe so. I wonder what people like Obi Wali, the arch-proponent of "African literature in African languages only" would say now if they were to hear that there are writers who write their novels in languages like Flemish and Italian and who unapologetically refer to themselves as African writers. Clearly there is more to it than language and style—it is most importantly about tradition.

It would not be farfetched to argue that the metaphysical empire has swallowed up the younger generation of African writers to such an extent that they themselves cannot see the fallacy of defending African writing in Flemish or Italian while arguing against writing in African languages. But more importantly, is it really possible to divorce language from a literary tradition? Certainly not in the case of English literature, where the growth of England as a nation, and Englishness as a culture with a canonized literature, are tied to the growth of the English language and colonial empire. There would not be an English literary tradition without the growth of the English language. At best there would be the oxymoronic sounding English literature in French/Francophone English literature, or Latin English literature.

For example, for the 14th century English power elite, French or Latin was the language of choice, while the majority outside the halls of power spoke English. In his essay, "The Use of English: Language, Law, and Political Culture in Fourteenth-Century England," W. M. Ormrod delineates this disjuncture between the official language of power and one's mother tongue:

The elite, represented by the royal family, the members of the central admin-istration, the senior judiciary, and at least a proportion of the high nobility, all knew how to speak French in one, two, or (occasionally) all three[35] of its forms and continued to use it regularly as a means of oral communication until (and, for certain purposes, well beyond) the end of the fourteenth cen-tury. Conversely, the lower ranks of the polity, the gentry and bourgeoisie, had already become Anglophone by the end of the thirteenth century; their knowledge of French was now largely pragmatic, needed only for the pur-poses of understanding administrative and accounting documents and for occasional dealings with the enemy when they joined the king on campaign abroad. (753)

It was not until 1362 that King Edward III passed a law in which English became the official language, replacing French as the language of instruction. The statute is explicit in its reasoning—it was so that "every man of the said realm may better organize his affairs without offending the law, and better keep, save, and defend his inheritances and possessions" (Ormrod, "Use of English," 756). Consequently, the king's laws could not exist in French: they had to exist in a language understood by the people. Ormrod points out a nationalist angle to the Statute of Pleading:

> French military aggression was represented as a form of cultural imperialism: drawing on a discourse employed by Edward I, the Crown several times in the mid-fourteenth century claimed, for the benefit of political audiences in England, that the French intended to wipe the English language from the face of the earth. . . . the royal declaration on the use of English was not solely or even principally about proper access to justice but rather about the reinforce-ment of a particular sense of political and cultural identity in a kingdom that had just emerged successfully from the throes of a major war with France. (780–81)

Linguistic nationalism, the idea that a government could not negotiate as an equal using the opponent's language, was the official argument. However, if nationalism was a bulwark against French aggression, then it had to be solid-ified at home.[36] By the time Samuel Johnson wrote about the need for stan-dardized English in order to propagate Englishness, writers like Shakespeare had already set the English language on the rails of a literary tradition. He could write that "[t]he chief glory of every people arises from its authors" and

"I shall not think my employment useless or ignoble, if by my assistance foreign nations, and distant ages, gain access to the propagators of knowledge, and understand the teachers of truth; if my labours afford light to the repositories of science, and add celebrity to *Bacon*, to *Hooker*, to *Milton*, and to *Boyle*" (92). In other words, the English language had to fight for its survival against the dominant French and Latin: as Johnson understood, writers were the best carriers, defenders, and propagators of English culture.

For writers like Helon Habila, who begin their literary clock with Ngugi, Achebe, and Bessie Head, who were born into the metaphysical empire, so to speak, to talk of African languages is to be atavistic. They do not have the earlier examples of writing in African languages, and they are not in conversation with this literary history, or English literary history and language politics, for that matter.

But in other ways, the language debate has shifted away from an English-only consensus to one that calls for a more democratic space where different languages can coexist. By a democratic space I don't mean just the kind of ahistorical leveling that Habila invokes, I mean one that recognizes that all languages are equal but some are more equal than others—a hearkening back to the hierarchical order in George Orwell's *Animal Farm*. For these groups of writers, without access to resources often reserved for those writing in English, the Internet has become the place where they can allow languages, European and African alike, to meet.

In February 2015, Ankara Press, a Cassava Republic Press romance imprint, produced a Valentine's Day anthology. The anthology featured romance stories originally written in English and then translated into the author's mother tongue. From a distance, there is some irony that the translations were originally written by African writers in English and then translated mostly into African languages. But a closer look reveals several exciting developments that herald yet another epoch in African writing. The anthology was digital and free to download. At the same time, both the original stories and their translations were read aloud and the recordings made available along with the stories online. Of course, the fact that these were romance stories written by established post-Makerere writers shows a changing attitude toward popular forms of writing. As the editors explained in their introduction,[37] Ankara Press showcases romance "with African settings, storylines and characters" with the purpose of "counter[ing] the one-dimensional view of life as portrayed in many romance novels." In describing the anthology itself the editors explained that "romance in Africa takes place in multiple languages and we wanted to reflect that in this collection. . . . This anthology therefore becomes a much truer representation of romance in Africa as we can hear and see what romancing in different languages might sound like and mean."

Capturing the shifting tide away from an English-only consensus, the 2015 Kwani Literary Festival in Nairobi was entitled *"Beyond the Map of English: Writers in Conversation on Language,"* and featured writers and critics discussing how they experience language as writers. At the 2015 Kwani Festival prizes for the inaugural Mabati-Cornell Kiswahili Prize for African Literature were awarded. It was a convergence of institutions and individuals from many backgrounds: cofounded by Lizzy Attree, the director the Caine Prize and myself, primarily funded by the Kenyan-Indian owners of Mabati Rolling Mills, a roofing company in Kenya, with an awards ceremony under the roof of a literary journal that publishes primarily in English, and with awards going to multiple Tanzanians. In putting together the prize, I have come to learn just how under-resourced the production of literature is in African languages. A language spoken by over 100 million people has only two or three literary prizes and journals. If Kiswahili, spoken across East and Central Africa, an official language in Tanzania and a national language in Kenya, is doing so poorly when it comes to nurturing a literary tradition that goes back to the 18th century, how about languages spoken within nations? Yet it seems to me that something has shifted: whether it is mere largesse from well-fed English language writing African writers, or something more fundamental, remains to be seen.

This is a good point to disclose that I am not merely approaching the question of the African novel, its false historical foundation, and its politics of language and identity from a critic's distance. I raise these questions from the inside out, as one intimately involved in the African literary tradition. I am a scholar and writer heavily invested in that tradition. In addition to cofounding the Mabati-Cornell Kiswahili Prize for African Writing, I also write poetry, fiction, and political commentary.[38] So when I raise the question of language, I am heavily implicated by having so far written all my published works in English. I too am a victim of the English metaphysical empire that trapped us from the moment we started kindergarten. And while I raise the question of translation, my novels have been translated into German and French but not into a single African language. As I raise the question of publishing and distribution, my books have been published for the East African market by East African Educational Books (built on the foundation and structure of British educational publishing), but in Western Africa by the independent Cassava Publishing House and in Southern Africa by Kwela Books, both working against the model of educational publishing. And when in the last chapter, I consider how the post-Makerere writers are challenging the form of the realist novel, I do so as the author of two detective novels, and as someone who is asked at any reading or interview why I chose that form.

And on the missing South African literary epoch in African literary criticism? As a writer I have to wrestle with what feels like a phantom leg; I can feel the literature used to be there but I cannot account for it in my writing. And as a literary scholar, it is even more galling—how and why did we allow for African literary criticism to not account for the full literary history? And what else are we missing? Why don't we read early slave narratives as early African memoirs?[39] Why can't we read early Ethiopian writing within the African literary tradition? Shouldn't *The Life and Struggles of Our Mother Walatta Petros: A Seventeenth-Century African Biography of an Ethiopian Woman*, written by the Ethiopian emperor Galawdewos and translated for the first time by Professor Wendy Belcher in 2015, be part of every African literature survey course? Why did it have to take several centuries before the book could be translated into English? And how long before it is translated into other African languages?

When I finally found my way to Makerere University for the 2015 Writivism Festival and gave a lecture on African writing and African languages at the national theater where years before my father's play had been performed in 1962 to celebrate Uganda's independence day, I felt I had a glimpse of the earlier conference and what it means to be a part of a generation of writers. We were celebrating the 1962 conference but it was more of an homage— what mattered most to us was the moment we were creating—the present and the future. Yet we remained tethered to the Makerere generation and the language question. It has become a question to be addressed at every gathering we have. And with the language question comes early South African writers writing in African languages—there is no running away from it. For the writers, contending with the early African writing is part of growing one's imagination, and for the scholar one of working within a truer and broader African literary tradition. And that in turn will allow us to look at past and present-day diaspora writing within an African literary tradition. To put it another way, literary criticism of the African novel in English has been sitting unbalanced, on a two-legged stool. My wish here is to have the African literary tradition sitting on a three-legged stool. What follows then is a fleshing out of the questions I have raised in this introduction.

In chapter 1, "No Shrubbing in the English Metaphysical Empire, Please: A Question of Language," I am primarily interested in the various ways Makerere and post-Makerere African writers have responded to the language question in African writing. I look at Chinua Achebe and Ken Saro-Wiwa, who argued that English was the best language for national and Pan-African literature, and then at Ngugi Wa Thiong'o and Daniel Kunene, who tied decolonization to African writing in African languages. I conclude the chapter by considering how post-Makerere writers including Chimamanda Adichie have answered the question of European versus African languages and the role translation has played and can play in African literature.

In chapter 2, "Amos Tutuola: Creating the African Literary Bogeyman," I examine how and why Tutuola's editors used his poor English usage to foreground his "nativeness" and thereby heighten the appeal of his novels. I consider the aesthetic costs and opportunities of noninterventionist editing in Tutuola's *Palm Wine Drinkard*. I look at how early critics emphasized his poor command of English, and his biography as a peasant/colonized native, as the lens through which to analyze the content and aesthetics of his writing.

In chapter 3, "Africa's Missing Literary History: From A. C. Jordan's Child of Two Worlds to NoViolet Bulawayo's Fractured Multiple Worlds," I look at the aesthetic and political shifts within the African literary tradition starting with early South African writing. I specifically look at how A. C. Jordan in *The Wrath of the Ancestors*, Chinua Achebe in *No Longer at Ease*, and NoViolet Bulawayo in *We Need New Names* address questions of whiteness and identity, gender, national and international citizenship, and colonialism, decolonization, and contested globalization. I demonstrate that it is possible to read early South African literature within the African literary tradition and that contemporary African literary criticism cannot be complete without it.

In chapter 4, "Manufacturing the African Literary Canon: Costs and Opportunities," I look at how African writers, their Western publishers, and literary critics came together to create and canonize the African political novel. Using Sol Plaatje's *Mhudi*, I look at the consequences of writers and critics working from a literary and scholarly imagination that is not aware of the fuller literary tradition. I also look at the rapidly changing publishing landscape as major and independent African publishers establish popular fiction and romance imprints and respond to the digital age.

In chapter 5, "Toward a Rooted Transnational African Literature: Politics of Image and Naming," I explore the extent to which old and emerging literary debates deny or enable the reader to translate literature across boundaries of time, culture, time, gender, sexuality, class, and language. Thinking through the writings of Aminatta Forna, Bulawayo, and Adichie, I ask: What critical tools and concepts are we to use to look at contemporary African literature in relation to its tradition? Transnationalism, the globalectic, or Afropolitanism? Diaspora/Black Atlantic, or globalization and its discontents?

## CHAPTER 1

# No Shrubbing in the English Metaphysical Empire, Please

## A Question of Language

Is it right that a man should abandon his mother-tongue for someone else's? It looks like a dreadful betrayal and produces a guilty feeling. But for me there is no other choice. I have been given this language and I intend to use it.

—Chinua Achebe, "English and the African Writer"

One wonders what would have happened to English literature for instance, if writers like Spenser, Shakespeare, Donne, and Milton, had neglected English, and written in Latin and Greek simply because these classical languages were the cosmopolitan languages of their times. Literature after all, is the exploitation of the possibilities of language.

—Obiajunwa Wali, "The Dead End of African Literature"

"Repeat after me. The red lorry went round the red bend," one of my older brothers turned English pronunciation teacher would say to me.

"The led rolly went lound the led bend," I would attempt.

"Try again, repeat after me—The red lorry went round the red bend."

"The led rorry went lound the led bend."

"Okay try this—She sells sea shells at the seashore," my brother, would move on, bemused, I like to think now.

"See shells she cells at the she sore." I would fail once again.

I don't remember at what age the practice finally paid off and I could say, "She sells sea shells at the seashore" and "the red lorry went round the red bend" without making a mistake—what we termed "shrubbing." We used shrubbing to describe the confusion of those who mixed their L and R, and mishmashed their "S" sounds. We made fun of "shrubbers" without mercy. There were no adults to defend shrubbers, or to ask us why it mattered so much how one pronounced words in a language that was not our mother tongue. No one bothered to ask what African language we spoke and applaud us if we spoke it well. All languages have word play and tongue twisters, but I doubt any have as high a premium as the one we put on English.

I was working against the grain of my mother tongue; the Gikuyu language does not have the "L" and "S" consonants. By running interference in my English pronunciation, Gikuyu had become a problem language. As teenagers, shrubbers, no matter how handsome or beautiful, had difficulty finding someone to date them.

In a postcolonial but not yet decolonized Kenya, English was all around us—the president addressed the nation in English, the two major newspapers were in English, and most of the programs on TV were in English. The legal system was in English, with black judges and lawyers wearing blonde wigs, just like their British counterparts. The books we read were all in English. English was what mattered.

At Tigoni Primary School, every morning we stood outside our classrooms and a teacher would inspect us for cleanliness—shorts and dresses were to be ironed, hair short and combed if you were a boy, and neatly braided if you were a girl. Fingernails were expected to be short and clean, black shoes polished and socks pulled up and neatly held in place by rubber bands. One could be punished or sent home for being untidily dressed. And from the moment we set foot in the school compound, only proper English was allowed. To be found speaking your own language was punishable by caning and wearing a sign, "I am an Ass," all day.

But if we did speak an African language, or our mother tongues, we were warned by our teachers and the prefect, "do not speak vernacular in school" and to report on each other; we would say, "so and so was speaking vernacular." Vernacular to us simply meant backward, vulgar, of the common village people. To speak of vernacular African languages was to already concede the debate.

Nothing much has changed. I visited Tigoni Primary School in the summer of 2017. Displayed outside every classroom were 29 rules and regulations. The second one was "Vernacular Speaking is PROHIBITED." Terms such as *vernacular, native, indigenous,* and so on carry their dual usages with them. For example, looking at the Oxford English Dictionary, *vernacular* means: "Of a language or dialect: That is naturally spoken by the people of a particular country or district; native, indigenous." But it also means, "Of a slave: That is born on his master's estate; home-born." *Native* means being "born to a place, natural," but to be "a member of an indigenous ethnic group. Freq. with a suggestion of inferior status, culture, etc., and hence (esp. in modern usage) considered *offensive*." And *indigenous*: "Inborn, innate, native."

*Ethnic* in the United States means "a member of a group or subgroup regarded as ultimately of common descent, or having a common national or cultural tradition; *esp.* a member of an ethnic minority." But historically it also meant "a person who is not Christian or Jewish; a heathen, a pagan." *Local*, as in African local languages, "Of, relating to, inhabiting, or existing in a particular place or region."

In this sense to say vernacular, local, or native languages recalls an opposite global cosmopolitan world that produces world literature. English, a global language. French, a global language. Swedish? Chinese? Russian? In translation they are world languages. That they are world languages, capable of producing world literature, is not in doubt in the popular and critical imaginations.

With some of my friends, I formed a clandestine Gikuyu-speaking group, not so much because we advocated for African language rights, but because it was the language that came naturally to us, and it was another law to be broken. Kiswahili was taught, but as just another subject—no other Kenyan languages were taught. In school, all my classmates had English first names— Helen, Judith, Philip, Tom, and so on. It was the normal thing and I, who went only by my Gikuyu names, Mukoma Wa Ngugi, was seen as an outlier, because statistically I was. And even now, some Kenyans still express surprise that I do not have a Christian or English name. I was lucky (or not so lucky, depending on who was asking me about my lack of an English name) that my father had from an early age seen the abnormality of baptizing African children with English names. He himself had changed his own name from James Ngugi to Ngugi Wa Thiong'o, and also started writing fiction in Gikuyu.

Whereas for me I could get a fix of Gikuyu at home, some children grew up speaking only English at home. I know many Kenyans who are now my age who have lived in Kenya all their lives speaking only English—and not just any English, proper Standard English, and if they went to an international school to boot, with a slightly British accent. We are talking about the 1970s and 1980s, 10 to 20 years after independence—decolonization meant colonial education by black teachers.

Two or so years after I had graduated from Ngenia Secondary School, I went back to ask my English and history teachers for a letter of recommendation—I was applying to US colleges. Naturally, I walked around the school but before long I noticed a student tailing me. "Come on, man—why are you following me around?" I asked him. In English, of course.

He was a shrubber. And he wanted me to say something in English.

"Your Engris is famoush alound here," he explained. A deep feeling of incomprehension, and defeat mixed with joy and shame, came over me. I am still haunted by that encounter. Why was it that somewhere in a village school in Limuru, Kenya, two decades after independence, or more aptly two decades into decolonization, it mattered more how well we spoke English than what we meant? Well, this was our linguistic inheritance. Our parents had gone through the same violent language and culture shaming. In the essay, "Recovering the Original," my father narrates an incident from his colonial primary school:

> He lay on his tummy on a high table in the assembly hall with all the students and staff present. Two teachers held his head and legs and pinned him to the table and called him monkey, as the third whiplashed his buttocks. No matter how horribly he screamed and wriggled with pain, they would not let him go. Scream Monkey. Eventually the shorts split and blood spluttered out, some of it on the shirts of those who held him down, and only then did they let him go. He stood up barely able to walk, barely able to cry, and he left, never to be seen in the precincts of that government school or any other again; I have never known what happened to him. His fault? He had been caught in the act of speaking Gikuyu in the environs of the school, not once, not twice, but several times. (13)

What does it mean that generations coming after continued to record similar experiences of language trauma? What does it mean to a literary tradition to have several generations who identify their languages with shame, wrongdoing, and fear?

My father's language awakening did not happen until after his Makerere generation had already cemented the idea that African writing, Pan-African writing that is, ought to be in English. By then it had become the norm for his generation to propagate English and Englishness, and bring up children in English language–only households. Within the logic of an English metaphysical empire, it was not strange that a foreign language could matter so much that it would affect my dating life and social standing in a small rural town called Limuru in Kenya. Or that how high I climbed up the upward mobility ladder was going to be determined by my command of English. The language question for me, as a converted and saved *shrubber* through the herculean efforts of my devoted older brothers, is deeply personal. I want to know why.

Chinua Achebe, in a 1965 essay, "English and the African Writer," had asked about language so painfully that every time I read it, I can feel the heartbreak: "Is it right that a man should abandon his mother-tongue for someone else's?" He went to answer it, "It looks like a dreadful betrayal and produces a guilty feeling. But for me, there is no other choice. I have been given this language and I intend to use it" (30). In the past, as many others have done, I used to read his essay as an unapologetic defense of English, a callous dismissal of African languages. Thus, in *Decolonising the Mind* (1986) Ngugi does not see the anguish behind Achebe's words. He writes that, for Achebe, "the possibility of using mother-tongue[,] provokes a tone of levity in phrases like a 'dreadful betrayal' and 'guilty feeling;' but that of foreign languages produces a categorical positive embrace" (7). Levity assumes a certain belittling of the question, but if you reread the essay as Achebe trying to justify his writing in English, the statement is anguished. And when Achebe writes that "I have been given the language, and I intend to use it"—this becomes not so much a declaration, but more a matter of willing himself to do something that is unpalatable to his imagination.

There is a similar pained anguish in what Ama Ata Aidoo terms as "pathos" in "To Be an African Woman Writer—an Overview and a Detail," her presentation at the 2nd African Writers Conference in 1986, where the languages of African literature was one of the central questions. She writes:

> We experience some sadness—though mixed with some positive emotions—at the mere confrontation with the notion of African women and writing. Nothing really tragic, nothing really worthy of jubilation either. Certainly however, there is no denying the pathos and wonder in being an African (and a woman) with the sensibilities that are struggling ceaselessly to give expression to themselves in a language that is not just alien but was part of the colonizer's weaponry. . . . There is pathos in writing about people, the majority of whom will never be in a position to enjoy or judge you. And there is some wonder in not letting that or anything else stop you from writing. Indeed, it is almost a miracle, in trying and succeeding somewhat to create in an aesthetic vacuum. (512)

Here she captures the pained anguish that could be mistaken for defiance in Achebe's essay. The idea of writing in a language formerly deployed to defeat your own language is bad enough. But writing to and for a people most of whom will not have access to it is tragic, and yet she writes on. However, this act is one of ambivalence, one that cannot be fully celebrated. That could not have been an easy realization, much less one to acknowledge and share publicly.

Certainly, calling for writing in African languages as part and parcel of decolonization resonated with intellectuals and political activists in and out of Africa. But for the writers it was more personal. The question of writing in English for a Swedish writer, for example, might be a pragmatic question, but for an African writer it is not just pragmatic, even though it is often presented that way. Imagine writing a book that those closest to you, your father, mother, relatives, and friends, cannot read. Add a colonial education that removed you from your language and your culture, a colonial culture that turned African cultures into emblems of backwardness, and yet both language and culture are still alive and you meet them in your day-to-day interactions. What was a logical call, that African languages are as viable as European languages, would have come across to Ngugi's fellow writers as accusatory.[1]

What was it that made it impossible for the Makerere writers to simply say—No thanks, my parents gave me my language and I intend to use it?[2]

## ENGLISH IN AFRICA THROUGH COLONIAL EDUCATION

Colonial education was not designed to produce African intellectuals equal in philosophy and science to the Europeans. It had the express purpose of producing Africans who would function as junior partners to whites in running the colonial machinery. In his essay "Educating the 'Native': A Study of the Education Adaptation Strategy in British Colonial Africa, 1910–1936," Michael Omolewa writes:

> [T]he foundation of the Western education in Africa was laid by Christian missionaries who were eager to use literacy training to introduce Christianity and win converts to their religion. The missionaries also used Western education to train Africans as catechists, messengers, and other positions needed to assist them in realizing the social and economic development and transformations desired by the European missionaries and their agents. Merchants and traders also required qualified personnel to handle their business transactions. (268)

The "pyramid educational system," as Ngugi calls it,[3] by design would produce more writers like Tutuola with only a partial grasp of English, and fewer writers like Achebe who had mastered English.[4] Tutuola, true to the nature of colonial education, ended up working as a blacksmith in the British colonial army during the Second World War, and later became an office messenger.

However, the colonial educators did not see themselves as creating an educational system that would contribute to the exploitation of Africans; to the contrary, the Africans were being given the kind of education that suited their level of civilization. It was taken as a given that Africans were to be weaned from an inferior civilization. But it could not be done all at once. Colonial education was supposed to produce Africans in balance with their primordial culture and the modern civilized world. One driving force for this educational mission was the Phelps-Stokes Fund, an American foundation heavily involved in education in British colonial Africa.[5] In a 1923 essay, "The Phelps-Stokes Fund and Educational Adaptation," W. Carson Ryan Jr. summarized the educational philosophy of the Phelps-Stokes Fund this way:

> Next to agriculture the commission places as the most important activities for education the "simple handicrafts required in the kraals and villages." Every teacher is to be taught the special forms of hand skill required for his community, not merely for economic ends, but because of the necessity of hand training for all. *Preparation for home life and for recreation, recognition of the language rights of the natives and of the need of a medium of inter-tribal communication* [emphasis mine], adaptation of the conventional school subjects to the needs of the environment, and the use of the movable school, farm demonstration, and other devices that have proved valuable in American efforts at educational adaptation, are also stressed by the commission. (281)

Education therefore was seen as functional and not meant to fulfill the existential needs of the African mind.[6] Schools were for producing agriculturalists who could do maintenance work around the villages while maintaining a healthy level of hygiene. African languages were not meant to carry learning; they were not to carry math, physics, or philosophy, they were to facilitate functionality and remain purely communicative. In other words, the relegation of African languages to the purely social realms with no hope of growing with new technologies and advances in philosophical thinking was a matter of deliberate policy.[7]

The fear that Africans would feel alienated from Western culture was a central concern. Thus, in a later essay on colonial education, but one that captures the principles and arguments over African languages, "The Place of English in African Education," Norman H. MacKenzie who taught at the University of Rhodesia could call for initial teaching to be in African languages because to fully immerse Africans in English without the anchor of their mother tongues would lead to alienation. He argued that "however diligently [Africans] work, they are like a man with a grafted skin, where the delicate sensitivity of the nerves has not yet grown again, so that his contact with his surroundings is uneasy and coarsened" (221). He was not calling for a bilingual education, but rather one in which English was generous enough to allow Africans to feel a sense of continuity with their culture:

> [If] the study of vernacular languages in secondary schools is indeed providing a strong tap root for our African pupils, then it is at our peril that we sever it. Whatever place we allot to English, it must not insulate the African from his native soil. As teachers of English we must therefore take it upon ourselves to discover whether in fact the vernacular studies in our schools are being as salutary as they could be, whether they are serving to show the pupil that his school education is not a preparation for certificates but for society. (222)

There is no mistaking that for him African languages were junior partners. African languages were not going to be taught because of their own intrinsic worth, or for Africans to be bilingual, but rather to facilitate a smoother transition to English. African languages, like education, were being discussed within the framework of functionality—to the extent they aided or hindered the acquisition of functional English. In a way, colonial education was running afoul of Samuel Johnson's dream of an "epic metaphysical empire" in which British texts would eventually become "classics" to formerly colonized peoples (Beach, "Creation of a Classical Language," 119). The English metaphysical empire was predicated on the natives mastering not only the language but also its texts.

## ADAPTATION, ENGLISH AND UPWARD SOCIAL MOBILITY

In the same way that in 1831 the English reformer William Cobbett[8] had called for the democratization of learning as a way to safeguard the rights of the poor and as a tool for upward social mobility, so did the Africans. Therefore, attempts to use African languages in the classroom were greeted with suspicion. For one, it was clear from the beginning that English was the language of upward social mobility. English, and the education that came with it, was the only way of getting something out of colonialism. Oyekan Owomoyela, in *Amos Tutuola Revisited*, argued that "fluency in the colonial language was arguably the most persuasive [way] of demonstrating one's qualification for elite status in the colonial scheme. It also was an emblem that announced one's insider status with regard to the culture of the masters" (3). It was the Europeans who did not want to see alienated Africans that were advocating for African languages to have a (somewhat minimal) role in the educational system. Africans, by contrast, wanted full English immersion. They wanted to master English because it was the only way out of poverty and an inferior culture and into a superior culture and way of life.[9] For Simon Gikandi the decolonizing Africans "wanted African children to be taught English so that they could have access to the institutions of colonialism, so that they could read Shakespeare in the original without having to rely on translations and adaptations" (*Maps of Englishness*, xx). The anticolonial struggle then was for greater access to, not the doing away with, colonial structures and institutions. To fight for more English and less African languages in the educational system was seen as a contribution to the anticolonial political struggle—but within a consensus of African cultures as representing the past, and English culture in the service of the future.

The colonial educators justifying the use of adaptation did not see it as a political question. MacKenzie, for example, advanced the argument that it was because Africans knew their languages were inferior that they preferred to learn the more superior and useful English. He did not consider the larger political issue of the colonizer and colonized engaged in a struggle of subjugation versus independence:

> Think of this for a moment as it affects the young African, growing up in a world in which the Nature which his tribal elders respected and feared is being unceremoniously driven towards serfdom. He is eager to take his place as a junior leader among his own people. At school a study of his vernacular will lead him backwards into a past with which he has generally scant sympathy, the very vocabulary and style having changed since the dignified days of his grandfather. In literature it has little of distinction to offer him. . . . Through English, on the other hand, he can have access to innumerable sources of vital knowledge—on politics and health, on scientific and technical matters (manuals about horse-power instead of legends about hares)—and a religion which will at any rate stand modern investigation better than his own. No

wonder the impatient African scholar calls out for more and more English, and Africans tend to regard any fostering of the vernaculars as a cunning political plot to fence them off from the broad streams of knowledge, wealth and power which issue from the perpetual springs of the great languages. ("Place of English," 217)

The idea that English was the passport out of an inferior African culture was a cornerstone of colonial education. It was an idea that was actively promoted and used to justify why African languages, though not to be completely abandoned, were ultimately not as useful as English. MacKenzie was arguing that Africans were in agreement with this premise and therefore saw the adaptation of African languages in schools as an attempt to deny them a full education. For MacKenzie, the starting and ending point was what colonialism had already created. Albert Memmi, in *The Colonizer and the Colonized*, made the observation that the colonizers first created the conditions of poverty among the Africans and then turned around and accused the Africans of being poor because they were lazy.[10] In this instance, colonial education had created the conditions under which Africans would see English as the language of power, and African languages as inferior. There were real material and educational gains in mastering English and none in mastering an African language within the colonial system.

MacKenzie also raised the question of whether Africans should write in their own languages, or in English. On the meeting between African and Western languages, he argued for English being the language of African literature for a number of reasons:

[L]ucrative jobs are open to a man whose native speech does not tether him to his own impoverished environment. Secondly, publishers cannot afford to provide extensive literatures in five hundred distinct languages, in each of which the demand will not even guarantee a recovery of printing costs. Moreover, small tribes cannot hope to find within their meager membership (so few of whom have had the best education anyway) the numbers of authors or even translators who could provide first-class material for the publishing houses. In English we can draw upon a wide and varied field. (217–18)

MacKenzie saw English as the language of employment and social advancement, as serving to unify Africans across different ethnicities and languages, and that those ethnicities without large numbers would be without resources with which to develop their languages. Thus, he anticipated the arguments that would be deployed by African writers such as Chinua Achebe and Ken Saro-Wiwa, who advocated for English to remain the language of African literature after decolonization.

## MAKERERE WRITERS AND THE LANGUAGE QUESTION IN THE AFRICAN LITERARY TRADITION

Like other educated Africans, writers were the immediate victims of the adaptation policy of using African languages as the language of instruction in the first few years of school, followed by an introduction of English. By the time they terminated their education, be it after primary school or the university, English had become for them the language of the intellect and imagination—the language of aesthetics. When asked why he did not write in Yoruba and instead used English, Tutuola answered, "I did not write in Yoruba because when I started writing, we did not take our language and our custom seriously. Anything that is good in the farm is *Onyibo*. You have Ope Onyibo (Pineapple), emo ebo (rabbit) etc, etc. No, I prefer my own culture" (Ajayi, *Amos Tutuola*, 158). He had imbibed the colonial lesson in which African languages could discuss mundane day-to-day living but not carry on serious discussions.[11] Ken Saro-Wiwa, in "The Language of African Literature: A Writer's Testimony," captured this unbalanced linguistic duality:

> When I went to primary school in 1947, I was taught in my mother-tongue during the first two years. During the other six years of the primary school course, the teaching was done in English, which soon imprinted itself on my mind as the language of learning. Khana was the language of play, and it appeared in the class timetable once or twice a week as "vernacular"— wonderful, story-telling sessions in Khana. We spoke Khana at home, and we read the Bible at church in Khana. It was enough to make me literate in Khana to this day. (153)

For Saro-Wiwa, Khana was the language for the lesser orature while English was for higher learning. In colonial education, African oral stories did not have any artistic merit[12] and hence were not worthy of any scholarly attention.[13] And yet, as scholars were to show, orature was an art form, what Linda Hunter called verbal arts in her study of Hausa orature's aesthetics that include rhythm, metaphors, meta-language, and so on. The term "orature" was coined by Pio Zirimu to show "utterance as an aesthetic means of expression" and to free it from the "literary colonization of orality."[14] But orature remained orature and was meant to be expressed in African languages, something that while aesthetically equal to the written was also something from the past. English was the language of the literary, and as I argue later, for the Makerere writers it was also the language for the urgent task of decolonization. By the time the African writers were getting ready to write their first novels and poems, it was already assumed that English was going to be the language. So Ngugi, who would later take the Wordsworthian line of writing in the "language of men," wrote his first major literary works in English.[15]

For the writers gathered at the Makerere Conference, it was Obi Wali who stood on the wrong side of literary history by questioning the conference title, "African Writers of *English Expression*." Ngugi captures the irony well when he writes in *Decolonising the Mind* that as a student with only two short stories in English, he was welcome to attend the conference whereas neither "Shabaan Robert, then the greatest living East African poet with several works of prose and poetry to his credit in Kiswahili, nor Chief Fagunwa, the great Nigerian writer with several published titles in Yoruba, could possibly qualify" (6). Indeed, Obi Wali's opening gambit was to ask why Amos Tutuola, a major African writer, was not only not invited but also not even discussed in the plenary sessions. He suggested the reason was "partly because [Tutuola] has gone out of line winning acclaim overseas for using that kind of English expression that is non-Ibadan, and non-Makerere" (281). That is, his usage of English, embarrassing and uneducated, did not reflect the goals of the educated writer well versed in standard acceptable English.

Wali went on to assert that because African writers have borrowed from the European tradition both in form and content, "African literature is a mere appendage in the main stream of European literature" (282). It had become European literature with African themes. He also argued that the majority of Africans were locked out of the enjoyment of works in European languages. Wali argued that "less than one per cent of the Nigerian people have had access to, or ability to understand, Wole Soyinka's *Dance of the Forest*. Yet, this was the play staged to celebrate their national independence, tagged on to the idiom and traditions of a foreign culture" (282). Wali had raised a central question, which would later resonate with Ngugi: For whom was the African writer writing?

Wali was aware of some of the arguments articulated by those like Mac-

Kenzie who felt that African languages could not provide a growing future, one that would ensure a literary tradition. In the "The Dead End of African Literature," he argued "of course all the old facile arguments would arise again—the multiplicity of African languages, the limitation of the audience to small patches of tribal groups, questions of orthography, and all the rest of them" (283). But to him these were not reasons to abandon African literature; they were challenges that could be overcome:

> I believe that every language has a right to be developed as literature. There is no part of the world where a false literary unity has been attempted in the way that we are doing today in Africa, not even in Europe. The problem has always been met by the technique of translating outstanding literary achievements into other languages, especially the more widespread and influential languages of the world. (283)

For him it was in the meeting of those challenges that a literary tradition would grow. Invoking the fight for English by English writers, he mused:

> One wonders what would have happened to English literature for instance, if writers like Spenser, Shakespeare, Donne, and Milton, had neglected English, and written in Latin and Greek simply because these classical languages were the cosmopolitan languages of their times. Even though a man like Milton could write even more easily in Latin and Greek, he did his major works in his own mother tongue without playing to the gallery of international fame. Literature after all, is the exploitation of the possibilities of language. (283)

In the eyes of Wali, if African literature were to grow, the only viable language for the African writer was an African language. Otherwise, even attempts to Africanize European languages so that they carried an African worldview would lead to a dead end; it would be African European literature. Wali also argued that if African writers should write in African languages, so should African literary critics. He stated, "what I am advocating here is not easy, for it entails a good deal of hard work and hard thinking . . . It would force some 'leading' critics to go in for the hard school of African linguistic studies, a knowledge of some of the important African languages, before generalising and formulating all kinds of philosophical and literary theories" (283). If literature and its criticism are symbiotic, one cannot survive without the other. For Wali, African literature in African languages could not thrive if its criticism was in European languages. The question of African literary criticism and language had not yet become a central issue among the critics, but if more and more literature were to be written in African languages, the implication was that criticism in those languages would follow. Sounding like Samuel Johnson and the idea that "the chief glory of every people arises from its authours" (*Dictionary of the English Language*, xxvi), Wali concluded his essay by arguing that the very future of African languages depended on African writers:

> The main reason for the study of a language is that it contains great literature—or some form of literature. This was what led scholars like Eliot and Pound to the study of oriental languages in their poetic experiments early in this century. There is little doubt that African languages will face inevitable extinction if they do not embody some kind of intelligent literature. The best way to hasten this extinction is by continuing in our present illusion that we can produce African literature in English and French. (335)

If a language does not have intellectuals working in it, it cannot grow, and that is precisely what colonial education had done. It had educated intellectuals who, divorced from their language, would essentially grow that body of literature that was to become known and organized under the category of commonwealth literature. African languages without writers, philosophers, and scientists—without the whole intellectual class working in them, would atrophy and become social languages.

The language question was already embedded in literary texts written in English, whether it was in the characters sometimes expressing themselves in an African language, or proverbs translated into African languages. Obi Wali's opening salvo forced the Makerere generation to consciously confront the language question and account for their language choice in a way they had not done before, with one group making the argument for African writing in English and the other for writing in African languages.

On one side of the debate, the writers made arguments that were in an inverse relationship with those like Samuel Johnson who had argued for standardization of English in England.[16] In Africa, English would unify an otherwise diverse people speaking multiple languages; English is the carrier of a rich culture and civilization and therefore more desirable than African languages; and English is indispensable to upward social mobility. At the same time, the debate over languages in Africa repeated the class dimension of the debate in England: Standard English was becoming the language of the elite, and African languages were to be spoken by peasants and the poor. Furthermore, English was the official language of the government, the courts, and education.

The same arguments used to advocate for English becoming the language of the English people over Latin and French were mirrored by those advocating for the use of African languages. A national literature cannot be in a language alien to that culture, particularly when that language has been imposed through conquest. By extension, decolonization in the language of the colonizer would be a contradiction. Literature and the official businesses of government ought to be in the languages that the majority of the people can understand.

## THE CASE FOR AFRICAN WRITING IN ENGLISH: A NATIONAL AND PAN-AFRICAN LANGUAGE?

The justifications for English came in several interconnected streams flowing into the abundant ocean of English philology. The first echoed MacKenzie's notion that because of linguistic diversity, English could serve as a unifying language—and not just within individual countries with multiple ethnicities but between peoples from different African countries. And closely related to this is the argument that English is the language that made it possible for diverse Africans to unite in struggle. African writers also argued that English was an international language of power and it was in Africa to stay—it was only pragmatic to use it. These writers also believed that English could be Africanized to carry an African experience, and that ultimately the language the author chooses to use is a personal choice with no social and cultural ramifications.

On English and unity, Achebe writes that English, for the most part, "did bring together many peoples that had hitherto gone their several ways. And it gave them a language with which to talk to one another" ("English and the African Writer," 28). Ken Saro-Wiwa, though writing his essay in 1992, followed Achebe and argued that, coming from a small ethnicity that he considered exploited and colonized by the larger ethnic groups, English empowered him because those from small minorities could communicate with each other and with everybody else ("Language of African Literature," 54). Conversely, writing in Khana or Igbo would contribute to ethnic tensions, something he felt Ngugi was doing in Kenya.[17] For Saro-Wiwa, just like Achebe, English also made it possible for him to be more Pan-African. Thus, he concluded his essay by saying, "I am content that this language has made me a better African in the sense that it enables me to know more about Somalia, Kenya, Malawi, and South Africa than I would otherwise have known" (157).

Mphahlele had also advanced a similar argument in his rejoinder to Wali. He asked:

> [S]upposing we met at Makerere to discuss African literature in the indigenous languages, what common language would we have which would help us understand the books being discussed? How many writers, even if they all wrote in indigenous languages, would have understood what was being talked about in connection with vernacular texts? What would be the common problems to talk about, such as we had as writers of English? And the problems we discussed are real, and are based on the reality that is African English literature, even though Wali thinks that it is an illusion to think of producing African literature in English and French. It is no use trying to wish this volume of writing out of existence. ("African Literature and the Universities," 337)

For Mphahlele, there was a part of African literature already existing in English. It could not be unwritten. In fact, for him English was the language best suited for the anticolonial and antiapartheid struggles. Speaking specifically of the growth of English and its own fight for survival against Latin and French, he argued that writers like Milton and Shakespeare had no

> need to abandon English because these writers were not committed in a struggle against colonialism . . . they were not discriminated against in the way a black man is today. The English did not need to organize a variety of tribes speaking different languages against a colonial or fascist power. Latin and Greek were not spoken by the man-in-the-street when Shakespeare and Milton wrote. These languages were scholastic fossils. English and French have become the common languages with which to present a nationalist front against white oppressors. Where the white man has already retreated, as in the independent states, these two languages are still a unifying force. By stages, each of the various states will need to find an African official language for itself. The African languages will need to develop a technical terminology and a vocabulary that meets the needs of systematic analytic contemporary thought.[18]

There was a bit of glossing over the reality of English speaking in Africa. In colonial and decolonizing Africa, English was a language spoken by small groups of a black educated elite, at most probably numbering in the thousands. As I discussed in chapter 1, English in Africa was the language of a much smaller elite and was then functioning very much like Latin and French in 13th century England. And if indeed English in decolonizing Africa was a unifying force, it was bringing together a small African elite. In other words, peasants and workers would not have been able to follow the 1962 conference proceedings, or discussions by the political elite about their future. Mphahlele also ignored an important point—English grew through use, not as an aftereffect of political development. Only a language in use can develop the "technical terminology and a vocabulary."

And yet Mphahele's point had merit. In critiquing the English language writers, Wali and later Ngugi missed just how Pan-African the Makerere literature was to become. Africans were getting a sense of larger Africa through the African Writers Series. For them, Anglophone writing was not antithetical to pan-African identity. Simon Gikandi captured this feeling of an African identity in his essay "Chinua Achebe and the Invention of African Culture":

> I have never met Chinua Achebe in person, but every time I read his fiction, his essays, or critical works, I feel as if I have known him for most of my life. For if the act of reading and re-reading establishes networks of connections between readers, writers, and context, and if texts are indeed crucial to the modes of knowledge we come to develop about subjects and objects and the images we associate with certain localities and institutions, then I can say without equivocation that I have known Achebe since I was thirteen years old. (3)

There is a certain familiarity that Africans from different countries share at first meeting that is hard to quantify. We have read some of the same books—thanks to standardized educational practices inherited from colonial education. It may vary from country to country, but I can say I don't know any African my age who went to secondary or high school who has not read *Things Fall Apart* or *The River Between*. And thus, African writers become national writers in nations outsider their own. My father has written about an encounter with an Achebe fan at Jomo Kenyatta airport in 2010, as he and I were on our way to a Kwani Festival organized around the theme of intergenerational writers. Chinua Achebe had just passed away. In a newspaper tribute to Achebe entitled "The Achebe I Knew," my father recounts:

As he and I walked towards the immigration desk, a man came towards me. His hands were literally trembling as he identified himself as a professor of literature from Zambia.

"Excuse me, Mr. Achebe, somebody pointed you out to me. I have long wanted to meet you."

"No, no I am not the one," I said, "but here is Mr. Achebe," I added, pointing at my son.

I thought the obvious youth of my son would tell him that I was being face-tious. But no, our professor grabbed Mukoma's hands grateful that he had at last shaken hands with his hero. The case of mistaken identity as late as 2010 shows how Achebe had become a mythical figure, and rightly so. He was the single most important figure in the development of modern African literature as writer, editor and quite simply a human being.[19]

As I remember it, it was an awkward but funny and pleasant meeting that lasted not more than a few minutes. We shook hands, laughed, and bid each other farewell. And Wole Soyinka, too, as noted by my father in the same article, has also been mistaken for Achebe. I, on the other hand, have been mistaken often enough to be Achebe's son to make me doubt my paternity.

My brother Tee also wrote a newspaper essay[20] as a tribute after Achebe's passing. In "Anthills of the Aberdares: How Achebe Lost His Lunch," Tee narrates how he, my father, and Achebe had driven to rural Kinagop in Kenya, and while there they decided to get some nyama choma (roast meat). Achebe was amused by how, far away from Nairobi and the university, "ordinary people in a hamlet deep in the interior of Kenya" recognized him as they shouted his name. But all does not go well:

> One middle-aged man, however, after greeting Achebe, made himself comfortable at the table, helping himself to copious amounts of meat from the large tin tray. "Your book, *The River Between*," he told Achebe with his mouth full, "is quite some story." He gathered meaty bones into his corner of the tray before raiding further afield for more succulent pieces.

Beyond the humorous nature of these encounters, they point to a larger Pan-African identity, one where a Zambian in a Kenyan airport is pleasantly shocked by running into Achebe—but not surprised enough to think it impossible.[21] Or, Achebe in a rural part of Kenya is still recognizable, or to use Gikandi's term "familiar." Yes, only a small educated number of people could truly access the politics, aesthetics, and philosophies in English. But even for those who could not, [22] it still mattered.

## LANGUAGE AND THE AFRICAN EXPERIENCE

On whether English could carry the African experience, these writers argued that it could in two ways—one was Africanizing English, and the other was doing violence to English. For Achebe, "The African writer should aim to use English in a way that brings out his message best without altering the language to the extent that its value as a medium of international exchange will be lost. He should aim at fashioning out an English which is at once universal and able to carry his peculiar experience" ("English and the African Writer," 29). In other words, English could be Africanized.

This was a position that Ama Ata Aidoo takes when in an interview she said of her English usage "I like the way I handle English. It has to do with my background. I haven't tried to speak the Queen's English. I've tried to always let the flavour of my African background come through in terms of the idioms and so on" (James, "Interview with Ama Ata Aidoo," 2). Ngugi does not miss the irony of Africanizing English—he notes that for him and his fellow writers at the Makerere Conference "the only question that preoccupied us was how best to make the borrowed tongues carry the weight of our African experience by, for instance, making them 'prey' on African proverbs and other peculiarities of African speech and folklore" (*Decolonising the Mind*, 7).

Achebe saw Tutuola as a practitioner of an English language forced to carry African experiences, but with the condescension that Tutuola was an unconscious writer. In order to draw a distinction between language handled by "a natural" and that of the conscious writer, Achebe offered an example from *Arrow of God* where one of the characters, the Chief Priest, is explaining to his son why it was necessary "to send him to church." The Chief Priest says:

> I want one of my sons to join these people and be my eyes there. If there is nothing in it you will come back. But if there is something there you will bring home my share. The world is like a mask, dancing. If you want to see it well you do not stand in one place. My spirit tells me that those who do not befriend the white man today will be saying *had we known* tomorrow. ("English and the African Writer," 29)

He then went on to render the passage in language that had not been used consciously—that is, he offered a free rendering of the passage without consciously trying to Africanize the English language:

> I am sending you as my representative among these people—just to be on the safe side in case the new religion develops. One has to move with the times or else one is left behind. I have a hunch that those who fail to come to terms with the white man may well regret their lack of foresight. (30)

The new rendering is notably dry. It lacks the heavy tone of the first and the proverb with the intriguing image of a *dancing mask*. The first passage to my ear makes the speakers sound old and archaic and I see an image of a wise old African man—akin to the noble wise Native American in Western movies. But, regardless, for Achebe it was possible to write well and Africanize English.[23]

The other alternative to Achebe's gentle Africanizing was what Zimbabwean writer Dambudzo Marechera saw as doing battle with English." On his language use, he said he never thought about writing in his Shona language because

> Shona was part of the ghetto daemon I was trying to escape. Shona had been placed within the context of a degraded, mind wrenching experience from which apparently the only escape was into the English language and education. The English language was automatically connected with the plush and seeming splendor of the white side of town. . . . I was therefore a keen accomplice and student in my own mental colonisation. For a black writer the language is very racist; you have to have harrowing fights and hair-raising panga duels with the language before you make it all that you want it to do. (*House of Hunger*, 7)

In a racially segregated and not yet independent Zimbabwe, his language had become a source of shame for him, a language he associated with poverty. And over the ghetto fence and in the rich white neighborhoods, English represented class and upward social mobility. The only way English could carry his Shona experiences was if he deracinated it first.[24]

## LANGUAGE AS CHOICE

The writers advancing the argument that language was a choice divorced culture from language, and saw language as a purely communicative tool. For

Ken Saro-Wiwa, English was "a worthy tool, much like the biro pen or the banking system or the computer, which were not invented by the Ogoni people but which I can master and use for my own purposes" (155–56). And as recently as May 2014 Soyinka offered a variation of the choice argument. When asked by the interviewer whether Ngugi's position on languages was vindicated, he answered, "I believe that each writer must decide in which language he or she is most comfortable; it applies not only to Africans—to former colonial societies, it applies even to writers who deliberately choose a foreign language in which to write—because that sense of distance exercises their imagination in a way that their own language should not."[25] Here, Soyinka was arguing that, along the lines of seeing one's home from a distance, a foreign language is like a fresh eye that lets people see things they would not have otherwise seen using their mother tongues. But he did not address what it means for the foreign language to keep growing at the expense of one's language.

Mphahlele for his part did not see the distancing that Soyinka later articulates. English could carry the African experience as authentically as an African language. In his response to Obi Wali, he wrote: "I believe a writer has a right to choose his medium, and it is hard on him to predict doom and a cul-de-sac for him when he has only just begun, relatively speaking. Why can he not be authentic, simply because he is using a foreign medium? He is bringing to the particular European language an African experience which in turn affects his style. There will naturally be conscious and unconscious imitation in the beginning, but if he is worth his salt, he will continue to clean up his style and eventually evolve something of his own" ("African Literature and the Universities," 338). It is not clear what he meant by imitation—did he mean imitation of European aesthetics? Or that using English automatically meant imitation of English writing? But regardless, for him writing in English would lead to authentic African literature.

But those advocating the free choice to use a European language did not address the question of whether writers had a duty to their mother tongues. Instead, choice made languages seem interchangeable and transactional and with no consequences for literary tradition. Obi Wali, in his rejoinder to his critics, also agreed that writers should express themselves with the language of their choice, but he also pointed that there were consequences:

> I completely agree that a writer is free to choose the linguistic medium for his works, and that nobody has the right to bully him out of this. But I insist that any African writer who chooses to write in a foreign language must face the implications of his choice, the most important being that his works belong to

the literary traditions of the language of his choice, for he cannot eat his cake and have it. ("A Reply to Critics," 47)

The implication for Ngugi in particular was that English could not carry African culture. For him "language carries culture, and culture carries, particularly through orature and literature, the entire body of values by which we come to perceive ourselves and our place in the world" (*Decolonising the Mind*, 16). Much like Samuel Johnson, who centuries earlier had tied the English language to culture, identity, nationhood—as the essence of Englishness—so would writers like Ngugi, Daniel Kunene, and Nadine Gordimer tie African languages to decolonization, African cultures, and longevity into the future.

## THE PRAGMATISM OF ENGLISH AS A HISTORICAL REALITY AND WORLD LANGUAGE

Another argument deployed against writing in African languages was the pragmatism of English as an existing reality. English was at the helm and there was no undoing history. Calling for a recognition of present-day history, Achebe wrote:

> I have indicated somewhat off-handedly that the national literature of Nigeria and of many other countries of Africa is, or will be, written in English. This may sound like a controversial statement, but it isn't. All I have done has been to look at the reality of present-day Africa. This "reality" may change as a result of deliberate, e.g. political, action. If it does an entirely new situation will arise, and there will be plenty of time to examine it. At present it may be more profitable to look at the scene as it is. ("English and the African Writer," 28)

For Achebe and the others it was easier to work with the existing reality than what ought to be. But they did not say the same thing about the existing political situation. They spent their lives fighting the successive neocolonial dictatorships; Achebe ended up in exile and Ken Saro-Wiwa was hanged for agitating for the rights of the Ogoni people. Why is it that when it came to the politics of language, pragmatism dictated working within the existing reality, while other political questions demanded action that would put their lives in danger?

For them this was not a contradiction. If English was the language that made Pan-African communication possible, it was because it was the language of struggle. And it also gave them access to the international community in ways that African languages could not. English was useful in the national, Pan-African, and international fronts. As Achebe put it, English was an international language, the best vehicle for "a new voice coming out of Africa, speaking of African experience in a world-wide language" (18).

For the writers using pragmatism and existing reality as arguments, either one wrote in English to reach other ethnicities, races, and nations, or in an African language and reached only members of that language group. There was no discussion of translation as a real possibility. Ken Saro-Wiwa, coming from a much smaller and marginalized ethnicity, argued, "Were I writing in Khana, I would be speaking to about 200,000 people, most of whom do not read and write. Writing in English as I do, I can reach, hypothetically speaking, 400 million" (155). The Danish population in 1965 would have been around 5 million; Swedish, 8 million, while the Igbo would have been around 8.5 million, and the Yoruba, 50 million. If a larger audience were the only reason to write in a language, it would have made more sense for Swedish and Danish writers to write only in English.

Translation was either not entertained or seen as impractical. Even when Ken Saro-Wiwa said he was writing a novel in Khana so that his mother, who was not literate in English, could read it, he did not consider that it might get translated into English. He saw it as remaining locked in the small Khana language. And he made it clear that the novel was an act of mercy, as opposed to taking a stand for African writing in African languages:

> Writing in English has not prevented me from writing in my mother tongue. I am, indeed, working on a Khana novel at the moment, but that is not because I want to prove a point. I am writing this novel so I can offer it to my seventy-year-old mother. She is always reading the Bible—the only book which exists in the Khana language—and I would like to give her some other literature to read. But I am also writing this novel because I can self-publish it. (156)

That Saro-Wiwa wrote his serious works in English for a wide audience, and a personal novel in Khana, shows that English was the language he wanted to work in. This was unlike Ngugi, who argued, as we shall see later, that "[a]n African writer should write in a language that will allow him to communicate effectively with peasants and workers in Africa—in other words, he should write in an African language."[26] Saro-Wiwa made it clear that he was not taking a political stand on language. He never saw Khana as a viable language, and he does not advance the idea that the Khana book could be translated into English. A discussion on translation, of how it could be done when you had people speaking different languages in the same room, or how creative one would have to be when translating between African languages, some mutually intelligible and others sharing the same noun class systems, was not considered. When translation was brought up it was to make a case for further writing in English, with the idea that the English work would then be translated back into African languages. Mphahlele, for example, wrote:

> Inasmuch as a book in an African language can be translated into English or French, there is no reason why Chinua Achebe's *Things Fall Apart* cannot be translated into Igbo or Yoruba or Hausa, or why Wole Soyinka's plays cannot be translated into any African language. There will thus be no reason why any language should wait for its own people to write originally in it in order to develop it as a literary medium. A writer must choose the medium that suits him best. ("African Literature and the Universities," 338)

He did not address the fundamental question of why write in a second acquired language first, and then translate back into one's language. Like Achebe, he took it for granted that English was the language of African literature and, in a moment of generosity, he conceded space for African languages sometime in the future.

For writers like Nadine Gordimer, it was important to first concede the principle that African literature should be in African languages in addition to European languages. For her the structural impediments to writing in African languages, barriers such as publishing and distribution, were very real. But they were not reason enough to argue that therefore African literature should be in English. In her forward-looking essay, "Turning the Page: African Writers on the Threshold of the Twenty-First Century," she categorically stated that "[w]e cannot speak of taking up the challenge of a new century for African literature unless we address the necessity to devise the means by which literature in African languages becomes the major component of the continent's literature. Without this one cannot speak of an African literature" (7). In other words, for her the idea of an African literature existing solely or mostly in European languages was not the way to grow an African literary tradition into the 21st century and beyond. It was an oxymoron—and the way to overcome it was to find ingenious ways to overcome the structural issues.

In the same essay she asked, "How shall we press for a new policy and structure of publishing and distribution, so that writers may write in African languages and bring pleasure and fulfillment to thousands who are cut off from literature by lack of knowledge of European languages? How shall we make the function of writers, whose essential gesture, the hand held out to contribute to development, is in the books they offer, something recognized and given its value by the governing powers of the twenty-first century?" The answer she gave was that "[w]e have to begin now to concern ourselves with the structures of society that contain culture, and within which it must assert its growth" (8). The problem was not in the principle of the centrality of African languages to African literature, but rather in the inability and unwillingness by the various actors in the production of culture to change the structures.

## ACHEBE AND TRANSLATION AS A POSSIBILITY

*Things Fall Apart* has been translated into over 50 languages, making it the most translated African novel. But as I said in my introduction, there is no authoritative Igbo translation. How is it that Africa's most celebrated novel has not yet been translated into the author's original language? Or why did Achebe not translate it himself? The answer is scattered in a number of interviews. In a 1991 interview with *Conjunction*, Bradford Morrow asked him whether the novel has been translated into Igbo. He answered "no" and then went on to say that it "shows, perhaps, that we are not ready for the novel in the Igbo language. I've written some poetry in Igbo and intend to do other things. But no matter what, I can assure you that the literature we have created during the last forty years in Africa had enormous influence which would have been much less if we had all retreated into our own little languages" (13). For him the absence is also the proof—because the novel has not been translated yet, it means that the language, or the Igbo people, are not equipped to handle the translation. And when he calls African languages little languages it is hard not to believe that he did place a higher premium on English than on African languages. There is irony in the fact that the AWS published African novels translated from French into English, with Achebe as the advisory editor.

In a 1994 *Paris Review* interview by Jerome Brooks, Achebe advanced another reason—that written Igbo had been standardized to create a language that could not "sing" and therefore "there's nothing you can do with it to make it sing. It's heavy. It's wooden. It doesn't go anywhere. We've had it now for almost a hundred years so it has established a kind of presence; it has created its own momentum among our own scholars" (255). He went to say that in his self-translation he would use his own dialect of Igbo. He extended the same argument in a 2008 *Economist* write-up celebrating 50 years of *Things Fall Apart*. He told the *Economist* that "his next project will be to translate 'Things Fall Apart' into his native Ibo [Igbo] for the first time" but "not the Union Ibo that was imposed on southern Nigeria in the early 1900s by British missionaries bent on religious conversion and the distribution of the Bible."

But even when Achebe acknowledged that translation was a possibility and something he himself wanted to do, he still believed that English was better suited for the novel, and Igbo for poetry. In the *Paris Review* interview quoted above he said, "When I write in the Igbo language, I write my own dialect. I write some poetry in that dialect. Maybe someday I will, myself, translate *Things Fall Apart* into the Igbo language. Just to show what I mean, though for me, being bilingual, the novel form seems to go with the English language. Poetry and drama seem to go with the Igbo language" (256). There is no reason to believe that English is better suited to the novel than Igbo, or Russian, or Chinese. One can argue whether the novel can carry African art forms such as orature, what the African literary scholar Linda Hunter calls verbal arts, because its stylistic devices such as repetition might not work in the novel. But there is no way to substantiate this claim that is first fueled by a belief that the novel is a higher form than poetry, and that English is a higher language than Igbo.

At the same time, Achebe saw himself as having transformed English in order for it to carry Igbo culture allowing "English and Igbo to hold a conversation, and see how you can tell a story that happened in Igbo in this dialect of English." In a 2008 interview Professor Joyce Ashuntantang asked Achebe about the translation of *Things Fall Apart* into Igbo:

> The book is almost like a mysterious presence. It is about taking the story back from English to the original language in which the events happened—because I had sort of taken the story from its roots and created a language, a dialect of English. This was my own invention. This I can now see, because I

kept worrying about what word would suit what; I kept worrying about how to translate a proverb so that its dignity would be maintained. . . . Now I want to go back and do it the other way and see what happens. Again, like before I have no idea whether it would work or not.[27]

For him, then, this would not have been a translation as we understand it, where it is a novel in a different language and carrying the world of a different culture being translated into another language and culture. It was going to be an experiment on how languages carry the same meaning differently. Yet translation of *Things Fall Apart*, and for African literature written in English, cannot be a simple act of restoration, of returning to the original, of recovery even. Whatever his ideological approach was going to be, faithful or imaginative, imitative or loose, the original English language would have already transformed the Igbo content.

## THE POST-MAKERERE GENERATION OF AFRICAN WRITERS AND THE LANGUAGE QUESTION

In her introduction to *A New Generation of African Writers: Migration, Material Culture and Language*, Brenda Cooper captured some of the difficulties of using an English language formerly deployed as a colonial cultural tool. For her, English is "steeped in imperialist and patriarchal tropes and symbols" and therefore the younger generation of writers "are challenged to find an English into which to translate their more than one culture, language and knowledge base without being sucked into some of those older tropes and imperial metaphors" (1). But it's not just language, and the historical baggage it carries, that African writers writing in English have to contend with; there is the question of the disjuncture between the language of the literature and literary tradition. For Cooper, when V. S. Naipaul said that the "the English language was mine; the tradition was not" what tradition meant here was "the deep meanings of metaphors and associations that the dominant culture shares with the insiders" (4). Can English, given the short time it has been in Africa, be said to be so well entrenched as to carry the deeper meanings of metaphors and associations found in Igbo or Yoruba culture? After all, Yoruba culture and Yoruba language have been in tandem for hundreds of years.

For the early South African writers, not yet having suffered the alienation from their languages that came with colonial education, writing in African languages and then getting translated into English was the norm. For the Makerere writers, the consensus was writing in English, with the question of African languages arising later to disturb their politics and imaginations. And looking at it from the vantage point of today, we can trace the threads into fully formed arguments.

Discussions around the language question for the post-Makerere writers can largely be seen in the anecdotal forms of tweets and Facebook posts—we do not as yet have the sustained analysis from the post-Makerere generation of the language question that one finds in the early *Transition* issues. There are, however, three broad views that one can discern—those advocating writing in English who have followed the Achebe idea of Africanizing English, those who actively oppose writing in African languages, and those who want to see the democratization of languages so that African languages can thrive alongside English.

## POST-MAKERERE WRITERS: ENGLISH AS THE PRIMARY LANGUAGE OF AFRICAN LITERATURE

The Makerere writers understood themselves as African writers using a colonial language to support decolonization and the African literary tradition, but they had a good command of their mother tongues. But, whereas the Makerere writers grew up speaking their mother tongues, for some of the post-Makerere writers, English is the only language they negotiate life in. They are African writers who grew up in Africa but cannot intellectually express themselves in an African language, even if they wanted to. For some, their parents actively encouraged them to speak English at home. But even those who have grown up speaking an African language, sometimes fluently, cannot write in it because the education system in former British colonies continues colonial language policies. The same attitudes that consider African languages as vulgar and incapable of carrying serious literature, science, and philosophy still inform education policies today. Only this time around, it is with the blessing of societies that have themselves internalized African language inferiority. Nigerian writer Chimamanda Adichie explained this in a 2008 interview with Ada Azado, when asked what her views were on writing in African languages:

I'm not sure my writing in English is a choice. If a Nigerian Igbo like myself is educated exclusively in English, discouraged from speaking Igbo in a school in which Igbo was just one more subject of study (and one that was considered "uncool" by students and did not receive much support from the administration), then perhaps writing in English is not a choice, because the idea of choice assumes other equal alternatives. . . . Although I took Igbo until the end of secondary school and did quite well, it was not at all the norm. Most of all, it was not enough. I write Igbo fairly well but a lot of my intellectual thinking cannot be expressed sufficiently in Igbo. Of course this would be different if I had been educated in both English and Igbo. Or if my learning of Igbo had an approach that was more wholistic.

Colonial education had divorced African languages from any intellectual work. For Adichie, English is reserved for serious issues and African languages for nonintellectual issues. She also brought up the question of audience and literature in Igbo:

The interesting thing, of course, is that if I did write in Igbo (which I sometimes think of doing, but only for impractical, emotional reasons), many Igbo people would not be able to read it. Many educated Igbo people I know can barely read Igbo and they mostly write it atrociously.

In other words, if you have a whole generation brought up with English as the language of intellect, can they read novels in African languages?[28] But if the literature existed in Igbo, speakers of Igbo would find innovative ways to access it. For example, when Ngugi's *Devil on the Cross* was published in Gikuyu (*Caitani Mutharabaini*), the literate would read to the illiterate. Currey in *Africa Writes Back* recalled how Ngugi "excitedly" told him and publisher Henry Chakava about how "new entertainment had entered bar life" where "[a] man literate in Gikuyu would read Ngugi's novel aloud to drinkers until his voice and glass run dry [and then] lay the novel page downwards on the bar until another drink was brought to him" (135). But, in any case, if churchgoing Africans are literate enough to read the translated Bible in their own languages, they are literate enough to read a novel. This is why the ostracized early South African writing needs to be restored to the African literary tradition: it gives a ready road map outside of the English-only consensus, out of the English metaphysical empire.

In an illustration of how knowledge can be transmitted from generation to generation, Chimamanda Adichie also echoed the negritude mantra of "Emotion is African, as Reason is Hellenic."[29] In this instance, emotion is to be expressed in African languages, and reason in European languages. In the speech that Adichie gave "at the ceremony to mark [the Nigerian state of] Anambra's Governor Willie Obiano's 100 days in office" in 2014, she was more explicit in connecting English to reason/literature and African languages to a traditional poetic past:

> I deeply love both English and Igbo. English is the language of literature for me. But Igbo has a greater emotional weight. It is the enduring link to my past. It is the language in which my great grandmothers sang. Sometimes, when I listen to old people speaking in my hometown Abba, I am full of admiration for the complexity and the effortlessness of their speech. And I am in awe of the culture that produced this poetry, for that is what the Igbo language is when spoken well—it is poetry.[30]

One cannot help but hear Samuel Johnson cheering the growth of the English metaphysical empire, declaring that indeed his labor has not been in vain. He would be uncomfortable with the idea of English being Africanized, or, in his view, vulgarized, but he would take comfort in the idea that the "Nigerian experience" places Standard English at the top of the language hierarchy. Johnson argued in his preface that even though meeting other languages would vulgarize the English through "mingled dialect, like the jargon which serves the traffickers on the *Mediterranean* and *Indian* coasts" it would in the end be "incorporated with the current speech" (15). Thus, for him, Adichie can "take ownership of English" as long as Standardized English is the starting point. It is almost as if the post-Makerere generations of African writers who advocate for writing in English are victims of a historical drama not of their own making.

To be fair, Adichie in the Azodo interview did call for African children to be taught African languages by their parents, before adding that, underlying the choice of English over Igbo, there "are deeper questions of self-esteem and fundamental pride in who we are" (3). And in her 2014 speech she does tie the loss of language to identity as well as to English only speaking children being locked out of their past and history. But for her English is the language of literature while African languages are useful to the extent they connect Africans to their history. Achebe ended his 1967 essay on English and the African writer by claiming that he had "no choice" and that he had been given the language and he intended to use it. Thinking through the language question 40 years later, Adichie went farther than Achebe to say that English had been domesticated enough to be her language, as a Nigerian living in Nigeria.

Where Achebe spoke of the dread that comes with betraying one's mother tongue before stating that he has been given the language and intends to use it, post-Makerere writers like Adichie have embraced English as their own. Achebe was Africanizing a foreign, colonial English—Adichie Africanizes English because she believes the language is hers. In the interview, she offered:

> I'd like to say something about English as well, which is simply that English is mine. Sometimes we talk about English in Africa as if Africans have no agency, as if there is not a distinct form of English spoken in Anglophone African countries. I was educated in it; I spoke it at the same time as I spoke Igbo. My English-speaking is rooted in a Nigerian experience and not in a British or American or Australian one. I have taken ownership of English.

The Makerere generation was taught Standard English and the aesthetic standards were British. For the post-Makerere writers, while the education system is in Standard English, the aesthetic standards are not British—they have access to literatures from all over the world.

At the opposite extreme of Adichie's pro-English but historically nuanced view of African languages, you have Adaobi Tricia Nwaubani, the author of the novel *I Do Not Come to You by Chance*. In a 2010 *New York Times* essay she actively argued against African literature written in African languages. "In Africa, the Laureate's Curse"[31] ostensibly called for new writing away from the Makerere canon, but she also argued that because Ngugi wrote in an African language, he should not be awarded the Nobel Prize for literature:

> I shudder to imagine how many African writers would be inspired by the prize to copy him. Instead of acclaimed Nigerian writers, we would have acclaimed Igbo, Yoruba and Hausa writers. We suffer enough from tribal differences already. This is not the kind of variety we need.

For her, writing in one's language exacerbates ethnic differences. Not even Achebe, who saw African literature in African languages as contributing to lesser ethnic literatures and writing in English as contributing to the higher cause of national writing, went as far as blaming African languages for civil strife.

## IF THE WRITERS WILL NOT, THEIR CHARACTERS WILL:
## THE LANGUAGE QUESTION WITHIN THE NOVEL

African writers writing in English inevitably deal with the language question intrinsically, within their novels. We see it playing out in how their characters and narrators respond to English versus their mother tongues. For example, in Achebe's *No Longer at Ease*, Obi suffers from all sorts of language anxieties while in England. The narrator, presumably speaking in Ibo, tells us that Obi

> spoke Ibo whenever he had the least opportunity of doing so.... It was humil-
> iating to have to speak to one's countryman in a foreign language, especially
> in the presence of the proud owners of that language. They would naturally
> assume that one had no language of one's own. He wished they were here to-
> day to see. Let them come to Umuofia now and listen to the talk of men who
> made a great art of conversation. Let them come and see men and women and
> children who knew how to live, whose joy of life had not yet been killed by
> those who claimed to teach other nations how to live. (57)

When he returned to Nigeria, his friends and relatives were annoyed that he did not display his close contact with the British through nasalized English (or in his dietary habits). They are disappointed that he returns as an Igbo, one who has been colonized like everyone else, but with nothing to show for his having lived in England.[32]

It is worth noting here that while women writers from the Makerere generation did not generate polemics on the language question to the same extent as their male counterparts, the question of language was discussed within their writing. The language question was an intrinsic and organic part of their characters navigating a decolonizing Africa. In so many ways, Ama Ata Aidoo's *Sister Killjoy* is a meditation on language—Sissie is very conscious of the place she occupies in the English language, one of ambivalence, and the place the English language occupies in her intellect and imagination. In her love letter to "My Precious Something" Sissie points out that "first of all there is this language. This language" that has enslaved her and shackled the messengers of her mind (112). For Sissie, while she can intellectually understand that language communicates and therefore English can get the job done, and love does not need a specific language because it is "beyond Akan or Ewe, English or French," the problem is how to carry life into the future, that is, to go beyond feeling and capture experiences that language presumably carries.

She says, "Time by itself means nothing, no matter how fast it moves. Unless we give it something to carry for us, something we value. Because it is such a precious vehicle, is time" (113). In other words, if a foreign language shackles her messengers, what of her will be carried into the future? To my mind this a literary animation of Ngugi's concept, in *Decolonising the Mind*, of language as "a carrier of culture" (15). If time needs something to carry into the future, if Sissie and her experiences are to live into the future, can it be in a foreign language? And, if it is, will it not always be shackled?

It is impossible to read *Nervous Conditions*, by Zimbabwean author Tsitsi Dangarembga, without being aware that the language question is at the center of how the characters relate. Whenever a conversation is in Shona or English, Dangarembga reminds us. The two languages become a veil through which Nyasha and Tambu attempt to communicate. As Tambu tells the reader, their conversations were "labored and clumsy because when Nyasha spoke seriously her thoughts came in English, whereas with me, the little English I had disappeared when I dropped my vigilance to speak of things that mattered (77). Or how strange it is for her that missionaries learn and value Shona when it is the English language that she herself craves:

> What I noticed, very early on, was that some of the missionaries were definitely strange, strange in the way Nyasha and Chido were strange when they came back from England. These missionaries, the strange ones, liked to speak Shona much more than they liked to speak English. And when you, wanting to practise your English, spoke to them in English they always answered in Shona. (104)

Like in Makerere writing, the characters in post-Makerere literature are almost obsessively aware of language as a marker of class in economic and social terms, class as in sophisticated and poised.

In Adichie's *Half of a Yellow Sun*, Ugwu is a peasant houseboy through whom we partially witness the disintegration of Nigeria into an ethnic nationalist war. Through him, we also see the psychology of English, its pull and attraction, at the same time that we see Ugwu as a victim of colonial education, which created a small educated elite and left the others to be functionaries in the colonial and now decolonizing Nigeria. When he gets to his "master's" house where he will be working, the first words he hears, "*Yes? Come in*" (4), are in English, a language that inspires admiration, asserts class difference, and keeps him from understanding the political discussions as the novel progresses. The narrator is very conscious of Prof. Odenigbo's English and Igbo and how they interact and interfere with each other—as markers of class and refinement. For example, on being first introduced to Ugwu, the master responds, "Oh, yes, you have brought the houseboy. *I kpotago ya.*" And the narrator observes, "Master's Igbo felt feathery in Ugwu's ears. It was Igbo colored by sliding sounds of English, the Igbo of one who spoke English often" (6).

Or conversely, when Odenigbo is speaking in Igbo and uses an English word, perhaps to show the level of diglossia where the educated unconsciously reach for whatever word comes most easily to them, the narrator makes remarks like "he said thirteen in English" (6) or "he said my good man in English" (8). Language becomes a source of anxiety for Ugwu and he begins to wonder whether "Master would send him back because he did not speak English well" (12).

In *Things Fall Apart*, the mastery of Igbo oral art is something to be showcased, the palm oil for eating words (Okafor, 24), as Achebe famously put it. But in Ugwu's eyes, it is English mastery that paints the Nigerian elite with a veneer of sophistication and intellectual nimbleness. On Ugwu first hearing the western-educated Olanna (wife to Odenigbo) speak English, the narrator takes us through the different kinds of English the Nigerian elite employ:

> He had always thought Master's English could not be compared to anybody's, not Professor Ezaka, whose English one could hardly hear, or Okeoma, who spoke English as if he were speaking Igbo, with the same cadences and pauses, or Patel whose English was a faded lilt. Not even the white man Professor Lehman, with his words forced out of his nose, sounded as dignified as Master. Master's English was music, but what Ugwu was hearing now, from this woman, was magic. Here was a superior tongue, a luminous tongue, the kind of English he heard on Master's radio, rolling out with clipped precision. (28–29)

Indeed, while some social conversations are held in Igbo, the intellectual conversations for the decolonizing Africans are in English. And Igbo is the language, not necessarily of a dynamic culture, but of tradition, a way of reconnecting to the past. The narrator tells us that "whenever Ugwu brought out the Kola nut, Master would say, 'Doc, you know the kola nut does not understand English' before going on to bless the kola nut in Igbo" (22). In *Half of a Yellow Sun*, from the beginning to the end, where Olanna gives us the last spoken sentence, "*Uwa m, uwa ozo*. When I come back in my next life, Kanene will be my sister," (541), the language question is always present.

Obi, in Achebe's novel *No Longer at Ease*, finds it "humiliating to have to speak to one's countryman in a foreign language, especially in the presence of the proud owners of that language" (57). But he can find comfort in that he will be going back to Nigeria where he can take for granted—and it is taken for granted—that he has a culture and a language. In fact, when he returns from Britain, his peers who remained at home and his elderly supporters are disappointed that he speaks to them in Igbo instead of the Queen's English. In Bulawayo's *We Need New Names*, the been-to (someone who has been or lived in a foreign country) is now an illegal immigrant, an undocumented worker, and an alien in the United States. And language takes on a new meaning, or rather adds another layer to the anxieties experienced by the characters in novels of the Makerere generation. The humiliation does not come from a fear of being seen as language-less and by extension nation-less. It comes from an acute awareness of one's accent as a basis of being misunderstood, and being judged, as a confirmation of the African stereotypes embedded in white America's view of Africa.

In a tragi-comedic scene that most African immigrants in the United States can relate to, Darling's aunt, Fostalina, wants to order a bra from the "Angel Collection." The white American saleswoman cannot understand her and the scene captures her escalating anger and shame as she tries different pronunciations and emphasis, and eventually she has to spell it out:

> It's A, Aunt Fostalina says. Her voice is a bit calmer. She has written the letter to the magazine to be sure.
>
> Okay, A as in *apple*—
>
> Not apple. A as in Anus, it's a different sound. N as in no. G as in God. E as in eat. L as in Libya. There you go, angel. Angel. Angel.

Finally, she manages to order and Darling tells us that after the call she has to tell the story,

> to someone who knows what you mean, who will understand exactly what you say, and that it is not your fault but the other person's, someone who knows that English is like a huge iron door and you are always losing the keys. (199)

And Darling observes that her aunt has "this look," that she doesn't know "whether to call it pain or anger, or sadness, or whether it has a name" (199). It's a look that, were she older, Darling might recognize as shame and a feeling of inadequacy if not outright racial inferiority.

This is my generation after all those years of practicing to say, "The red lorry went round the red bend," and finally finding out that it did not matter. We are accented where it matters most. Why the pain or anger? Or, to put it differently, why does it matter to Fostalina that her English is not immediately understood? After all, it is not her mother tongue. Richard the Englishman in *Half of a Yellow Sun*, who speaks fluent Igbo with an English accent in the same way Fostalina speaks English with an Ndebele or Shona accent, does not betray such anguished anxiety.

Zimbabwean novelist Petina Gappah's *Book of Memory* (2016) takes the language question within the text even further. In most Anglophone African novels, words in African languages are explained within the text or footnotes. But in the *Book of Memory*, words, colloquialisms, songs, sentences, and conversations in Shona are left unexplained. Ikhide Ikheola notes in his review that

> [t]his would not be a problem if one could easily Google them and get translations. Google does explain terms like Voetsek to the world, and Zimbabwe's history becomes accessible. . . . The reader however soon tires and curiosity grows into frustration as Shona songs and terms are too obscure for Google to translate or explain. In the confrontation between Shona and the English language, Shona loses.[33]

It is only frustrating if one expects to understand every single word, reference, historical allusion, and so on in a novel—a high claim even for a novel in a single language. Gappah's language use is better understood if one takes Édouard Glissant's "right to opacity" and extends it to languages. For Glissant, opacity is not just the opposite of transparency, or just the "right to difference" (190), it is a "focus on the texture of the weave and not on the nature of the weave and not on the nature of its components" and a letting go of an "old obsession with discovering what lies at the bottom of natures" (190). A better question is not whether the reader is locked out of the meaning of every single word, but whether the languages coming into conversation weave a texture that is aesthetically pleasing. For example, Memory, the main character, tells us about an inmate who, after having convinced the Zimbabwean government cabinet that she "could make diesel come out of a rock," gets richly rewarded, only to be thrown in jail after it is discovered she was tapping into a "tanker of diesel" behind the rock. During lunch Memory tell us:

> She belched and said, "Mudzimu wangu unoti ndinonada nyama."
> Synodia said, "You can tell the spirit that is in the wrong place. There is no meat for it here."
> She belched again and broke in to song, "Black September, wairamba kubire Charter Mukoma, wakatozibira watombodzu-nduza musuro Mukoma."[34] (205)

We get to know she is asking for meat from Synodia's reply to her. But we do not get to know the song, though we can tell it is a song about wanting. Black September tells us that there is a reference to Zimbabwe's political struggle in the song, or something disastrous. But the texture of the weave brings to us a woman we cannot reach in her madness, for whom meat, diesel, Black September all roll into one—our inability to enter her language contributes to our understanding her as a mad, lying truth speaker. Shona readers might get the full meaning of the passage, but I would argue that it does not make the aesthetic experience any lesser for non-Shona speakers.

More directly, Memory also gives us full treatises on the language question. On her relationship to Shona and why she writes her prison memoir in English, she explains:

> My spoken Shona is still fluent, but my writing is frozen at the age of eight, which is when I last wrote it in school. This is one of the consequences of a superior education, you see. In this independence hundred-percent empowered and fully and totally indigenous blacker-than-black country, a superior education is one that whites would value, and as the whites do not value local languages, the best educated amongst us have sacrificed our languages at the altar of what the whites deem supreme. So it was in colonial times, and so it remains, more than thirty years later. (52)

This goes back to Chimamanda Adichie's, Binyavanga Wainaina's, Chika Unigwe's, and my relationship to our mother tongues discussed earlier. English is the language of upward social mobility, of prestige, the marker of class. On prestige, Henry Blumenthal and Renée Kahane write:

> H(igh) and L(ow) is the linguistic representation of a class system. H, the prestige language, is used by, and therefore becomes of, a sector of society

which excels through power, education, manners, and/or heritage. L, the everyday idiom, is the language of the others, and is often used by H speakers in their non-H roles. . . . Socio-linguistically, H is always close to a foreign language since it functions as barrier between H and L speakers. (183)

Indeed, throughout the *Book of Memory*, *We Need New Names*, and *Half of a Yellow Sun*, African languages are not invoked to discuss philosophy or the stuff of high culture; they are used to express idioms, proverbs, folktales, and songs. There is also irony in who values and learns African languages. Memory also lets us know that Lloyd, the wealthy white man who adopts her, feels invested in Shona, writes fluently in it, and is involved in translating Homer to Shona.[35] This recalls Richard, the Englishman in *Half of a Yellow Sun*, who writes and speaks Igbo fluently. Since most African language study programs are in the West, with a heavy concentration in the United States, these characters are in a way fictionalizing the question of who studies, values, and benefits from African languages.

Sometimes the characters whose words are written in English are speaking English, while the writers employ italics, or spell out the meaning of a word spoken in an African language, or outright tell us what language a character is speaking. The narrator is conscious of what language is being spoken.

Binyavanga Wainaina, in his memoir *One Day I Will Write about This Place*, or in his short fiction, leaves us with no doubt that he is writing in English. Or for that matter, in both *Nairobi Heat* and *Black Star Nairobi*, perhaps to evade the language question, my narrator is an African American who then narrates in first person in English. Even then, I was conscious of the language question and Ishmael, the African American detective, is very much aware that he is being locked out of many things Kenyan by not speaking Kiswahili and he keeps vowing to learn.

## THE OTHER POST-MAKERERE WRITERS: WORKING ACROSS MANY LANGUAGES

In contrast to the post-Makerere writers who see themselves as primarily writing in English, differentiated by the degree to which the language question and African languages is present in their writing, there is a third group that actively seeks to create a democratic space for African languages. *Jalada Africa*, an online journal, best exemplifies the meeting between African literature, languages, and the Internet age. The Jalada Collective that produces the journal is composed of young writers: Managing Editor Moses Kilolo, Deputy Editor Novuyo Tshuma, Treasurer Ndinda Kioko, and other writer administrators are in their 20s and early 30s. Writer members of the collective include the 2013 Caine Prize winner Okwiri Odour; a brilliant young writer, Mehul Gohil, featured in the anthology *Africa 39*; and the poet Clifton Gachugua, whose first collection of poetry, *The Madman at Kilifi*, won the Sillerman First Book Prize for African Poets and was published by the University of Nebraska Press in 2014.

They are the generation that has grown up taking the Internet, e-mail, and social media for granted. In fact, *Jalada* has a social media manager. And whereas my generation inherited the language anxieties of the Makerere generation, their existing work points to a generation that is more confident, unencumbered by colonial and neocolonial aesthetics. The Makerere generation was composed of writers in their 20s and 30s who understood themselves as having a mission to contribute to decolonization; this generation sees itself as having the mission to create democratic spaces for African literature, languages, and, through Internet use, a Pan-African readership.

The 2015 *Jalada* language issue, which also carried podcast interviews with some of the contributing authors, aimed to create a meeting ground where languages would meet as material entities through the literature—side by side—and also engage each other through translation. In their call for papers they announced that

> [t]he anthology will be a celebration of language, featuring fiction, poetry, visual art and various essays on the very subject of language. Writers are asked to submit original works written in their own languages and provide an accompanying English translation. We also ask writers to feel free to treat language as a theme, where language can be a character, a topic in a story or even incorporate languages other than English as the theme in the story. Writers may also write in English or various Englishes.[36]

While in the end most of the writing featured was originally in English, there were conversations across various language borders—Lusophone, Francophone, English, and African languages. Translation is the very foundation of their approach, so that literatures from different languages can be in conversation. That is, they are normalizing African languages so that translation becomes a means for different African languages to be in conversation. In the spring of 2016, a short story originally written for *Jalada* by Ngugi wa Thiong'o was translated into over 70 different languages, 45 of them African. This came with practical challenges. Moses Kilolo, in personal correspondence, noted they had very few professional translators and had to work with a team of "younger writers who are not very experienced in translation [but] are taking up the challenge as well, and consulting widely in order to learn and do it well." And in terms of setting up structures, they are "encouraging other continent-based magazines to join [them] in providing such platforms to these writers."

To call for translation as an active agent in the growth of literary traditions also sends out a challenge to writers, scholars, and publishers who see African languages as being in the service of the more-useful English. Or, conversely, it challenges those who understand translation as most desirable when coming from European languages into anemic African languages desperately in need of a Euro linguistic and aesthetics transfusion. The *Jalada* collective then is challenging the idea of servicing English, and proving the feasibility of a democratization of linguistic and literary spaces. Translation among African languages, as opposed to English to African languages, has yet to be practiced and theorized into critical and popular acceptance. For *Jalada* to make Ngugi's *Ituĩka Rĩa Mũrũngarũ: Kana Kĩrĩa Gĩtũmaga Andũ Mathiĩ Marũngiĩ* ("The Upright Revolution: Or Why Humans Walk Upright") the most translated African language story is to claim a piece of literary history yet to be written.

More ambitiously, in 2016 *Jalada* conducted a *Jalada* Mobile Literary Festival, across five Eastern Africa countries. Kilolo, in an online interview with Praxis magazine, saw the festival as having "interrogated the place of African languages and translation in the 21st century, celebrated cultural diversity through multilingual performances and exhibitions, and revitalized cross-cultural interchanges between Africa and the world through writing, translations, and publishing in digital spaces" (Jalada Mobile Festival: Q&A with Moses Kilolo). For the Jalada collective the production of African literature means having African languages and writers in conversation. English still has a role to play, but the end goal is not to have cultural production be in English; rather it is to have African languages and writers be in conversation through translation.

However, the African language awakening among the post post-Makerere writers still has a long way to go before it can claim a space of coexistence with African writing in European languages. When setting up the Mabati-Cornell Kiswahili Prize for African Literature, Professor Lizzy Attree and I were immediately confronted by the absence of structures that are simply taken for granted when it comes to English writing, not just in Africa but worldwide. Most if not all colleges in the United States, for example, have a literary journal for undergraduate and graduate students. English and other literary departments have well-respected literary journals (not to speak of university presses). States and cities have their own regional prizes and often have state-sponsored cultural organizations that support writers. Writer residencies compete for prestige.

In *Decolonising the Mind*, Ngugi does not take into account just how absent these structures are. He does argue that the future of the African novel is

> dependent on a willing writer (ready to invest time and talent in African languages); a willing translator (ready to invest time and talent in the art of transition from one language into another); a willing publisher (ready to invest time and money) or a progressive state which would overhaul the current neo-colonial linguistic policies and tackle the national question in a democratic a manner; and finally, and most important, a willing and widening readership. (85)

But for him "it is only the writer who is best to break the vicious circle and create fiction in African languages" (85). Certainly, without writers there is no fiction. Yet he romanticizes the writers while underestimating the magnitude of the task ahead of them—that unlike the writer writing in English, who will find national and international publishers, mentors, reviewers, and critics, the path for the African languages writer is very lonely. For Kenyan writer David Maillu, only the already established writer as opposed to upcoming and young writers can pave the way for writing African languages:

> I am just thinking about the question of the local languages, and the relationship between the local languages, and the publisher, because although the writer can do whatever it is within his ability to promote this language or the other there is a second very powerful person, and that is the publisher. . . . Most of the books that I have read in Africa are published by British publishers and they do not want to hear anything about local languages. Therefore, it is very difficult for new writers to get published if they write in local languages. So I see the established writer as a very important tool in the promotion of these languages. (Petersen, *Criticism and Ideology*, 53)

But we still run into the same problems—how many established writers, say, in Kenya, that is, writers with enough national recognition as to set an example younger writers, are willing to follow? And how many of them are willing to commit to writing in African languages? For Kiswahili, with over 100 million speakers, there are only a handful of literary journals. And there are not more than five literary prizes for Kiswahili. For Gikuyu, my mother tongue, spoken by close to 7 million people, I can name only one journal, *Mutiiri*, launched by Ngugi in 2000 as a print journal, and now found online.[37] There are no literary prizes associated with Gikuyu. Publishers of literary texts in African languages outside of South Africa are few and far between. I do not know of a single journal that produces literary criticism in an African language, or any writer residencies that encourage writing in African languages. The point is, given a continent whose population exceeds 1 billion people spread out in 55 countries, even a hundred journals and literary prizes would still be pitifully inadequate. Without literary structures in African languages, there will be very few writers who are willing and able to write in African languages.

It cannot just be writers. There have to be literary critics setting up literary journals and schools of criticism, and educators and governments changing policy toward the teaching of African languages and creating economic opportunities in those languages—whether it's agricultural extension officers trained in the languages for the communities they serve, teachers trained in teaching African languages, or interpreters for national and international organizations, and so on. African languages have to move from being primarily social languages to vehicles of political and economic growth.

Whether consciously, through the language democratization work of *Jalada* and Cassava Press, or intrinsically, in text invocations, questions around the languages of African literature have been inherited by the post-Makerere writers from the Makerere writers. And if each generation of writers works from within their times, from a broad consensus within which arguments and debates are held, then for the post-Makerere writers the broad but contested consensus is that the language question is not going anywhere. No matter where one stands on the long spectrum of the language question, it cannot simply be ignored.

## CHAPTER 2

# Amos Tutuola

## Creating the African Literary Bogeyman

I am rather apprehensive of Mr. Tutuola's turning out a Problem Child. He promises a sequel. . . . I fear [however] that the public appetite for this line of fiction may be satisfied with one book.
　　—T. S. Eliot, cited in Bernth Lindfors, *The Blind Men and the Elephant*

We do, of course realize that it is not quite as good as it ought to be, but it is the unsophisticated product of a West African mind and we felt there was nothing to be done about it except to leave it alone.
　　—Peter du Sautoy, cited in Bernth Lindfors, *Early West African Writers*

Amos Tutuola, through his biography and his writing, illustrates how questions of African aesthetics were immediately caught up in the politics of material and cultural decolonization; but all within the web of the English metaphysical empire. Due to lack of school fees, he had managed only a Standard Six colonial education. Any randomly picked sentence in his most famous work, the *Palm Wine Drinkard* (*PWD*), published by the London-based Faber & Faber in 1954, reveals a poor command of English. The first sentence in the opening chapter, titled "The Meaning of 'Good' and 'Bad,'" reads, "I was seven years old before I understood the meaning of "bad" and "good," because it was at that time I noticed carefully that my father married three wives as they were doing in those days, it was not common nowadays" (17). It is not clear to me why bad and good are in quotation marks. And the chapter title and the construction of the sentence establish an infantile voice, even though we get to know that the narrator is an adult. The idea of three wives is both mitigated and judged by "it is not common nowadays," and the reader cannot be sure whether the ambiguity was deliberate or not. As a result of content always recalling language use, his usage of English became the lens through which his works were received.

Indeed, to draw out the issue of English as the language of African literature, Obi Wali built his essay, "The Dead End of African Literature," around the question of why Amos Tutuola was excluded from the Makerere Conference. After all, Tutuola had published *The Palm Wine Drinkard* to critical, albeit debatable, acclaim in 1952, six years before the publication of *Things Fall Apart*. Indeed, by the time *Things Fall Apart* was being published, Tutuola had written *My Life in the Bush of Ghosts* (1954) and *Simbi and the Satyr of the Dark Jungle* (1955). For Wali, Tutuola's exclusion was "partly[1] because he has gone out of line, winning acclaim overseas for using a kind of English expression that is non-Ibadan and non-Makerere" (330). That is to say, he was excluded for his use of uneducated, broken, non-university English, "vulgar" English.

Western literary critics mostly saw Tutuola's novels as authentic representations of African culture, but did so often in condescending and sometimes in racist terms. Cecil T. Lewis in his review of *Life in the Bush of Ghosts* told his readers:

> Take a modern Nigerian. Give him six years of formal education. Let him with rampant and febrile imagination enclose within a rudimentary fictional framework his tribal lore—a lore in which mythology and reality are often indistinguishable for those whose culture itself is a mélange. Result: a coupling of the predominantly primitive with outcroppings of sophistication in a book to delight the ethnologist, the psychologist, the theologist, the linguist. (116)

Lewis here went beyond paternalism—"rampant" and "febrile" made Tutuola out as a writer out of control and in a feverish state, one who cannot distinguish the real and imaginary, who cannot distance himself from his subject, and in the end only succeeds in writing a novel that captures his primitive state. Taken to its logical conclusion, a perverse delight for students of human nature and language was going to be derived from witnessing Tutuola's attempts at sophistication while learning about his primitive music, language, and religion. Lewis recommended the novel for all the wrong reasons. For Lewis, Tutuola's usage of English, what the poet Dylan Thomas in a positive but condescending review called "young English," authenticated the African content that Thomas had also termed as "bizarre."[2]

Africans going through decolonization felt that how white Westerners perceived them and Africa also informed how *PWD* was received. Where Western critics welcomed Tutuola as a major voice in African literature, albeit paternalistically, African critics were less enthusiastic and sometimes outright hostile. One has to employ emotive words such as anger and shame to describe Tutuola's reception by African critics. Charles Larson, in *The Ordeal of the African Writer*, concluded that "[r]eviewers were largely divided into two factions: English and American critics were captivated, enthralled by Tutuola's exotic story as well as his style; African critics, however were made uncomfortable by a fear that westerners would regard Tutuola as a 'typical educated African'" (3).

Right from the very beginning Faber & Faber wanted to authenticate Amos Tutuola's *The Palm Wine Drinkard* as the genuine product of an African. Once Faber & Faber established that *PWD* was the work of an African, this authenticity would be maintained by retaining and highlighting Tutuola's poor Standard Six English usage. In an attempt to make sure that the book was genuinely "African," Geoffrey Faber wrote to Daryll Forde, an Africanist anthropologist at University College, London, and said, "We have had submitted to us a highly unusual MS. about which we are anxious to get a line from an anthropologist familiar with the workings of the West African imagination. . . . we should like to know whether it has its roots in the common West African mind."[3] For Gail Low, in "The Natural Artist: Publishing Amos Tutuola's *The Palm-Wine Drinkard* in Postwar Britain," Faber's letter "represented the manuscript's anthropological value in no uncertain terms [and] portrayed *The Palm-Wine Drinkard* as offering metropolitan readers extraordinary insights to the West African mind" (22). That is, Faber wanted it certified that not only did a West African write *PWD*, but that it was also representative of the culture and psychology of the African—as perceived by the Westerner. Low concludes that "Faber saw their publishing investment as essentially of anthropological value" (22). Along the same lines, in a letter to Jocelyn Oliver,[4] Ann Faber wrote in part, "We have talked back and forwards about this story and have taken the trouble to discover whether it is likely to be genuine. We think it is and we are keen to take a chance on it."[5] *PWD* was genuine to the extent it is an artifact from African anthropology.[6] Faber & Faber were approaching questions of authenticity using a paternalistic, if not racist, lens. They had an idea of what African culture was like—alien, terrifying, and superstitious—and they wanted *PWD* to confirm that. *PWD* was, right from the beginning, not taken as a piece of fiction but rather as a cultural artifact clothed in the literary form of the novel.

## GRAMMAR AND AUTHENTICITY

If establishing *PWD*'s content as authentically West African was critical, so was preserving Tutuola's poor grammar. In the letter to Tutuola in which Faber & Faber told him of their decision to publish his novel, they referred to *PWD* as *The Palm Wine Drinker*.[7] However, Tutuola misspelled "Drunkard" as "Drinkard" in the body of the text and they made an editorial decision to rename it *The Palm Wine Drinkard* "because it was more colourful to use in the title" (Low, "Natural Artist," 23).[8] Changing the title from a grammatically correct rendering to one derived from Tutuola's misspelling in the text of the novel stresses the degree to which Faber & Faber wanted to establish *PWD* as a text written by an African native who had yet to fully learn English.

When in 1952 an editor at Norton rejected *PWD* because "it was not worth the confusion," presumably because of Tutuola's English use, its style and structure, Peter du Sautoy, a director at Faber & Faber, wrote back:

> We do, of course realize that it is not quite as good as it ought to be, but it is the unsophisticated product of a West African mind and we felt there was nothing to be done about it except to leave it alone. When I say unsophisticated, that is not altogether true, since Tutuola has been to some extent influenced by at any rate the externals of Western civilization. . . . Its interest is more anthropological than literary, but apart from being in the end a little tedious, it has got a certain quality as [a] piece of unusual writing. (Lindfors, *Blind Man and the Elephant*, 32)

Good publishers interested in the intrinsic value of the novel would have tried to polish that "certain quality" so it became central to the novel. However, to du Sautoy, any part in *PWD* that shows sophistication was a result of "Western civilization," while the anthropological was the result of African culture lacking civilization.

Tutuola himself wanted to write in Standard English and wished his English to be corrected. He wrote to Faber and Faber saying that "I shall be much grateful if you will correct my "WRONG-ENGLISH" etc and can alter the story itself if possible, of course it is not necessary to tell you as you are an expert in this work."[9] But in a 21 June 1951 reply, Faber & Faber stated, "Perhaps you would let me know, when you write, if you would wish to send printer's proofs to you in case you have any corrections to make; if so, it would be important that your corrections should be as few and as small as possible, owing to the expense of shifting type" (Lindfors, *Blind Man and the Elephant*, 118). On the face of it, Faber & Faber's response is standard—once the type has been set, it is expensive to make changes. However, the question is whether the editors should have been making allowances for Tutuola's unique and rather powerless situation. There is an argument to be made that in changing the title, and in seeing anthropological value in both the content of *PWD* and its language use, the editors were already recognizing the unique position of their writer—a position they were using to their advantage. They could choose when to treat Tutuola as a regular writer working on a standard contract, and when to treat him as a writer whose value lay in being a marketable African native. It made sense, then, for them to argue that Tutuola's mistakes were part of the aesthetic appeal. But in reality, his poor grammar was doing the work of authenticating his work as that of an African coming into English and civilization and it was best to leave it as it was. On 21 June 1951, Alan Pringle wrote to Tutuola about the editing process:

We propose therefore that our reader should go through the manuscript before it is set up in type, correcting what are evidently copying errors, accidental omissions, confusions or inconsistencies, but leaving intact all those expressions which, though strictly speaking erroneous, are more graphic than correct expressions would be. You can depend upon it that we have the success of the book at heart, and we hope you will be content to leave the matter to our judgment. (Lindfors, *Blind Man and the Elephant*, 118)

Looking at the facsimile of an original page from Tutuola's handwritten manuscript and the changes the editors made, Pringle did not keep his end of the bargain. He left the misspellings, "accidental omissions, confusions or inconsistencies" for the most part intact in the typeset version. Tutuola replied on June 27. After thanking Pringle for his letter, he wrote:

I am very glad to read in your letter that you will publish the M/S and also the letter points out about the correction of my wrong English etc., in conclusion, I leave everything for you to do as how it will profit both of us, and is no need of sending me the printer's proofs for corrections as you an expert in this field. (Lindfors, *Blind Man and the Elephant*, 119)

Right from the beginning, Tutuola, as a colonial subject, had less power in his relationship to the international firm of Faber & Faber. Second, aware of his own lack of education, he was not confident enough to make editorial demands. When asked by Pringle to sort out punctuation and syntax in the editing of *Simbi and the Satyr of the Dark Jungle*, Tutuola replied, "To the point you raised . . . as far as you know, I am not capable of writing English correctly and that I do not know so much where the commas and the full-stops should be, I am pleased how you put everything in good order" (Low, "The Natural Artist," 23). Tutuola, self-conscious of his poor command of English, was unwilling to assert his authorial rights. Therefore, he ended up abdicating them, giving room for Faber & Faber to leave his work deliberately uncorrected.[10]

## TUTUOLA AND ENGLISH LITERATURE INFLUENCES

Part of what du Sautoy called the "externals of Western civilization" was colonial education, the main reason Tutuola was trying to write in limited Standard English as opposed to Yoruba. The majority of Africans were not being educated to become thinkers in, and have a full command of, English language and culture, but rather to enable the smooth functioning of the colonial machinery. Just as peasant education in Romantic England produced good workers and Christians, colonial education produced Christian Africans who knew their place.[11]

The point here is that because he was a product of a colonial education in which only Standard English was the language of aesthetics, all the examples of English literature he would have come across would have been in Standard English. Bernth Lindfors in "Amos Tutuola: Debts and Assets" writes:

> Tutuola claims that he read only textbooks while in school but some of those would have been literary works. It is known, for example, that Aesop's fables were read in Nigerian schools in the 1930's and that John Bunyan's *The Pilgrim's Progress* was available in Nigeria in a simplified version as early as 1937 . . . he also told Eric Larrabee that he enjoyed reading Joyce Cary's *Mister Johnson* and Edith Hamilton's *Mythology* . . . (323)

By "simplified" Lindfors means that the English was standardized and the book abridged. John Bunyan, who wrote in everyday, colloquial English was at first seen as vulgar but the later "metaphysical Empire" saw value in literature carrying Englishness. Even though he wrote *The Pilgrim's Progress* in

1678, almost one hundred years before Samuel Johnson's dictionary, his book came to represent Johnson's nationalist and imperialist dream of the English language carrying the best of English culture. In "How Bunyan Became English: Missionaries, Translation, and the Discipline of English Literature," Isabel Hofmeyr argues that this was because the role philologists had played in promoting the English language as a carrier of culture had been replaced by literary critics who argued that literary works, widely read and accessible, were better suited for promoting Englishness:

> Despised in the eighteenth century as vulgar and un-English, Bunyan's language gradually became the desired model of Anglo-Saxon purity. This shift is apparent in changing editorial practices. Some eighteenth-century editions, for example, edited Bunyan's language to make it more polite. Hence, in one instance the phrase "O, they say, hang him, he is a turn coat" had been deemed to be too robust and was changed to "They tauntingly say, that he was not true to his profession." Nineteenth-century editions reversed these circumlocutions and reinstated Bunyan's original language. Critics also lauded the language of *The Pilgrim's Progress* as pure and accessible. . . . This view of *The Pilgrim's Progress* as a book whose language was accessible to all classes chimed in well with nationalist interpretations of English literature as a unifying factor and promoter of national consciousness. (109)

*The Pilgrim's Progress*, already widely read, debated, and translated into many African, Asian, and European languages, was rehabilitated from being an exemplar of vulgar English to a carrier of Englishness. The edition of *The Pilgrim's Progress* that Tutuola would have read was taught as a carrier of Englishness.[12] But it did not come with the history of contestation that surrounded the book, or that surrounded philological discussions around standardization. If Bunyan influenced Tutuola, then Tutuola would have been emulating the standardized, cleaned up, and pious Bunyan. Tutuola, when asked by Claudio Gorlier whether he studied English literature in school and whether that "influenced" his writing, replied: "Well, of course I can't say yes. The time that I attended school we did not know what was called literature" (Tutuola, Di Miao, and Gorlier, *Tutuola at the University*, 165). Along the same lines on whether he read Fagunwa, he said, "His town is far away from my own. Even when I was young like this [gesturing] when I saw his book at the school. They brought the book to the school, I read only one page. Then I gave it back to the owner" (165).

Yet most critics, including Bernth Lindfors, Oyekan Owomoyela, and Harold Collins, agree that his debt to both Fagunwa and Bunyan is obvious. However, it is more complicated than simply a question of influence: Bunyan might have influenced Tutuola, but Tutuola also Africanized Bunyan in style, content, and belief. Hofmeyr argues, that because many of the colonized societies would have had similar quest stories such as Bunyan's *The Pilgrims Progress*,

> the plot—which involves a movement from this world to the next—would probably have seemed unremarkable. In addition, it might have appeared as a failed half-story since it ended just at the point where the protagonist entered the next world and things promised to get interesting. Normally, in the West African tradition, the most exciting events would unfold here as the human hero pitted his strength and wit against that of the spirits, ancestors, and gods of the next world. Evidence of these types of interpretations can be seen from two West African novelists—D. O. Fagunwa and Amos Tutuola—who put matters right when they "completed" Bunyan's story in their novels by embedding it in a tale that moves from this world to the next and back again. ("How Bunyan Became English," 96)

The editors, by seeing Tutuola as simply writing folktales, failed to see that he was in conversation with the very nature of Englishness, and that he was extending and improvising over texts at the heart of the colonist's culture. This might not have changed their editorial desire for a native text, but at least they could have alerted the reader to the intertextuality of *PWD*. Then it would have been more difficult to dismiss Tutuola as "unsophisticated"—a code word for half-civilized. At the same time, it would have been more apparent that if a central text in English literature influenced Tutuola, he would not have wanted his work in anything but the best grammar. That is, while Tutuola wanted to carry African content, he did not want that content carried in ungrammatical English. African and Africanized content had to be in Standard English.

Tutuola's ambition was to preserve, carry, and practice a Yoruba essence in the same way missionary teachers presented Bunyan as preserving, carrying, and practicing an English essence. The contradiction was that he wanted his Yoruba essence preserved in the English language. Tutuola was aware of his limited command of English. Eric Larrabee in a review of the *PWD* writes that:

> After much thought, Amos has decided to attend evening classes to "improve" himself, so that he may develop into what he describes as a "real writer." "I am not telling the story as it is in my head all the time, but I cannot speak good English for them yet" is his moving self-condemnation. ("Palm-Wine Drinkard Searches for Palm Wine," 37)

Most writers talk about improving technique, experimentation, or other aspects of their writing—but not of improving their command of the language itself. For example, one can imagine Joseph Conrad telling a friend he is working on improving his English when he is unpublished and young, but not after he is established and world-renowned. Here Tutuola, a world-recognized author published by a top publishing house, is saying he needs to go back and learn to speak and write in Standard English.[13] With that kind of self-consciousness, he would not have the basis or confidence to argue with his editors or to participate actively in the editing of *PWD* and subsequent works.

At the same time, Tutuola came to see his work of preserving African culture as more important than grammar. Or, more correctly, he saw his language use as secondary to the more important and urgent work of maintaining an African culture under threat from Western civilization. He argued:

> So far as I don't want our culture to fade away I don't mind about the English grammar. Even my publishers tell that I should write as I feel. I should feel free to write my story. I have not given my manuscript for anyone who knows grammar to edit. Only my publishers do everything relating to Editing. (Lindfors, *Blind Man and the Elephant*, 143)[14]

Since his publishers had promised to take care of his grammar, he was free from what the peasant Romantic poet John Clare had called the tyranny of grammar.[15] Tutuola also did not see his limited education as necessarily a good or a bad thing, but as a handicap that had become part of his aesthetical appeal. A little later, he says:

> Probably if I had more education, that might change my writing or improve it or change it to another thing people would not admire. Well, I cannot say. Perhaps with higher education, I might not be as popular a writer. I might not write folktales. I might not take it as anything important. I would take it as superstition and not write in that line. (Lindfors, *Blind Man and the Elephant*, 143)

There are two things here in this self-evaluation. One is that for him his limitations are strengths as well as weaknesses. He has no reason to improve his education in such a way that it takes him away from his writing style. Second, he sees the pitfalls of education—it could very well distance him from his Yoruba culture from which he draws his inspiration, and which he hopes to preserve. Where another publisher might have pushed Tutuola to finish unrealized aspects of *PWD*, hence generating reimaginations over the plot or character development, Faber & Faber had essentially told Tutuola that his language flaws were part of his aesthetic appeal. Tutuola, too, came to see his minimal education and poor command of English as possible assets.

## EDITORIAL CHOICES: INTRINSIC AND EXTRINSIC EFFECTS

The editing decisions, or lack thereof, had immediate intrinsic effects (metaphors and images and other literary devices) and long-term extrinsic effects (reception, aesthetics and context) on Tutuola's writing. While the extrinsic effects may vary depending on the context in which the book is read, the intrinsic losses are a constant. These include inaccessible meaning because of grammatical mistakes that hinder meaning; lost authorial intention because deliberate use of language cannot be discerned from mistakes; and a narrative style that remains opportunistic, resulting in too much linearity and a narrator and characters that all sound the same. The following passage, from the section of *PWD* entitled "A Complete Gentleman," will help illustrate the intrinsic losses and justify my notion that the editors should have at a minimum corrected Tutuola's grammatical mistakes and standardized his English:

> I could not blame the lady for following the Skull as a complete gentleman to his house at all. Because if I were a lady, no doubt I would follow him to wherever he would go, and still as I was a man I would be jealous him more than that, because if this gentleman went to the battle field, surely, enemy would not kill him, or capture him and if bombers saw him in a town, they would not throw bombs on his presence, and if they did throw it, the bomb itself would not explode until this gentleman would leave town, because of his beauty. (207)

To the above excerpt from a facsimile of the original editing reproduced in *PWD*, the editors say they made only minimal changes. They changed *atal* to *at all*; collapsed *where-ever* to *wherever*; added *went* and *did*; and changed *see* to *saw*. For the most part, they left awkward phrasings, wrong word order, and run-on sentences intact. My argument is that the beauty of the passage is not rendered through the foreignness of his English, but in the semantics—a beauty that is so visceral that it can stop a war while undermining masculinity. The narrator later consoles himself with the knowledge that the Complete Gentleman is after all an evil skull:

> After I looked at him for so many hours, then I ran to a corner of the market and I cried for a few minutes because I thought within myself why was I not created with beauty as this gentleman, but when I remembered that he was only a Skull, then I thanked God that he had created me without beauty, so I went back to him in the market, but I was still attracted by his beauty. (207)

The word choice of beautiful over handsome in the passage highlights a beauty that is flawless—a beauty forged by nature. The Complete Gentleman is a flawless force of nature; even bombs will wait for him to pass before exploding. It is not feminized beauty—his is a sublime beauty. This sublime beauty contains the duality of being perfectly good and evil.[16] However, the reader by this time has been trained to be constantly in doubt about what Tutuola means; he or she can easily read *beauty* as meaning the lesser *handsome*. The complexity is lost.

Not only is authorial deliberate use of language undermined, meaning is obscure, leaving the reader to make educated guesses. For example, the Drinkard narrates, "if I were a lady, no doubt I would follow him to wherever he would go, and still as I was a man I would be jealous him more than that, because if this gentleman went to the battle field *surely, enemy would not kill him*" (207). What is the meaning of "and still as I was a man I would be jealous him more than that?" One reading is men go to war expecting to die or survive based on their fighting prowess. But the Drinkard feels that it is unfair that the Complete Gentleman's beauty guarantees his survival. In other words, he is jealous of the exceptionalism that greets him wherever he goes. Just like with the sublime beauty, this reading is not immediately apparent. The "I would be jealous him more than that" is just plain confusing. Rather than put in extra work just to learn that the Drinkard begrudges the Complete Gentleman his beauty for complex reasons, it is easier to keep reading.

Authorial irony is also lost on the reader. The Complete Gentleman is far from complete as all his body parts save for the skull are borrowed. Tutuola uses the word "complete" to describe something that has all its parts intact and at the same time, given the ensuing loss of parts, serves to undermine the completeness. In the absence of a reading that allows for the contradiction of being perfect and flawed at the same time, irony is lost. For it to be more visible, Tutuola would have had to deliberately call attention to it. Given that anything and everything can have metaphorical significance in *PWD*, deliberate highlighting or emphasis cannot be visible.

Harder to quantify is the relationship between the reader and the text. Suspension of disbelief, for example, is predicated on the reader being immersed in the text without leaving the text to wonder after what the author is actually trying to say. The experience of a constant stop and go while reading *PWD* takes the reader out of the flow of the novel. That leads to the author, as opposed to his narrator, being read as unreliable. In other words, because the flaws are so apparently not intended and serve no larger purpose other than showcasing Tutuola as a native novelty, the unreliability becomes Tutuola's and not the Drinkard's.

Yet, more deliberate use of conventional stylistic devices, varying sentence length, and strategic repetitions would have worked better. It is my contention that Tutuola's language use would have been equally if not more captivating when standardized. Here below is my rendering of the same passage used above in "straightened" English:

> I could not blame the woman for following the Complete Gentleman home. If I were a woman, I would have followed him to the ends of the earth. Even though a man, I was jealous of him. He was so complete, so perfect that even in battle, his enemies would not take him prisoner, much less kill him, bomber planes would not drop bombs. And if they did, the bombs would not explode until he left town. He was a complete beautiful gentleman.

Tutuola's use of images makes his language so physical, graphic, and startling that there was no need to publish him unedited in order to call attention to his work, or even his Africanness. He does not need the adornment of nativeness. His imagination, rendered in a language that lets it through rather than stands in the way, would have been "novelty" enough for those looking for a native writer and literary enough for those who wanted to engage with good writing. In a vivid passage found *In the Bush of Ghosts*, three ghosts are competing for the narrator:

So as he lighted the flood of golden light on my body and when I looked at myself I thought that I became gold as it was shining on my body, so at this time I preferred most to go to him because of his golden light. But as I moved forward a little bit to go to him then the copperish-ghost lighted the flood of his own copperish light on my body too, which persuaded me again to go to the golden-ghost as my body was changing to very colour that copper has, and my body was then so bright so that I was unable to touch it. And again, as I preferred this copperish light more than the golden light then I started to go to him, but at this stage I was prevented again to go to him by the silverfish-light which shone on to my body at that moment unexpectedly. (24–25)

The language here is very physical. There are no internal thought processes and one can imagine an editor asking him what was going through the narrator's mind. However, the loss of the narrator's inner thoughts or consciousness is compensated for by the sheer beauty of the different competing ghosts that try to entice him through their colors after an earlier attempt to get him through competing cuisines. A little later, the three ghosts immobilize him when they shine their lights on him at the same time. It is a vivid and arresting scene but the power is lost, not enhanced, by the interruptions caused by poor grammar and needless repetition. Tutuola's writing remains powerful in spite of his editors as opposed to because of them.

There is, however, an argument to be made that the editors at Faber & Faber were, at the moment they received and decided to publish *PWD*, condemned to err on either forcing Tutuola to write in an "English manner" or nativizing him. Having Tutuola first write in Yoruba and then translating him would have solved the question of grammar and authorial intention.

## CRITICAL RECEPTION: THE AFRICAN "NATIVE" WRITER AND TRANSLATABILITY

The critical reception that greeted Amos Tutuola's *Palm Wine Drinkard* revolved around several articulated and unarticulated concerns. The literary novel was being adapted from the West to carry African aesthetics—would its form be pliable enough? Related to this was the question of what role the African writer was going to play in the decolonization of Africa—and whether Tutuola's writing was part of the problem or part of the solution. The question of literary tradition was another central concern—could Tutuola and his poor command of the English language lay a solid foundation for a literary tradition or was it, hearkening back to Obi Wali, leading to a dead end?[17]

In addition to the extrinsic questions that were more concerned with Tutuola's relationship to European and African aesthetics, there were intrinsic questions that emerged from *PWD*. Was he merely chronicling Nigerian cultures by translating Yoruba folktales into English? Was *PWD* the work of a writer conscious of himself as a writer or the work of, echoing John Clare, a child of wonder? Was he a magical realist writer, or a folklorist? And to what extent was his English a detraction from or enhancement to the aesthetics in *PWD*?

The traditional approach to analyzing Tutuola has been to divide literary criticism between European and African critics. For example, Bernth Lindfors in *Early West African Writers* argues that for Western critics:

> [T]he *Palm-Wine Drinkard* was a highly original work written by an untutored but extraordinary genius [while] many educated Nigerians looked down upon Tutuola and fretted that his imperfect control of English would come to be regarded by the outside world as typical of Nigerian speech and writing. (53)

This division between the two streams of criticism hearkens back to colonial education. The colonial educators saw African languages as necessary accessories to the teaching of English so the African students would not become alienated from their cultures. Africans, on the other hand, viewed the teaching of African languages as detracting from the real work of mastering English because as the language of power it was the only way up the social ladder. Many found pride in their mastery of English and Tutuola's poor grasp of English was a source of shame. Tutuola was aware of this feeling of shame from the Nigerian educated elite in relation to his work, and he explains some of the negative criticism this way:

> Before, I don't know whether those people who were well educated were ashamed[18] of their own heritage. I wonder why they not want to write anything concerning their tradition. Even when the publisher passed the manuscript to the Yorubas who were in London by that time, to comment, or recommend, or say whatever they liked about the book, some said, "No, this is nonsense! They should not publish it." Yet some of them rec-

ommended that they should publish it—so many did. . . . Now the people who disrecommended this story are at the Universities of Lagos, Ibadan, Ife, and in the Eastern region. (Tutuola, Di Miao, and Gorlier, *Tutuola at the University*, 53)

Colonial education also portrayed African cultures as inferior, with nothing of aesthetic value, at least in relation to Western cultural production. African aesthetics were the byproduct of functionalism—masks were for ceremonies, drumming for communication, and dances and music were ceremonial as well. Folktales had the express purpose of teaching moral lessons to the young. Oyekan Owomoyela, writing on the Western versus African reception of *PWD*, spells it out this way:

> Nigerians and West Africans were confounded for yet another reason, that the praises showered on Tutuola were inconsistent with what they had been taught—often by the same Westerners whose selected authors included the likes of Aeschylus, Shakespeare, Milton, Moliere, Dostoevsky, and Arthur Miller—about what consisted good literature. They had been led to believe that creative writing required a mastery of language, adeptness at plotting, ability to create believable characters, and a clear idea of the theme(s) the work will convey. (*Amos Tutuola Revisited*, 102)

The educated African elite greeted the elevation of *PWD* to the level of literature with derision because it violated, in content, form, and language, aesthetic standards. To portray *PWD* as an aesthetic masterpiece was taken as further condescension toward African people by Westerners. Steven Tobias also draws a line between Western and African critics, arguing that whereas the Western critics "initially reacted quite favorably towards the book and praised it for its rich, albeit 'primitive,' adherence to Yoruba oral folk traditions, African critics were generally less favorable" ("Amos Tutuola and the Colonial Carnival," 66). The Nigerian elite were unhappy because

> a "primitive" book, written in broken English by a lowly messenger, was being lauded in European intellectual circles as the pinnacle of Nigerian culture. In particular, with Nigerian political independence nearly in sight in the early 1950s, Tutuola's world of bogey-men was one that most educated Nigerians would have liked to purge forever from global perceptions of their country. (Lindfors, 344)

In addition to language and content, there was the issue of decolonization. Nigeria was supposed to be moving to modernity. Nationalism in practice meant westernization that worked for Nigerians as opposed to benefiting the British. Tutuola was a throwback to the past that Nigerians were trying to leave behind.

Therefore, there is a solid base for dividing the African and Western criticism, not only because they are coming from two different cultures but also because culture was a battlefield between the colonized and the colonizer. However, I prefer to approach the criticism thematically because, firstly, the critical reception, whether African or Western, had two concerns as the starting point—Tutuola's use of English, and his "bizarre" content. Through him, critics erroneously assumed that what was at stake was African history, its role in the present, its authentic portrayal of the African mind, and the future of African literature.

Second, the divide between African and European literary critics is misleading: African critics did not all agree with each other about the reception of Tutuola, nor did the European critics always agree. Ultimately, what mattered was where each critic stood on the question of Standard English. For most critics, Standard English was the future; differences arose over how to make Standard English carry African content. The future was in modernization and westernization; the differences were over the role of African cultures within westernization.

Criticism of Tutuola therefore can be organized around several themes: the extent to which he was a conscious writer, the African writer as a political agent, the language of African literature, the extent to which Tutuola was laying a foundation for an African literary tradition, and, finally, Tutuola's style. On each of these concerns, Tutuola, like Clare, ended up being denied translatability—but with a twist. Not only was he not translatable to the Westerners engaged in anthropological readings of his work, he was also untranslatable to the African elite.

## TUTUOLA AS AN AUTHENTIC UNCONSCIOUS WRITER

When it was first published, Tutuola's *PWD* was read as a piece of anthropology or as forensic evidence to show the state of African psychology and linguistics. To those critics, his writing did not have literary merit or any intrinsic aesthetic dimensions to it: Tutuola was not a conscious writer; he simply transcribed oral stories to capture the real African mind and imagination. Cecil T. Lewis in his review of *Life in the Bush of Ghosts* tells his readers to:

> Take a modern Nigerian. Give him six years of formal education. Let him with rampant and febrile imagination enclose within a rudimentary fictional framework his tribal lore—a lore in which mythology and reality are often indistinguishable for those whose culture itself is a mélange. Result: a coupling of the predominantly primitive with outcroppings of sophistication in a book to delight the ethnologist, the psychologist, the theologist, the linguist. ("Primitive Verbal Fantasy," 116)

Lewis is not alone in seeing Tutuola's work in purely functional terms. Geoffrey Parrinder, in his introduction to *My Life in the Bush of Ghosts*, declares that the "anthropologist and the student of comparative religion will find here much of the unrecorded mythology of West Africa. There are themes running through the book, as to the nature of death, fear and disease" (13). In the larger colonial framework, white people generally saw Africans as lacking in civilization and being childlike.[19] For example, Selden Rodman, in a 1953 *New York Times* review of *PWD*, wrote:

> If you like Annia Livia Plurabelle, Alice in Wonderland and the poems of Dylan Thomas, the chances are you will like this novel, though probably not for the reasons having anything to do with the author's intentions. For Tutuola is not a revolutionist of the word, not a mathematician, not a surrealist. He is a true primitive. And the pleasure of a sophisticated reader will derive from his un-willed style and trance-like narrative is akin to the pleasure generated by popular painters like Rousseau or Obin . . . only a dullard who has trapped his childhood under several mountains of best-selling prose could fail to respond to Tutuola's naive poetry. (15)

For Rodman,[20] the joy of reading Tutuola is in the unconscious writing. Tutuola has no writer's agenda, no style or viewpoint he is trying to get across, he just slips into a trance and transcribes words onto a page. To appreciate Tutuola, readers have to tap into their inner child. "Naivete" and "child-like," suggesting an unconscious writer, are staples in the early criticism of Tutuola. This line of criticism ended up legitimizing the colonial project, just as the early criticism of Clare sought to naturalize class structures.

The misreading of Tutuola as an unconscious writer was a result of using a European aesthetic standard to critique African aesthetics. Eric Larrabee, in "Palm-Wine Drinkard Searches for a Tapster," took the Eurocentric aesthetic standard of literature a step further and questioned whether Tutuola could be called a writer at all:

> As an exercise in imagination, try to conceive of an author who (1) probably has never met another author, (2) owns no books, (3) is not known to his daily acquaintances as an author, (4) has no personal contact with his publisher, (5) is not certain where his book is on sale, and (6) does not think of himself as an author. (13)

This assumption is erroneous on several levels. If Tutuola's sources are in orature, and if it is true that, as Tutuola himself acknowledged, a kernel of what was to become the *Palm Wine Drinkard* was narrated to him by an old man[21] (a palm wine tapster himself), then we can say that he was in contact with an artist of orature. Larrabee did not consider folktales and the art of storytelling as valid source material for the written text. Indeed, for many critics, closely related to the question of whether Tutuola was a conscious writer was the extent to which his writing was original or plagiarized. There were two strands: that he copied or transcribed from oral stories and therefore should not claim sole authorship, and that he plagiarized stories written in Yoruba by Daniel Fagunwa.[22]

For Harold Collins, Tutuola "adapts his folk material freely for his own purposes" (*Amos Tutuola*, 54). Collins demonstrates this using the episode of the "Complete Gentleman," arguing that, while it is true the story exists in various forms in other cultures,

> Tutuola has contributed a great deal of elaboration on the willful beauty's fascination with the handsome stranger and that stranger's extraordinary beauty. . . . [The] Drinkard's careful "investigation to the skull's family house," the conditions of the lady's imprisonment, the exciting rescue with its transformations and Drinkard flying through the air with her, the subsequent removal of the noisy cowrie from the lady's neck, and the cure of her dumbness and lack of appetite. (55)

It seems to me that Collins is right in seeing him as adapting[23] *PWD* from already existing stories. That is, Tutuola takes the oral story and improvises over it. It becomes an inspiration. Bernth Lindfors, in *Critical Perspectives on*

*Amos Tutuola*, writes that Tutuola "admitted that he always enjoyed hearing and telling folktales" (279) and quotes Tutuola on various occasions telling interviewers that "stories exist objectively and he merely sets them down" and after feeling "written out" he planned to return to his hometown "to rest and draw fresh inspiration from listening to old people re-telling Yoruba legends" (280). It is undeniable that he is greatly indebted to Yoruba folktales. This does not constitute mere translation, or plagiarism, because he imposes his imagination over the folktales to create a work different in form and content.

Larrabee's suggestion that a man who owned no books could not be a writer was, again, a narrow application of European aesthetic standards. Tutuola, in contrast, was aware that orature could serve as a literary source. Lindfors argues that Tutuola, both in school and much later, would have come across Western writing[24] that would influence his own style. In the essay "Amos Tutuola: Debts and Assets," he states that

> at least twenty-six school books classified as "General Literature" were published in Yoruba between 1927 and 1937, and that many others have been published since. Moreover, in recent years Tutuola has acknowledged that there are many stories like his written in Yoruba and has admitted in a letter that he read *The Pilgrim's Progress* and *The Arabian Nights* in 1948, just two years before *The Palm Wine Drinkard*. (323)

A little stretch of imagination, or even a little generosity, on the part of critics such as Larrabee would have allowed them to take into account that the standard of authorship they were using was not universal but rather rooted in a European tradition.

Whereas in the earlier essay his argument was that Tutuola was not an artist by virtue of having no exposure to literature, Larrabee in a later essay, "Amos Tutuola: A Problem in Translation," maintained that Tutuola had no notion of himself as a writer. He wrote, "Tutuola simply does not see himself as we see him as a recognized writer or even, in our terms, as a writer at all" (41). He continued on to argue:

> Though we, in this country, can speak of the alienation of the artist, it is difficult for us to imagine an alienation so complete that the artist does not even know that he is an artist. In the first place, Tutuola does not think of himself as the creator of his stories. Stories exist objectively; he merely sets them down. When I asked him if he planned to write more, the question had no

meaning to him. "But there are many stories," he said. In the second, he has no internalized standards by which to measure his own virtues; he does not "know" what it is he seems to us to know. We attribute merits to him on which he cannot very well congratulate himself, since neither he nor those whom he normally encounters are aware of them as merits. (42)

For Larrabee, Tutuola is a conduit through which oral stories are set down in writing. Tutuola is not conscious of himself as a writer and he does not consciously manipulate language. Talking with Tutuola about his critical reception and the praise of his technique has no meaning to Tutuola because his labors are natural. And Tutuola does not exercise his imagination over the folktales; instead, he just transcribes them.[25]

At the most basic level, Larrabee's charge that Tutuola did not think of himself as an author has no meaning unless critics are to take authors as the final authorities on their work. Tutuola's own statements directly contradict the suggestion that he did not think of himself as a writer. Like most writers, Tutuola had a creative process that he followed. In his second lecture in Italy, he said:

> Now, if I want to write a book first of all, before I start, I collect materials. I sit down and think, for many days: how or what can I write? By the way, what title should I give my story? I will think all that. Then, I begin to make a sketch. Sometimes I cancel that sketch. Another idea will come to my mind. Then I write another sketch, until I get to the words that I require. (Tutuola, Di Maio, and Gorlier, *Tutuola at the University*, 49)

Here, he was describing the process of writing, from research, to brainstorming, to working through multiple drafts. Later in the lecture, he was more precise about the creative process:

> If you want to become a writer, you should be able to endure the hardships of it. To begin a story is very, very difficult, because you do not know what to write immediately. You'll be confused. Sometimes I stand up, begin to walk up and down, thinking in memory what to write. And then I sit down, raise up my head. What will I write? How could I begin this story? With what? Then, later in a week or two, the idea will come to my mind. Once I form the first page of the story, then everything is okay. What will come to my mind

is just like a vision, as if I am seeing what I am writing. And by that time I'll go ahead. So, writing needs strong imagination and endurance. If you cannot endure, I don't think you will be a good writer. (52)

Equally important to having a strong imagination is a writer's ability to endure. I do not think Tutuola was referring to physical deprivations—he meant the ability to go through the difficult process of germinating an idea and the torture of using one's imagination to turn that germ into a story. In other words, writing is hard work—both mentally and imaginatively.

## READING TUTUOLA THROUGH HIS PHYSICAL LOOKS AND BODY LANGUAGE

Tutuola's early critics, mostly Western, were obsessed with the physical demeanor of the writer. What they saw as primordial or infantile language for them translated into a primordial or infantilized man. His body language and demeanor became part of the reception. Harold Collins titled the first chapter of his otherwise serious treatment of Tutuola "The Shy Yoruba." He described him as looking "rather like our Afro-Americans" and added that it should not be "surprising since many of our black Americans have Yoruba ancestors" (*Amos Tutuola*, 23). In a swift move, Collins glossed over the violent slave trade that disrupted African societies while at the same time revealing his audience to be white Americans, hence "our Afro-Americans." Here, Collins was telling the Western reader that the shy Yoruba, writing "devilish tales" in strange English, was already familiar if read through the filter of "our Afro-Americans." Tutuola's physical looks as deployed here were not mere descriptors; they established racial hierarchy.

The Nigerian Correspondent[26] whom Collins relied on to draw his composite said that Tutuola "looks like a thousand other junior government clerks. He seems much younger than his thirty-four years. His speech is slow and diffident, and his manner shyly polite" (35). For the correspondent, Tutuola was not an individual, but rather a type of African—his age could not be deciphered, and he was easily lost in a sea of colonized workers. Is it possible that his speech was slow and lacking confidence only when speaking English? The Correspondent did not tell the reader. On Tutuola's shyness, Larrabee said the following:

I had asked to have an interview with the author at the U.S. Consulate, which may have been a mistake, for he was painfully shy and probably suspicious of my motives. The conversation was uncomfortable and inconclusive for both of us. It only occurred to me later that he might never have been interviewed before, and I wonder what he made of it all. ("Palm-Wine Drinkard," 13)

It did not occur to Larrabee that he might have been a terrible interviewer—instead, the blame for the painful interview is on Tutuola alone. Second, at the height of British colonialism and Nigerian nationalism, interviewing him in the U.S. embassy should have been reason enough for Tutuola to be suspicious of his motives. As an interviewer, Larrabee also failed, in that he did not put his subject at ease. To conclude his portrait of Tutuola, he wrote:

I went to the Labour Department later, to get him to sign my copy of his book, and found him seated in a corner in his loose-fitting uniform, asleep. I had to get to him past row on row of bespectacled Nigerians, sitting at their desks in bureaucratic self-satisfaction and palpably annoyed at the breach of decorum in a white man's calling on a messenger. He asked me what I wanted him to write and then, after signing the inscription he said: "I think, when you reach there, the U.S.A., you write a letter to me." I said I would, but why did he want me to? "So I know you not forget me." ("Palm-Wine Drinkard," 14)

Larrabee is conscious of his whiteness as a symbol of power in a colonial setting and this reads like a white man's fantasy of a first meeting with Africans. He walks across a sea of Europeanized Africans, all of them eager for his attention and annoyed when he instead chooses to recognize the lowly messenger boy. Of course, the messenger boy in his native bliss, in a "loose fitting uniform," is fast asleep. It is interesting that for such a detailed passage Larrabee did not tell his reader what Tutuola inscribed. Instead, what he chose to tell the reader was that Tutuola wanted a letter from the West so as not to be forgotten. The way the passage is constructed, Tutuola is a child begging for recognition from a parent. A child is shy, so is a native, and so is a peasant in the face of an adult from the superior race and class. Shyness, self-effacement, diffidence are not merely descriptors of Tutuola as an individual, but words that capture the relationship between the colonizer and the colonized, the powerful to the less powerful. At the same time, they tell us how the colonizer viewed the colonized.[27]

## THE QUESTION OF LANGUAGE—YORUBA IN ENGLISH?

Criticism of Tutuola and his non-Standard English revolved around whether he was writing in Nigerian pidgin, transcribing Yoruba into English, that is, transposing Yoruba linguistic rules to English grammar, or whether he was attempting to write in proper English and fell short. In "Amos Tutuola: Debts and Assets," Lindfors[28] sees Tutuola's English as being deeply influenced by Yoruba:

> Unorthodox constructions such as "I had no other work more than to drink," "I could not do any work more than to drink," "he had no other work more than to tap," and "we did not know other money, except COWRIES" are taken directly from Yoruba. ( 316)

Johnson Babasola, in a 1954 letter to the editor, disavowed Tutuola, accusing him of "largely translating Yoruba ideas into English in almost the same sequence as they occur to his mind (Lindfors, *From West Africa*, 31). Rejecting the idea that Tutuola is writing in pidgin or a dialect, A. Afolayan, in a 1971 essay, "Language and Sources of Amos Tutuola," argues that Tutuola's language was Yoruba English, "in the sense that it represents the expression of Yoruba deep grammar with English surface grammar of Yoruba systems and/or structures in English words" (194). Indeed, at the 1962 Makerere Conference one of issues on the table was how to carry African thought and culture from African languages into European languages. The conclusion reached, according to Obi Wali, was that an African writer should "think and feel in his own language and then look for an English transliteration approximating the original" (283). But Wali argued that transliteration will lead to a dead end because the "'original' which is spoken of here is the real stuff of literature and the imagination, and must not be discarded in favor of a copy which, as the passage admits, is merely an approximation" (283).

Tutuola, however, was not thinking about moving from an original to a copy; he understood his process as one in which the original was also the copy, or rather where the original was in the copy—he understood his process as literally creating an English language that was also Yoruba. In this way, he would be able to preserve the original Yoruba meaning and flavor. To explain his "changing the Yoruba dialect into the English language," he said:

I use the way the Yoruba speak their language in English as well, though it is wrong to use it in English. Though it's not good, or correct grammar, but I use it like that. For example, in English, they say, "When I saw that I could not go . . ." But you know when the Yoruba say something, or look at something, or think to do something, we say, "When I saw that I would not be able to go . . ." That is wrong in English for those who are well educated. It is wrong, they won't use it like that. But that is the Yoruba dialect, the way we speak. It is wrong, but I use it. They understand what I mean by that. (Tutuola, Di Miao, and Gorlier, *Amos Tutuola at the University*, 50)

However, the problem is that he did not know enough English to make this happen. In the example he gives above, I do not see much difference between "When I saw that I could not go" and "When I saw that I would not be able to go." He sees the former as the correct English version and the latter as the nonstandard, Yoruba-rendered English. As fragments, pending context, there is nothing fundamentally different between the two.

Unlike translation, where meaning or rhythm might be lost, in transliterating Tutuola argued that he could stay as close to the Yoruba original as possible. An audience member in his Eighth Lecture at the University of Turin asked him, "But do you have a problem of how English can express what you are saying?" Tutuola responded:

Look we have so many tales and other stories, which if you would tell them in English wouldn't be good at all. Just like Fagunwa's stories. Fagunwa was a M.A. in English. Yet he wrote all his books in the Yoruba language. After that, one man, Wole Soyinka, trying his best, translated one book into English, but it was not good. The taste had been lost. . . . so, well, I try my best not to affect my stories in English. Though it's not my own language I adopted, I try my best to use it in a way that it does not affect my story. (Tutuola, Di Miao, and Gorlier, *Amos Tutuola at the University*, 148)

In translation terms, what Tutuola is doing is creating a trot where the words and sentence structure in the source language are matched in the same order as in the target language. It is from the trot that the translation can then be done. Taken this way, Tutuola's writing functions like an incomplete translation. He knew enough about the movement from Yoruba to English to know that nuances would get lost in translation. But he did not know enough of the target language to consciously and effectively manipulate it so that the Yoruba original was not lost in translation.

## THE QUESTION OF TRANSLATION

As I have argued, for Tutuola, English was the language of power. He had come to believe in the superiority of English over Yoruba. Jare Ajayi, in *Amos Tutuola: Factotum as a Pioneer*, quotes Tutuola as telling him, "I write for foreigners and for my town's people who can read me" (159). At the same time, his publishers preferred his own brand of English rather than the standardized English that would emerge from a work professionally translated from Yoruba. The result was Tutuola writing in the best Queen's English he knew. And English was the language best suited to carry literature. Ajayi gives an instance where Tutuola portrays English as the language for serious matters and Yoruba as the language of play:

> [I]n Italy when he told his interviewer that in those early days "we'd take English to read something important—or what people who could speak English thought to be very important. That influenced me to write my first book in English." (x)

He had imbibed the colonial lesson in which African languages could discuss mundane day-to-day living but not carry on serious discussions. Equally important is that colonial education also drove a wedge between writing and speaking African languages. Ajayi argues that another reason for Tutuola's reluctance to write in Yoruba was that even though fluent in spoken Yoruba, "he had not fully mastered its literary nuances enough to pursue a writing career in it—his scuttled education and little teaching of Yoruba at school then being responsible" (159). The question, however, remains—would it not have been easier to struggle in a language in which he was orally fluent and intimate with rather than one from which he remained alienated in terms of speaking and writing?

The question of Yoruba language, although always present, either in his transliterating into English, or in translating back into Yoruba, was tangential rather than central. Beyond his determination, it is clear that he was already translating from Yoruba to English, only the original was not set down on paper but coming directly from his mind. He tells Ajayi, "English give me a lot of problem. But I did not let it disturb (hinder me). I always have Yoruba-English dictionary with me when I am writing my stories" (159). The question of translation did come up when a Nigerian deputy director of education asked Tutuola to translate *The Palm Wine Drinkard* into Yoruba so that it could be used as a school text and for general interest. In a letter to his publisher Tutuola stressed that the Yoruba translation would not "affect the one published in English etc., in any way as there would be no single word to be used in it in English as it is for those who cannot read English" (Lindfors, *Blind Man and the Elephant*, 122). Yet the idea of Tutuola first writing in Yoruba and then having his works translated into Standard English did not arise for his publishers. Faber & Faber would not have wanted to lose his "broken" English—the marker of his nativeness.

Tutuola did write *Ise Baba Osi* in Yoruba, which he himself translated into English to become *Pauper, Brawler, and Slanderer*, published in 1987 by Faber & Faber. However, there is no question that his preferred language was English—not Standard English but rather his English, as he wielded it. Yet translation would have solved all the English language problems while allowing for Tutuola to be a deliberate writer, as opposed to being as unreliable as his narrator.

But there is another sense in which Tutuola is not translated—he is not seen as a serious writer wrestling with important political and aesthetical issues. He is in this sense denied translatability. Walter Benjamin, in "The Task of the Translator," writes:

> Translation is a form. To understand it as such means going back to the original. Because the original, in its translatability, contains the laws that governs the translation. The question of a word's "translatability" is two-fold. It can mean: will the work ever find its proper translator among all its possible readers; or—and more to the point—does it, by its nature, permit translations and therefore, given the significance of the form, demand it? (298)

For Benjamin, translation as form means that translation has its own sets of rules and aesthetic goals. The first concern is more about the process, the effort of finding the translator best equipped to translate a particular work. His second concern is more about the content and form of the original—does the original contain within it qualities that make it translatable? As Benjamin explains:

The less the quality and dignity of its language, the greater the element of communication, the less it offers to translation. A text that offered nothing but communicable sense, far from providing the occasion for a model translation, would defeat translation altogether. The higher the nature of the work, the more translatable it is even at the most glancing contact with sense. (306)

In the more literal sense of the word, Tutuola's editors denied him translatability by insisting that he write in ungrammatical English, as opposed to first writing in Yoruba and then having his writing translated into English. But it was Tutuola's early critics who denied him metaphorical translatability, regardless of whether they were applauding or deriding him. As a native writer, he was anthropologized as representing both the African mind and African cultures. Reading Tutuola was therefore an exercise that never reflected back on the reader. In addition, by being denied political metaphor, he was seen as having nothing to say outside of transcribing Yoruba stories. Yet to ask his fellow Nigerians to take a second look at their cultures was important because at a minimum it raised the question of what role African cultures were going to play in decolonization.

## TUTUOLA, THE AFRICAN LITERARY TRADITION, AND LANGUAGE

In an interview after Tutuola gave a Palermo University lecture,[29] Professor Claudio Gorlier asked Tutuola a series of questions, including "What does the word tradition mean to you? What is your relationship with tradition: How have you been faithful to your tradition?" Tutuola replied:

When I wrote *The Palm-Wine Drinkard*, this was the main improvement with the book gave to our tradition. I mean, my writing also improved our tradition and customs much. Because so many in my town, so many Yoruba people like Wole Soyinka, Kole Omotoso, and so many writers like them began to write stories about our tradition, customs, and so on. So, by that time, our tradition continued to exist and maybe to improve. (Tutuola, Di Miao, and Gorlier, *Tutuola at the University*, 160)

Gorlier did not mean literary tradition—and Tutuola was talking about tradition as culture, in an anthropological sense. However, at the same time, there is in the question and answer another register—one of a literary tradition; a tradition in which Tutuola sees himself as a central figure in that he influences writers like Soyinka, Omotoso, and, by extension, Chinua Achebe.

Ato Quayson, in *Strategic Transformations in Nigerian Writing*, warns that attempts to find continuities between African orature and literary novels can "become amenable to a positivist anthropological harvest in which details are read directly from cultural backgrounds to fictional world and back again" (2). Consequently, African literature becomes "a receptacle or mirror of culture" (2). It becomes a case of authentication, a defensive maneuver that simply ends up defining African literature in opposition to European literature. At the same time, there is the danger of totalizing African culture, something of which Tutuola himself was aware. Gorlier, in the same interview quoted above, asked Tutuola, "Do you consider Nigerian literature as epitomizing the rest of the African continent? I understand that this is a very general question. But when we, as outsiders, as Europeans speak of Africa, we often speak of it as an abstract, very general notion. Do you think it's legitimate to say 'Africa'? . . . In other words, do you look at Africa as a whole—as a whole of different realities, different countries?" (Tutuola, Di Miao, and Gorlier, *Tutuola at the University*, 157). Tutuola responded, "Oh yes. Yes. Well, I cannot say only Nigerians write stories, but each African country writes stories according to their surroundings, culture, or things like that. So we do the same thing in Nigeria" (157). Even more so, it is possible to make the same argument for the different cultures within Nigeria. The point is not to authenticate African literature in opposition to European literature, or to seek uninterrupted "continuities between oral traditions and writing in English" (Quayson, *Strategic Transformations in Nigerian Writing*, 4), but to try and immerse Tutuola in a literary tradition that does not deny either influences from his Yoruba orature and English written literature as filtered, and distorted by, colonialism in Africa.

Eliot's definition of literary tradition is useful as a point of departure precisely because it also the departing point for Ato Quayson's and Abiola Irele's discussions of African literary tradition and Amos Tutuola. T. S. Eliot, in "Tradition and the Individual Talent," writes that tradition

> cannot be inherited, and if you want it you must obtain it by great labour. It involves, in the first place, the historical sense, [which] involves a perception, not only of the pastness of the past, but of its presence; the historical sense compels a man to write not merely with his own generation in his bones, but with a feeling that the whole of the literature of Europe from Homer and

within it the whole of the literature of his own country has a simultaneous existence and composes a simultaneous order. This historical sense, which is a sense of the timeless as well as of the temporal and of the timeless and of the temporal together, is what makes a writer traditional. And it is at the same time what makes a writer most acutely conscious of his place in time, of his contemporaneity. (38)

For Eliot, tradition is earned by present-day writers immersing themselves in the works of previous generations, as each of those generations have done. Yet the present is not the sum total of the past; books get lost, original manuscripts burned, yet by virtue of having been read they remain active ghosts, contributing to the "historical sense." My understanding of this is that the past is the past, and yet it is contained in the present and writers have to be aware of both. It means that each generation of writers is not starting from scratch, and at the same time it frees enough from the past to create something new. A poet practicing a literary tradition means that tradition is not just in the past but in the present as well and at the same time setting the stage for the next generation—it cannot be complete or singular since by definition it exists as a debate between the voices of the present and those of the past.

Ato Quayson sees Eliot's view of tradition as a contradiction in which on the "one hand the literary tradition is perceived as monolithic while on the other it is seen as open to change and mutation" (*Strategic Transformations in Nigerian Writing*, 4). However, it does not need to be a contradiction, if we take a contradiction to be more than a statement sitting in opposition to become a dialectic containing opposing truths that need not be reconciled. I think it is true that just like aesthetics, what constitutes a literary tradition can be pressured to appear monolithic—so we end up with minor and major literature. Or, in thinking about missing early South African literature, we end up with a whole literary epoch suppressed. However, these designations cannot undo the existence of the tension between what is designated major and minor, for example—since the literature is there and each generation of critics can rescue the minor into the major.

Eliot writes, "We dwell with satisfaction upon the poet's difference from his predecessors, especially his immediate predecessors; we endeavour to find something that can be isolated in order to be enjoyed. Whereas if we approach a poet without this prejudice we shall often find that not only the best, but the most individual parts of his work may be those in which the dead poets, his ancestors, assert their immortality most vigorously" (38). For

Eliot, writers must not only produce in their present times, but also do it with an acute awareness of the past. Consciously or unconsciously, the writer cannot escape the present, or the past for that matter. In a way, it is better for the writer to be conscious of both the present and the past to better manipulate them, but that writers are always part of a tradition is a given. The idea of a writer's tradition is therefore a paradox, one that gives freedom to create by keeping the work tethered to the past, or rather in conversation with past work. However, the writer writing in the present is not just mutating tradition into other directions. To write within a tradition is to not only give present writing historicity but also to give the past new meanings and originality. The present reveals more of the past. What is original is not necessarily new, and the mutation is not only into the future, but also into the past. But the question remains, how in a situation where orature and literature meet is the critic not to seek out the "individual parts" in the work at hand in order to find where orature "assert[s] its immortality vigorously"?

One has to remove Eliot's useful definition of tradition from its European roots for it to become applicable to Tutuola, whose tradition is partly located in orature. Abiola Irele, in *African Experience in Literature and Ideology*, argues that

> [t]he interest of the formal approach to the study of oral literature resides in the possibility it offers of establishing a valid typology of African oral literature, derived from internal evidence gathered from the representative texts across the continent, so that through such evidence we may arrive at some conception of an African literary aesthetic which not only informs the traditional literature but also exerts an influence, either directly or indirectly, on the new writing. (20)

In Tutuola, the influence of the Yoruba oral tradition is direct. In Tutuola, perhaps more than in any other African writer, the oral tradition is being translated and improvised upon—the Yoruba oral tradition meets the European tradition proper—or, rather, in Tutuola we see an attempt to have a European form carry not only African content, but the form of orature as well.

But in the end, though, brave as it is, his attempt fails. He could not fully actualize Achebe's mastery of the language in order to bend it to the will of the African experience, nor could he fully actualize Ngugi's call for writing in African languages, because psychological, social, and economic handicaps stood in his way. Writing from this halfway place, writing from the space between the two cultures where none has been fully actualized, came with a cost. This space is not a hybrid space where agency can be found. In the case of Tutuola, this is a literal and literary space, a gap. In a figurative in-between space, Tutuola should have been able to draw from both cultures, and even multiple cultures, becoming a cosmopolitan symbol challenging single definitions of culture. But in this literal space of half-knowing the English and yet being Yoruba, he is simply not able to carry the science, philosophy, history, and aesthetics of Yoruba culture.

On Amos Tutuola and his command of English, Irele in *The African Imagination: Literature in Africa and the Black Diaspora* writes that

> [O]n the specific point of language, the limitations of Tutuola are limitations and constitute a real barrier, sometimes even a formidable one, both for him as an artist, and for his readers. Tutuola obviously does not dominate his linguistic medium and there is no pretending that this is an advantage. The truth is that we arrive at an appreciation of Tutuola's genuine merit, in spite of his imperfect handling of the English language, not because of it. (183)

This is quite a different statement from earlier critics who saw Tutuola as a native-child genius. For those critics, Tutuola wrote in spite of his native background, and it was because of this that they appreciated his writing. Irele was simply arguing that Tutuola's use of English actually stood in the way of his writing. And not just for the reader, but also for Tutuola as a writer. His imagination did not benefit from wrestling with English; rather, the expression of that imagination became dulled.

For Irele, it is pointless to argue over what Tutuola's writing would have looked like or how it would have been received had he written in Yoruba. Irele's main concern is that

> [t]he very pressure of the Yoruba language upon the peculiar idiom which Tutuola wrung out of the English language may have a fascination for some of his foreign readers, but it is not, to my mind, a satisfactorily creative tension between the two languages that it produces, but rather an imbalance, and a resultant break between the content of his work, and its medium of expression which must be considered a serious shortcoming. (183)

In *Things Fall Apart*, one could argue that Achebe's use of English is in a "creative tension" with Ibo language and culture. His English, inflected with proverbs, which he calls "the palm-oil with which words are eaten," contribute to a tension of the English language carrying Ibo culture. *Things Fall Apart* is in essence written in "Africanized" English, one that is attempting to carry a worldview that it ordinarily does not carry. But in Tutuola's case, the tension that might have arisen between Yoruba and English had he been deliberately "doing violence" to English is lost to his inability to imaginatively impose himself over English. His poor command of English ran too much interference to the extent that artistic deliberateness and choice are not discernible.

## CHAPTER 3

# Africa's Missing Literary History

## From A. C. Jordan's Child of Two Worlds to NoViolet Bulawayo's Fractured Multiple Worlds

Now White people never wait for the formal questions as to whence and why they have come, especially when the object of their visit is known. So, soon as he arrived, the Bishop went straight to the point.
—A.C. Jordan, *Towards an African Literature*

In 1900 Mr. Green might have ranked among the great missionaries; in 1935 he would have made do with slapping headmasters in the presence of their pupils; but in 1957 he could only curse and swear.
—Chinua Achebe, *No Longer at Ease*

Well, go, go to that America and work in nursing homes. That's what your Aunt Fostalina is doing as we speak. Right now she is busy cleaning kaka off some wrinkled old man who can't do anything for himself, you think we've never heard the stories?
—NoViolet Bulawayo, *We Need New Names*

In popular and critical reception of African literature, the tendency has been to start Africa's literary clock with Chinua Achebe's *Things Fall Apart* (1958) and, when most generous, with Amos Tutuola's *The Palm Wine Drinkard* (1952). And sometimes the chronology starts with D. O Fagunwa's *Ògbójú Ọdẹ nínú Igbó Irúnmalẹ* (1938), which was written in Yoruba and translated into English as *The Forest of a Thousand Daemons* by Wole Soyinka in 1968. But, as with Tutuola, Fagunwa is seen as a precursor to the modern African novel. Yet as I showed in my introduction, long before Achebe and his generation of African writers, there was an established literature originally written in English, or in African languages and then translated into English, in South Africa. Thomas Mofolo, who was later to be known for the epic novel *Chaka* (written in 1909, but only published in 1931), was the author of the first novel in Sesotho, *Moeti oa Bochabela* (1907), translated into English as *Traveller to the East* in 1934.[1] R. R. R. Dhlomo wrote in both English and isiZulu—*An African Tragedy* being first published in 1928 and *UNomalanga kaNdengezi* in 1934. Samuel Mqhayi's isiXhosa book, *Ityala Lamawele* (*The Lawsuit of the Twins*) was published in 1912. A. C. Jordan's *Ingqumbo yeminyanya* (1940) was translated as *The Wrath of the Ancestors* in 1964.

And outside of writers writing in African languages there were those writing in English such as Sol Plaatje (*Mhudi*, 1930). These writers are not usually discussed within an African literary tradition, or read as having set templates of writing in African languages and translation that the Makerere writers could have followed. Instead, like Tutuola and Fagunwa, they are invoked as bridges between orature and literature. In *No Longer at Ease*, Achebe sends Tutuola a nod when, in a passage detailing a conversation between the Chairman and Obi, the narrator notes that their "conversation ranged from Graham Greene to Tutuola" (45). The fictional Chairman and Obi, just like literary critics, do not seem to be aware of Mofolo, Jordan, and other South African writers.

In a book central to the field of African literary criticism, *The African Experience in Literature and Ideology* (1981) by Abiola Irele, there is no sustained discussion of the early South African writers even though he has a chapter on the language question. And in discussing the relationship of orature to the literary, he notes in passing that "in some African literatures there has been a direct development from the oral to the written within the indigenous language itself, and it's obvious that in these cases, as regards both themes and internal features, a structural connection exists therefore between the 'old' and the 'new'" (20).

In the *Cambridge Companion to the African Novel*, literary critic Olakunle George, in his essay "The Oral-Literate Interface," looks at how orality has driven African literary aesthetics, how the "interaction between orality and literary takes shape in the creative imaginations and literary production" (17) in writers such as Fagunwa, Ayi Kwei Armah, Chinua Achebe, and Ngugi Wa Thiong'o. He briefly discusses Mofolo's *Chaka* but only to set up his larger argument on orature in the literary texts. M. Keith Booker introduces his essay, "The African Historical Novel" by giving Mofolo's *Chaka* recognition as an "early reminder of the historical development of sophisticated, large scale social and political organization in Africa, completely apart from European intervention" (141). And then he just as quickly moves on to discuss the works of Ngugi, Achebe, Nadine Gordimer, Zakes Mda, and others.

Certainly, how orality figures in the rise of the African novel deserves constant study. In fact, Olakunle's essay, by rejecting the linear oral to literary trajectory, where orality is phased out as the literary takes hold, and instead showing orality as a continuing aesthetic device in the writings of the Makerere writers, is making a serious intervention—orality lives on in the literary. The problem is when our sole entry point into the African literary tradition becomes the "oral-literate interface." Thus, writers such as Tutuola become the bridge between orature and the Makerere generation, while early South African writing is simply excluded from African literary criticism and history. We immediately privilege the African novel in English instead of seeing it as disrupting and then burying the South African literary tradition of writing in African languages, followed by translation into other languages. What I am taking issue with is our starting the African literary clock in the wrong literary epoch. Imagine an English literature where the modern period is simply absent from literary criticism and history; where it is so outside the consciousness of the living present that there can be no intertexuality with the postmodern novel.

As I argued in my introduction, it is not that examples where such studies have been undertaken are lacking. For example, in *Relocating Agency: Modernity and African Letters*, Olakunle George looks at D. O. Fagunwa, his aesthetics, and the choices that Soyinka undertook in his translation of *Ogboju Ode Ninu Igbo Irunmale* into *The Forest of a Thousand Daemons: A Hunter's Saga*. He also looks at Tutuola in relation to both Fagunwa and Soyinka. The point is not that such studies do not exist, but that African literary criticism as a field does not see early South African writing, and by extension early writing in African languages, as part of the African literary tradition. In British literary studies, for example, scholarship around romanticism is by definition conscious of the Enlightenment even when the focus is on Wordsworth or John Keats. In African literary studies it is possible to study the Makerere writers as aesthetically and ideologically independent from what the Comaroffs term the Afro-Modernists, the early South African writers and early African writing in general.

The questions I am asking in this chapter are straightforward ones. What does it mean for the African literary tradition when there is an absence of sustained critical readings of African writing before the Makerere writers? That the Makerere writers, instead of being read within an already existing literary tradition, are read as the originators of the African realist novel? What does it mean for a literary tradition if the contemporary writing of Chimamanda

Adichie and NoViolet Bulawayo, for example, are not read within a literary tradition of the African novel that starts with the South African writers?

What I would like to do here, then, is to read early South African writing within an African literary tradition. I will do that by looking at three novels that exemplify the rise of the African realist novel from early South African writing of the early 1900s through the early 2000s: A. C. Jordan's *The Wrath of the Ancestors* (published in 1940 as *Ingqumbo yeminyanya*), Chinua Achebe's *No Longer at Ease* (1960), and NoViolet Bulawayo's *We Need New Names* (2013).

Also drawing upon other literatures from the three literary eras, I want to look at how these three authors responded to colonialism, decolonization, and contested globalization; and also to questions around whiteness and identity, gender, and national and international citizenship. I want to look at their aesthetic and political concerns in a rapidly changing world as colonialism was revealing its final form of apartheid in South Africa, at decolonization with hints of neocolonialism in Nigeria, and the contradictions of "arrested decolonization" in Zimbabwe and failed world citizenship in the United States. In other words, I am interested in the various aesthetic and political shifts within the African literary tradition.

I also want to be mindful of the cultural critic Keguro Macharia's contention that "the ways the literature is 'cut,' often generationally, as opposed to, say, by formal strategies or even political affiliations (think modernism, romanticism, the Harlem renaissance), makes it even more difficult to imagine a [African] 'literature.' After all, what does the continual production of generation do if not simply tether anthropological time to literature (via coincidence)?"[2] Instead of thinking generationally, I want to think about what makes these three writers representative of three different literary epochs. The categorization of pre-Makerere, Makerere, and post-Makerere is not without problems. For example, between Makerere and post-Makerere, there is the writing of Tsitsi Dangarembga, and Dambudzo Marechera, for example. One can certainly make the case that they were writing from neocolonial Africa.

I am also not trying to write out women writers from the Makerere generation. For writers like Ama Ata Aidoo, there was an urgent crisis within African literary criticism—an absence of African women writing—that while women were writing, literary critics were silencing them out of the African literary tradition. Aidoo, in her Stockholm essay, writes that in addition to having to write in English, "it is especially pathetic to keep on writing without having consistent, active, critical intelligence that is interested in you as an artist (or creator)" (514). Florence Stratton, in her book *Contemporary African Literature and the Politics of Gender*, writes of Kenya's Grace Ogot who like Ngugi was writing in her mother-tongue, Dholuo, that her

> stance on the language issue is not essentially different from Ngugi's . . . In 1983 she stated that she was prompted to start writing in her first language by her mother's remark on the publication *The Graduate* that "If only you could write in Luo you would serve your people well." She also indicates that she has remained committed to writing in Dholuo so that her work "can be read by all my people" and her language preserved and not "swallowed up by English and Kiswahili." (59)

Ogot's decision has not, however, generated any of the interest or debate that Ngugi's resolve did a few years earlier to begin writing in Gikuyu. The debate has, in fact, been characterized as a wholly male affair, and Ogot's act has been negated by the absence of critical commentary on it (59).

Indeed, Ngugi's *Decolonising the Mind* does not discuss any African women's writing in English, or African languages for that matter, with very few exceptions like Micere Mugo on orature and her collaboration with Ngugi on the play *The Trial of Dedan Kimathi*. To be fair, though, he did, shortly after Ogot's death in 2015, recognize her contribution to writing in African languages. He acknowledged that, while they disagreed politically, "She was very present at the dawn of Anglophone Kenya Literature, and established herself as one of the major founders and makers of the Kenya modern literary tradition." He noted that they had turned to writing in African languages around the same time, and that the "esthetic in her books in Dholuo and English will continue to shine for generations to come."[3] But the larger point of a primarily masculine Makerere literary production still stands.

So there are other ways of drawing lines and networks within African literature—*Mhudi, Nervous Conditions, Americanah*, for example. Or *Traveller to the East, Sister Killjoy, A Question of Power, We Need New Names*. By putting Bulawayo in conversation with Jordan and Achebe, I am simply drawing out and showing the costs of cutting out early South African writing from the African literary tradition. And, if I succeed, I will also be showing how much richer and vast the African literary tradition can be if we allow it to reach back in time to, say, early Amharic writing and across space to accommodate diaspora writing.

In pre-Makerere writing, the writings of Thomas Mofolo and A. C. Jordan are concerned with synthesis. That is, the coming of the European has not yet bloomed into an irreconcilable apartheid. At the same time, African cultures are not only confidently alive but are also resisting. The answer for these writers becomes synthesis—not just coexistence but strategic borrowing and melding. As R. L. Peteni, in his introduction to *The Wrath of the Ancestors*, wistfully told his readers, the novel shows that "disaster can be averted only by the willingness of opposing forces to work together for mutual comprehension of the legitimate claims of tradition and modernity" (10).

*The Wrath of the Ancestors* is a novel about the internal dynamics of a culture about to be overrun by another one. The word *about* carries a lot of weight. From the vantage point of knowing the history that followed, of knowing how a brutal colonialism mutated into a grotesque apartheid, we know the tragedy about to befall the Mpondomise. The history of a brutal apartheid and colonialism that we know is coming gives us dramatic irony. But the people in the world of the novel do not know this. The Mpondomise are a nation living inside the belly of a growing nationalism. They are still holding to their language, culture, and laws—granted, colonial culture and laws carry more power.

In the novels of decolonization, the question is not retention of the nations but rather how to live together within the colonial boundaries. For the Makerere generation, synthesis is no longer possible and decolonization becomes the answer, but it is one full of contradictions and they usher in economic, political, and aesthetic neocolonialism.

In the post-Makerere novel, the contradictions of a decolonizing state where the Obi Okwonkwos took over the colonizer's seat means that the betrayal of African nationalism is complete. As globalization becomes more and more contested, the contradictions of decolonization have ripened. So Darling, the narrator in *We Need New Names*, becomes a subject of the black government and global politics and capitalism. At the same time, the culture she is born into is itself an inchoate amalgamation of multiple Zimbabwean and Western cultures. What then are the continuities and discontinuities across the three literary epochs? By looking at how Jordan, Achebe, and Bulawayo treat religion and culture, compromise, resistance, and survival, and the politics of gender, language, and aesthetics, it becomes possible to draw out a African literary tradition that is truer to the African literary clock.

## WHITENESS, SYNTHESIS, DECOLONIZATION, AND DISJUNCTURE

*The Wrath of the Ancestors* is both a political and romance drama. Zwelinzima, a missionary-school-educated young Mpondomise prince, is in love with Thembeka, a teacher in training at Lovedale Missionary School. Mthuzini, her fellow student, is in love with her, and for this he will eventually betray Zwelinzima to his uncle, Dingindawo, who had killed his brother, the rightful heir to the throne. When it is finally discovered that Zwelinzima is alive and therefore the rightful heir, his uncle plots to destroy him. There is a parallel love story between Mphuthumi, Zwelinzima's best friend and advisor, and Nomvuyo, who also serves a counsel to her best friend, Thembeka. But what propels the novel forward is the tension between the vision of the Western educated and Christianized Zwelinzima and his people, who have as yet to be westernized. Thembeka is too westernized for her people and she is, with the machinations of Zwelinzima's uncle, isolated and hated. In the end Zwelinzima cannot reconcile his vision with that of his people; he moves too fast, too soon in implementing changes. But when he capitulates to the demands of tradition and agrees to marry a second wife, Thembeka, already traumatized by being rejected by the Mpondomise people, comes undone and commits suicide; Zwelinzima follows her over the cliff. The politics of colonization, the clash between the two cultures, in a very personal way leads to their undoing.

The first agent of westernization we meet in the novel is an old white man that we get to know only as the Bishop. He is an idealized character who understands Africans even as he wants to convert them to Christianity. When an emotionally tortured Zwelinzima comes to him, torn between continuing with his education and fulfilling his historical role to assume the chieftainship, the Bishop tells him:

> My son, though I am White man, I have lived among Africans for a long time and I have a deep respect for some of their customs. I know that among your people the wishes of the dead—especially of a parent—are sacred. Of course it is a praiseworthy thing that you should wish to further your studies and I commend you for it. But on the other hand, I think it's incumbent upon you—nay, I go as far as saying it is your solemn duty to go and serve your people. (50)

The Bishop does see that there are some customs worth respecting. The operative word here is "some," meaning that there some customs he accepts and others that he rejects. He therefore opens up the possibility of synthesis—you can be an educated African, even a Christian, and still be part of and contribute to African culture. And the use of *my son* to address Zwelinzima? It is both literal and figurative. That is, just like any other African elder, the Bishop means that he sees Zwelinzima as his son, and as a representative of God on earth, a Father, Zwelinzima, a son of God, is also his son.

Indeed, throughout the novel, the older missionaries become father figures to the African characters, and their roles and that of African elders in the society are interchangeable. Take the moment where Mthuzini is brokenhearted after Thembeka rejects him. Taking a walk in the middle of the night, he stops under the "great cross on the gateway leading to the church" (69). On cue, a streak of light and Father Williams materialize, his "torchlight shining full in Mthuzini's face" (69). The symbolism is clear that Father Williams is bringing a light sanctioned by God to Mthuzini . The narrator describes Father Williams as "always [having] showed an interest in the welfare of those who worked under him, especially young teachers who regarded him as a father" (69). And a little later, Father Williams asks, "What is troubling you, my son?" Mthuzini replies, "Nothing, Father" (69). And Father Williams replies, "My son, I am your father. You need not be afraid to speak to me. I know you are not happy" (70). And pointing to the issues of gender and the infantilization of women that I discuss below, Father Williams promises, "I shall do my utmost to show this child [Thembeka] her proper course," but cautions him not to be too optimistic as he might fail to "persuade" her as well (70). Mthuzini refers to Williams with a capitalized Father but given that he wants help for love, a very earthly need, Father Williams, the messenger of God, and the earthly elderly respected father, become one.

At the same time, unlike in the literature of decolonization, where the power of whiteness is often destructive, in *The Wrath of the Ancestors* the power of whiteness acts as a deterrent to crime. Already worried about murdering Zwelinzima, getting caught, and being tried by the laws of the "White man" (113), Dingindawo has to change his plans any time the power of whiteness comes into play. And, for Zwelinzima, having a white man travel with him through hostile country serves as body armor. The narrator tells us "the cunning Dingindawo was a snake. From the moment when he learnt that there was a white man in the car bringing Zwelinzima, he had begun misgivings about his plans" (135). His plans foiled, he lets Zwelinzima assume the chieftainship and lives to kill him another day. The implication here is that "White man's" law is literally keeping order in ways that African law cannot;

because it has the powerful colonial machinery behind it, African law and justice, or crime and disorder, defer to it.

In the novel, both white and black characters seem to want to go out of their way to accommodate each other. The Bishop goes to see an old man by the name of Gcinizibele (Zwelinzima's adoptive father) to discuss Zwelinzima's future, but there is a question of "customary formalities," so we read, "Now White people never wait for the formal questions as to whence and why they have come, especially when the object of their visit is known. So, soon as he arrived, the Bishop went straight to the point" (59). Gcinizibele "knowing the ways of the White people . . . dispensed with the customary formalities and adapted himself to the manner of the visitor" (59). One can interpret this to mean that because it is the African who adapts, it shows a power imbalance between Africans and whites. But that is if we are using postcolonial tools of agency and the subaltern. If we simply picture the scene as rendered, it becomes one of give and take. The Bishop is in the home of Gcinizibele surrounded by Gcinizibele's people. Gcinizibele does not have to be confrontational; he is in control and so he cedes some ground to the Bishop. And the Bishop is representing the interests of Zwelinzima, and not his own.

Obi Okonkwo is the grandson of the Okonkwo in Chinua Achebe's *Things Fall Apart*. When, in Achebe's later novel, *No Longer at Ease*, we first meet Obi Okonkwo in a decolonizing but not yet independent Nigeria, he is on trial on corruption charges. The "white man's" law that Dingindawo feared in *The Wrath of Ancestors* has caught up with him and he sits before a white judge, William Galloway. This is to the collective disappointment of the whole community, because unlike the great Okonkwo and his selfwilled heroic acts, Obi's education in England was sponsored by his community through the Umuofia Progressive Party. As a character, identified only as a member of the party, angrily says, "We paid eight hundred pounds to train him in England . . . and now we are being called together again to find more money for him" (5). Obi did not start out corrupt—it is the circumstances of decolonization that turn him against himself and the principles he stood for. But because of the psychology of the colonized, or rather the political economy of the colonized, he has no choice but to be part of the corrupt machinery. His people demand it; colonialism has made it the only possible, and more importantly desirable, position, and Obi rides history like a wave all the way to prison. In decolonizing Africa, he is both agent and victim.

In *The Wrath of the Ancestors* there was hope for reconciliation and synthesis, room for the dream of two cultures meeting to mutual benefit, conquest and colonialism notwithstanding. For a reader like myself, brought up on a steady postcolonial diet, there is something jarring about reading a novel where missionaries are seen as having a positive role to play, where they are not figured as cultural agents of imperialism no matter their benevolence. This is because in the world of the decolonizing novels, the fact of the missionary as an agent of colonization has become clear. For example, in *Things Fall Apart*, Reverend Brown is drawn sympathetically, as one able to synthesize both cultures along the same lines as Jordan's Father Williams. But he cannot last long because colonialism, which is to say conquest, does not run on a benevolent give and take. The rabidly racist Reverend Smith replaces him. Together with the equally racist District Commissioner, they make the perfect colonizing team—one on the military-political front and the other on the cultural front. In their thinking, African civilizations have nothing to offer.[4] In *No Longer at Ease* and the decolonization novel, the colonizer is the colonizer—there is no hope for synthesis.

The white characters in both *Thing Fall Apart* and *No Longer at Ease* are for the most part caricatured—that is, they are official mouthpieces for uncomplicated racist and racialist philosophies. Mr. Green, Obi's boss, has a very uncomplicated understanding of Africa and Africans. He believes that "over countless centuries the African has been the victim of the worst climate in the world and of every imaginable disease. Hardly his fault. But he has been sapped mentally and physically. We have brought him Western education. But what use is it to him?" (4).

But Mr. Green's brand of colonialism has been meeting resistance over the years to a point where whiteness no longer invokes fear. The narrator tells us of an incident involving Mr. Jones, a feared inspector of schools, who had at one point "thrown a boy out of a window" (73) in the 1930s. This time around he slaps a headmaster who "had learnt the great art of wrestling" and in the "twinkling of an eye Mr. Jones was flat on the floor" and the whole school runs away because to "throw a white man was like unmasking an ancestral spirit" (74–75). Bringing us back to the present, the narrator explains that, "In 1900 Mr. Green might have ranked among the great missionaries; in 1935 he would have made do with slapping headmasters in the presence of their pupils; but in 1957 he could only curse and swear" (121).

White characters in the decolonizing novel are shown to have a perverted love for Africa that is conditional on Africans accepting their place. As Obi observes of his boss Mr. Green, "They said he had put in his resignation when it was thought that Nigeria might become independent in 1956. . . . It was clear that he loved Africa, but only Africa of a kind: the Africa of Charles, the messenger, the Africa of his garden boy and steward boy. He must have come originally with an ideal—to bring light to the heart of darkness, to tribal headhunters performing weird ceremonies and unspeakable rites" (121). The tables have turned. It is now Obi who voices Mr. Green's vision with a mixture of pity and condescension. Recalling Conrad's *Heart of Darkness*, he narrates how Kurtz, like Mr. Green, was led by the single desire to "exert power for good," but where Kurtz "succumbed to the darkness," Green had succumbed to "incipient dawn" (121). Ironically, as Byron Caminero-Santangelo argues in his book, *African Fiction and Joseph Conrad: Reading Postcolonial Intertexuality*, Obi is closer to Kurtz than he thinks. For Caminero-Santangelo, "[b]lind to their real conditions of existence not only are Obi and Kurtz unsuccessful in their efforts to improve conditions in Africa, but they themselves ultimately denigrate and come to embody the forces against which they define themselves" (33). Obi, then, like the nationalists of decolonization who would usher in the dictatorial neocolonial African state, ends up being corrupted by the very forces he understood himself as resisting.

When we first encounter Darling in NoViolet Bulawayo's *We Need New Names*, in Zimbabwe before she makes her way to the United States, she is on her way from the poverty-stricken Paradise to the wealthy and white Budapest suburb where she and her friends hope to find some guavas. In Budapest, they encounter our first white character, a 33-year-old woman who is visiting her "dad's country" for the first time. She is wearing a chain with a map of Africa on it (9). She is eating what appears to be a donut or a slice of pizza in front of the starving guava-hunting children. When she, to the horror of Darling, throws away the remainder of the food into a dustbin, Darling tells the reader, "We have never seen anyone throw food away, even if it's a thing." And to top it all off, she has been on a diet, one she terms the "Jesus diet" (10). Later, after she has taken photos of them, the children hurl insults at her. Darling for one recalls the food she has just witnessed her throw away. And the woman looks at them, "puzzled" (12).

What is interesting in this meeting is that without historical context, it comes across like a comedy of errors. But hearken back to *The Wrath of the Ancestors*, where hope of synthesis was still alive. Then to the world of *No Longer at Ease*, where that hope of synthesis has been revealed to be false, where a dying colonialism is still bitter and racist, where independent Anglo-Africa is turning into what Ama Ata Aidoo, in *Our Sister Killjoy*, calls a "neocolonial outfit" (90). The descendants of Zwelinzima and Father Williams, meeting in present-day Zimbabwe, are each propelled by history, even when they themselves in that meeting do not recall it as such. They merely act it out.

This history of racial oppression and resistance boils over later in the novel when black people start taking over white-owned farms. And, unlike in the literature of synthesis and decolonization, we see for the first time whites rendered powerless. Both Father Williams and Mr. Green have the British army and economic might behind them. The white Zimbabwe farmers in the novel are powerless, and, in their powerlessness, taunted and humiliated. A group of black men and women invade a house owned by whites. They kill the woman's little dog after passing it around like they "are playing netball" (118). They serve the man of the house with what appears to be an eviction or appropriation notice. When he protests, saying that he owns the land, the leader of the gang tells the crowd, "somebody please tell this white man that this is not fucking Rhodesia," and then turning to him tells him, "Know this, you bloody colonist, from now on the black man is done listening, you hear? This is black-man country and the black man is in charge now. Africa for Africans" (120).

In *The Wrath of the Ancestors*, in a confrontation between whites and blacks, it is the African who is afraid because the power of the law and violence favor the colonizer. In *We Need New Names*, power has shifted to the black nationalists. As the gang enters the house, Darling captures the white couple's helplessness this way: "The white man and woman remain standing there near the guard like sad plants; maybe they are afraid of the weapons and that's why they don't try to stop them or follow them inside" (121).

When Darling immigrates to the United States, *We Need New Names* introduces a whiteness that could not have possibly existed in *The Wrath of Ancestors*, or in *No Longer at Ease*. Earlier in the novel, through the staff of NGOs in Zimbabwe, Darling had introduced some of the well-meaning whites who fail to see the larger national and international politics at work in the poverty-stricken faces of the children. When they deliver food, they do not see the children as human beings but rather as curious little things to be photographed without considering that they might be "embarrassed by [their] dirt and torn clothing" (45). In the United States, Darling now gets to hear their patronizing rationale through the voice of a white woman who she meets at a wedding. In spite of the happy occasion, she tells Darling, "Africa is beautiful . . . but isn't it terrible what's happening in the Congo? Just awful," and then goes on to talk about the "rapes, and those killings. How can such things even be happening?" (177). Darling narrates:

Then she lifts her head like she has remembered something important. Now, Lisa, up there, my niece, one of the bridesmaids, the tall one, real, skinny redhead—she is going to Rwanda to help. She's in the Peace Corps, you know they are doing great things for Africa. (178)

And with that "her face is looking much, much better, like the pain from earlier is going away" and she goes on to tell her that last summer her niece taught at an orphanage in South Africa. And she and others had donated clothes, pens, crayons, medicines, and candy (178). Her troubled conscience at the rapes and killings in the Congo is assuaged vicariously through her Peace Corps volunteering niece.

One can draw a line across the African literary tradition that starts with Father Williams through to Reverend Brown and Reverend Steven, finally resting with the hapless NGO volunteer. Alternatively, the 1900s Mr. Green in *No Longer at Ease*, the one who would have been a great missionary, recalls Father Williams in *The Wrath of the Ancestors*. Following the progression of Mr. Green into the world of *We Need New Names*, what does the Mr. Green of the 21st century look like? And the answer that emerges is that he would have been an NGO worker—a Bob Geldof figure holding a sack of maize flour.

## RELIGION AND CULTURE: HOPE, DISILLUSIONMENT, MOURNING, AND MELANCHOLY

In *The Wrath of the Ancestors*, white and black culture can coexist and learn from each other. In *No Longer at Ease*, what it means to be African, and what is African culture, is under debate. Yet in spite of their differences they both see African cultures as traditional and westernization as the modern. From the introduction to *The Wrath of Ancestors*, we read that for Zwelinzima, "The clash of his modern ideas and the traditional beliefs of his people mirror the clash of the western way of life with African custom and tradition" (12). The back cover to *No Longer at Ease* in part reads, "Forced to choose between traditional values and the demands of a changing world, he finds himself trapped between the expectations of his family, his village, and the larger society around him." But in *We Need New Names* there are no old and new worlds, modern and traditional; Darling's world has in it the fractured and multiple cultures of Zimbabwe and the United States as the starting point.

In the *Wrath of the Ancestors*, Zwelinzima is the ideal chief—one who works within the orbit of colonialism but carves a space within it. He forms several committees, farmer associations, and a committee to write a constitution. He is interested in world affairs and listens to his trusted friend who cautions him about "African chiefs [who] ride round the countryside with a huge retinue of men to usurp from their constituents" (169–70). His wife, now titled Nobantu, Mother of the People, forms a child welfare and home improvement society, becomes a patron for tennis and netball, and would "invite Girl Guide and Boy Scouts to the Royal Palace" (171). His constituents come together and buy him a car because he needed "a pair of feet" so that he could discharge his many duties; the car affectionately comes to be named "Ndawo-Zonke" or "Mr. Everywhere" (171).

But there is a problem: the ideal chief is also too eager to abandon what to him are retrogressive African cultural practices for his people. For example, he wants to "exterminate goats" because they are the currency of "diviners and medicine men" (185). His argument is that without the currency, the medicine men and healers will be out of business and the people will realize as life goes on that they were simply lying, and with that, turn to the real doctors of the West.

Zwelinzima's people also believe that he should marry a woman from royalty as opposed to the commoner they see Thembeka to be. They also hold equally strongly that, because it was his father's death wish that he marry royalty, he has to follow through. But as a Christian, he is opposed to polygamy. He decides to go and visit a fellow chief who has faced a similar problem; he advises him to play along with some of these cultural practices to avoid alienating himself from the people. This chief tells him a story about how "against his own beliefs, he had to submit being treated by a medicine man" so that his followers would believe that he been "strengthened and made immune to witchcraft" (188).

The solution then put forward by the chief is that he reconsider his commitment to marry only one wife, a core tenet in his Christianity, and marry a second wife from royalty. For the people, this proposal would allow for the coexistence of the white culture and African culture. Zwelinzima refuses, and soon after the fissures between the two cultures break wide open. The Africans stop sending their children to school, but the teachers go behind their backs and entice the students back to school. At this point the angry parents attack the school, beating up the teachers and taking their children home. Enter Father Williams, who travels to the Mpondomise, where he meets a headman who explains the situation to him:

> We praised you and your people too soon for the light you brought, Mfundi-si, not realizing that through your religion and your education our children are learning to lose the respect for the customs and traditions of their fathers. . . . But at least we still have a way of saving our children while they are still young, and, by taking the action we have taken, we are saving them. (239)

Father Williams does not reply but the narrator tells us that "[h]e who had until now flattered himself that he understood the Black Man realised the he did not know him at all" (239). Later, his misunderstanding of the Mpondomise leads to the death of an elder who is killed while protecting him from revolting youth. Father Williams's life is spared only when African women come to his rescue, offering their bodies as shields. The people's revolt against Zwelinzima and Father Williams is not offered as a critique of colonialism and Christianity—it is a critique of youthful violence, of those elements in society that reject the modern for the retrogressive, of those that see synthesis as a threat to their existence. And even where colonialism is mentioned, it is in passing.

In *No Longer at Ease*, Christianity is here to stay. It is a question of the nature of that Christianity. Will it be uncompromising and self-righteous, or can it coexist (not synthesize) with other cultures? Obi's father, Isaac Okonkwo, is a devout Christian, or, as the narrator puts it, he was not "merely a Christian; he was a catechist" (66). The Igbo culture he tries to ignore keeps pulling him back. Obi wants to marry his girlfriend but she is an Osu, meaning that she comes from a "forbidden caste" (82). His father objects and Obi reminds him that they are Christians and it should not matter. His father replies, "We are Christians . . . but that is no reason to marry an Osu" (151). For Isaac, the idea of being shamed by the community for his son marrying an Osu, and his grandchildren being shunned to an extent that they will not find anyone to marry them, overwhelms his Christian principles.

Before Obi was born Isaac had already forbidden his wife from narrating folktales to their children, saying, "We are not heathens. . . . Stories like that are not for the people of the Church" (66). When Obi is ridiculed in school for not knowing a single folktale, his mother immediately teaches him one—and when called upon again to narrate one a few weeks later, he confidently recited it and "even added a little touch to the end which made everyone laugh" (68). Igbo culture is still immediately around Obi. That is, he has easy access to that which he had lost. Even though the decolonizing world in *No Longer at Ease* is one in flux, that which has been lost to the colonizing culture can still be known to Obi.

For Freud, "mourning is regularly the reaction to the loss of a loved person, or to the loss of some abstraction which has taken the place of one, such
as one's country, liberty, an ideal, and so on" ("Mourning and Melancholia,"
243). In melancholia, "one cannot see clearly what it is that has been lost,
[and] is in some way related to an object-loss which is withdrawn from consciousness, in contradistinction to mourning, in which there is nothing about
the loss that is unconscious" (244). The Makerere writer can be said to be
mourning—they know what they have lost, whether it is language and culture, or land and nation. And their writing is an attempt to recover a lost
known object. For the post-Makerere generation, they do not fully know the
language they have lost, and have no direct memory of the land and nation
that belonged to their parents. Examined through this lens, Obi in *Things Fall
Apart* is in a state of mourning, and Darling in *We Need New Names* is in a
state of melancholia, whether at home in Zimbabwe or abroad in the West.
But Zwelinzima cannot yet mourn his culture or country because he still has
them—he is just in the process of losing them.

The Christianity in *We Need New Names* no longer carries the quiet and
deadly colonial dignity of Father William, or the sacrificial kind espoused
by Obi's father, Isaac. The Christianity in Bulawayo's Zimbabwe is chaotic,
loud, and bordering on the caricature. For example, Darling narrates that,
"On the Mopane is a big sign with an arrow that points upwards, towards our
church. Beneath the arrow are these words: "HOLY CHARIOT CHURCH OF
CHRIST—IT DOESNT GO BACKWARDS, IT DOESNT GO SIDEWAYS, IT
DOESNT GO FORWARDS. IT GOES UPWARDS, TO HEAVEN. AMEN"
(32). The service itself is led by Prophet Revelations Bitchington Mborro and
a group of evangelists that Darling describes as "look[ing] like something else
with the colorful crosses emblazoned on their robes, their long sticks with the
hooks at the ends, their bald heads glimmering in the sun, the long beards;
you can just tell that they are trying to copy the style of those men in the
Bible" (34–35). The woman leading the singing is described as having a voice
worse than a cat's (35). The service itself is one chaotic affair that culminates
in an exorcism. When the possessed woman is brought in by a group of men,
the Prophet "points his stick at the pretty woman and commands the demon
inside her to get the hell out in the name of Jesus. . . . Prophet Revelations
Bitchington Mborro prays for her like that, pinning her down and calling to
Jesus and screaming Bible verses. He places his hands on her stomach, on her
thighs, then he puts his hands on her thing and starts rubbing and praying

hard for it, like there is something wrong with it" (41–42). This is not gentle, albeit racist, Christianity in the novel of decolonization.

And once Darling is in the United States, what becomes of Christianity, of religion and God? God is leveled—his church is mentioned in passing together with liquor stores and Chinese hair stores. Darling finds a new god whose religion is consumerism. She narrates that while in Zimbabwe, hungry and angry, they had forsaken their God:

> But when we got to America and saw all that food, we held our breath and thought, Wait, there must be a God. So happy and grateful we found his discarded pieces and put them together with the Krazy Glue bought at the dollar store for only ninety-nine cents and said, In God We Trust too now, In God We Trust for real, and began praying again. At McDonald's we devoured Big Macs and wolfed down fries and guzzled supersized cokes. At Burger King we worshipped Whoppers. At KFC we mauled bucket chicken. (240–41)

In Zimbabwe they had the God of desperation, and paradise was hell. In the United States, they find a racist and classist God of plenty living cheaply in Wal-Mart.

## STRATEGIES OF COMPROMISE, RESISTANCE, AND SURVIVAL

In *The Wrath of the Ancestors*, Dingindawo at the slain elder's funeral says in reference to the women who saved Father William's life, "The calamity that the woman of Jenca averted by her courage might well have had more serious results than the assassination of Hamilton Hope at Sulenkama. It must be remembered that Mhlonto was not fighting against missionaries, but against the colonial government" (245). This is a rare admission of the larger brutal historical processes at work in the novel. The narrator is referring to a real historical event where revolting Mpondomise people led by Chief Mhlonto killed Hamilton Hope, a British magistrate, and his party. Historically there was a communal price to pay for Hope's death. Clifton Crais in his essay, "Of Men, Magic, and the Law: Popular Justice and the Political Imagination in South Africa," notes "people paid dearly for the killing of a colonial official and a white man. The colonial state deposed chiefs, doubled the hut tax, disarmed men, and confiscated land" (50). It is this refusal by the narrator and

Dingindawo to see a link between missionary work and colonialism that is intriguing, because that is precisely what they mean when they say the killing of a white missionary would have brought down a calamity on the Mpondomise. But that is the point of the novel of synthesis, it is not yet too late—there is still hope if the missionaries, Western educated and Christianized Africans, and Africans still living within their culture can speak across their differences and learn from each other.

In *No Longer at Ease*, what is at stake in decolonizing Nigeria is the master's chair and what the characters are willing to do, or not do, in order to sit in it. Obi is on trial on corruption charges but he was not always corrupt. When he returns from England he finds a country where taking bribes is so much the norm that it is those who refuse bribes that are seen as naïve. But he has his scholarship to pay back, a bank note for his car, relatives who need money, and a girlfriend who needs money for an abortion. That is the story on one level. But as one digs deeper it becomes a story about Nigerian corruption within colonial corruption. That is, he is as much a victim of the very processes created by colonialism, even as he takes advantage of the opportunities. Take a discussion around work leave between Mr. Green, Marie (Green's secretary), and Obi. When Obi returns from a two-week leave, Mr. Green laments that an African like him who already "has too many privileges" should not be taking local leave because it was meant "to give Europeans a break to go to a cool place like Jos or Buea" (174). And then when Obi tells him he would be okay with the government abolishing local leave, Mr. Green goes on to say:

> It's people like you who ought to make the government decide. That is what I have always said. There is no single Nigerian who is prepared to forgo a little privilege in the interests of his country. From your ministers down to your most junior clerk. And you tell me you want to govern yourselves. (174)

Mr. Green, who believes that the English have brought the Africans civilization, cannot even contemplate that the English might be complicit in creating and propagating corrupt practices. But Obi is quick to remind him:

> It is not the fault of the Nigerians. You devised these soft conditions for yourselves when every European was automatically in the senior service and every African automatically in the junior service. Now that a few of us have been admitted into the senior service, you turn round and blame. (175)

The problem here for Obi is not the system itself that allows for work leave abuses to happen, or how it might work for the those in the senior service, or how it might not for those in junior positions. What decolonizing Africans want is precisely what the Europeans have. And that includes all the trappings of colonialism, from fancy cars to having housemaids and garden boys. Indeed, Obi, who can barely make ends meet, has a new car and a cook. As Fanon puts it:

> The national bourgeoisie of the under-developed countries is not engaged in production, nor in invention, nor building, nor labour; it is completely canalized into activities of the intermediary type. Its innermost vocation seems to be to keep in the running and to be part of the racket. The psychology of the national bourgeoisie is that of the businessman, not that of a captain of industry; and it is only too true that the greed of the settlers and the system of embargoes set up by colonialism has hardly left them any other choice. (120)

In a way, *No Longer at Ease* is a fictionalized account of the making of the national bourgeoisie. Obi has no choice; once the colonial system takes a hold of him he is canalized, herded at every turn into becoming corrupt. The only difference between decolonization and neocolonialism is that, in decolonization, Africans do not have the power of the law behind them. They cannot as yet corrupt the laws set up to protect colonial interests, and Obi cannot get away with breaking the law the way a white man would. The colonial machinery will only work for corrupt Africans when they take over the government and truly form their very own "neocolonial outfits."

For Benedict Anderson, the nation is an "imagined political community that is imagined as both inherently limited and sovereign" (*Imagined Communities*, 7). In *The Wrath of Ancestors* and *No Longer at Ease* it is this imagined community under negotiation, whether it is how to synthesize opposing cultures, or the process of decolonization. The Africans in *We Need New Names* are reimagining and re-creating what was already an imagined community. They are partly sovereign because in most instances you have geographical areas that are predominantly inhabited by that group (e.g., little Mogadishu in Minneapolis), but also limited because the national laws trump communal laws. These imagined immigrant communities can survive—the question that I think *We Need New Names* raises is whether they can thrive. This is not to say there are no individual successes within African immigrant communities, the question is whether they can be collective. Thus, they dream of a return that can only be a visit, but only if they are still legal and can therefore be allowed back into the United States. In *We Need New Names*, the processes that herd Darling into a forced settlement and eventually into forced immigration are too many and historical in nature, too removed from the oppressive present. As such, the narration is fragmented.

The opening chapter, "Budapest," in *We Need New Names*, reflects the brutal violence and poverty that rule the lives of Darling and her friends. As they walk from the poverty-ridden Paradise to the wealthy Budapest we learn that Chipo, Darling's 11-year-old friend, has been raped and impregnated by her grandfather. They decide to help her have an abortion using techniques they have learned from the TV show *ER*. Sbho tells them, "In order to do this right, we need new names" and then goes on to give them corrupted TV names from the show—Dr. Bullet, Dr. Roz, and Dr. Cutter (84). It's funny, almost a caricature until the reader realizes that there can be deadly consequences. Using a hanger, these children are about to attempt the abortion when Mother Love intervenes.

In "Budapest," we see that violence is always under the surface when they insult the white woman ostensibly for being rich, white, and for throwing food away. However, they are really being acted upon by history—that is, even though they cannot articulate it, they know that their poverty has something to do with whiteness, with the colonial oppression of yesteryear and the wealth before them. A little later, after they steal guavas, they come across a woman who has hanged herself and, after throwing stones at her, decide to take her shoes to go sell in order to buy some food (20).

But the children also dream. The children dream of being wealthy and of going abroad. Shbo points to a big house and says, "One day, I will live here, in a house just like that" (13). And Darling, right from the very beginning, keeps talking about going to live in America with her Aunt Fostalina.

> Then I look up at the sky and see a plane far up in the clouds. First, I am thinking it's just a bird, but then I see that no, it's not. Maybe it's a British Airways plane like the one Aunt Fostalina went in to America. (36)

But their dreams are more aware of the contradictions of the West and the African diaspora than in *No Longer at Ease*, where England is seen as a paradise. When they come across the woman hanging from a tree, Darling ties this tragedy to the United States by observing "a tall thing dangling in a tree like a strange fruit" (18). Even when they mispronounce Detroit, Michigan, as Destroyedmichygen, there is a knowing wink to the reader who is familiar with the economic devastation and corruption in Detroit, and eventual municipal bankruptcy. More pointedly, they are aware that the United States is not the paradise previous generations thought it was. When Darling tells her friends that she will be going to the United States, Bastard responds:

> Well, go, go to that America and work in nursing homes. That's what your Aunt Fostalina is doing as we speak. Right now she is busy cleaning kaka off some wrinkled old man who can't do anything for himself, you think we've never heard the stories? (17)

And true to Bastard's word, the America she finds is not paved with gold. In the night, she hears the "bang-bang-bang of gunshots in the neighborhood," and whereas in Zimbabwe she could walk freely, in the US she feels unsafe. But it is more than that. Darling tells us that, in her letters back home, she paints an ideal picture of the United and tells the reader the things she leaves out; a woman who drowns her four children in a bathtub, and people begging for money (190). This not the United States she had dreamt of.

Obi, while living in England, has a return date. Zwelinzima is at home. But Darling is an illegal immigrant and without the proper "papers" she cannot go to Zimbabwe to visit. She has been sentenced to stay in the US for as long as it takes for her to become legal. Aunt Fostalina tells her when she asks to visit home for two weeks, "Child, it's not like your father is Obama and he has the Air Force One; home costs money. Besides, you came on a visitor's visa, and that's expired; you get out, you kiss this America bye-bye" (191). Trapped, unable to return, the United States is turning into a dystopia.

In the chapter "How They Lived" she distills this dystopia to reveal the desperate lengths that people go to in order to come to America only to become laborers. Darling narrates, "For the visas and passports, we begged, despaired, lied, groveled, promised, charmed, bribed—anything to get out of the country" (242). Tshaka Zulu, who eventually loses his mind, stole all his father's cows and had siblings taken out of school, in order to pay for his way to the United States (242). And for all that, Darling writes they would never "be things we wanted to be: doctors, lawyers, teachers, engineers" (243). Instead, they "worked with dangerous machines" that took limbs and lives so that they can send a little bit of money back home. Darling cleans toilets and bags groceries. But this America does not just demand physical and mental sacrifices; it also tears them away from their culture:

> And then our children were born. We held their American birth certificates tight. We did not name our children after our parents, after ourselves; we feared if we did they would not be able to say their own names, that their friends and teachers would not know what to call them. We gave them names that would make them belong. (249)

Instead of well-adjusted immigrants whose worries are focused on balancing between maintaining their culture and assimilation, the brutal reality of being an illegal immigrant leads to mental disorders as we see with Tshaka and Uncle Kojo. Their black nationalism is not enough. These are not children of two worlds; they are the children of multiple histories that have spat them out. They cannot get back in, and madness becomes a way out.

## POLITICS OF GENDER ACROSS THREE AFRICAN LITERARY EPOCHS

Women are portrayed differently across the three literary epochs. In *The Wrath of Ancestors*, women have little political agency, in addition to being idealized—that is, while not angelic, they do no evil beyond gossiping. In *No Longer at Ease*, women characters have limited agency though they are more fully drawn. In *We Need New Names*, women have the center stage.

In *The Wrath of the Ancestors*, women are absent in meaningful negotiations. When the Bishop and Gcinizibele meet to discuss Zwelinzima's future, his adoptive mother is not part of the conversation. There is an assumption that his adoptive mother was listening in because, after the men decide that Zwelinzima should take the kingship but keep it secret in the meantime, we read that his foster mother sobbed as if the "Mpondomise had already come to take away her child" (59). The discussion about whom Zwelinzima should marry is also a discussion among the men. Even when they acknowledge intergenerational change where young men are free to marry whom they want, it is within patriarchy. Zwelinzima chooses his wife, or his people choose a wife for him (149–54). The older women do not have a say over the matter; instead, they facilitate the deceit so that male council members can view the candidates. Thus, the wife of the respected elder, Ngubengwe, invites her niece along with Thembeka to work in the kitchen and make lunch so the council members could secretly observe Thembeka in order to decide on her suitability to be queen:

> As these two young women went in and out of the room, waiting on them, these grave men gazed their fill. Little did Thembeka dream that she was the center of their attraction. Each councilor found some excuse to engage her attention as she passed . . . obviously there was something more selfish than their duty to their Chief that inspired them! (157)

The narrator refers to Thembeka as a "girl" in spite of being a grown educated woman now working as a teacher (66). In a way, the narrator's gaze is male, and his audience is not women, but men, young and old alike. Thembeka is the narrator's woman fantasy because a little later he tell us that "Thembeka was not the kind of girl who likes to have young men around her, only to keep them dangling between hope and despair" (67). In other words, she does not play around with men's emotions by leading them on.

Thembeka refuses to submit to cultural practices she sees as "cruel torture" and speaks in "condemnation of the practice of medicine-men who scarify babies' bodies and rub them with burning powders to protect them against witchcraft" (182). But she does not refuse as a woman; it is her Christian duty.

In *No Longer at Ease* women have more agency, but only as far as they lead to Obi's ruin. Clara is his beautiful British-educated girlfriend and for a time his fiancée. Her relationship with Obi appears to be equal, and she wounds his masculinity by trying to bail him out of debt. But she leaves the money she is giving him in the glove compartment of an unlocked car and it gets stolen. And, even worse, it is her pregnancy that leads to Obi needing money for an abortion. It forces him into his accepting what turns out to be his final bribe as he is arrested. And on top of being a woman, she is also an Osu—the final and absolute strike against her.

In *We Need New Names* the roles of the elders struggling to keep colonized and decolonizing communities together are taken over by women. Mother of Bones, Darling's religious grandmother; Mother Love, who functions like Paradise's godmother; and Aunt Fostalina—each in their own ways try to keep their families and people together in spite of the powerful forces of poverty and forced migration arrayed against them.

Whereas in *The Wrath of Ancestors* white women are largely absent except as benevolent, and mostly silent, nuns, in *No Longer at Ease* they are present, but only as not fully developed and at other times caricatured characters. For example, Marie Tomlinson, Mr. Green's secretary, while drawn sympathetically, is used by the narrator to reveal more details about Mr. Green. For example, she reveals to Obi that while Mr. Green "says the most outrageous things about Africans" he also "pays school fees for his steward's son" (119–20). The manager of Palm Grove is an old white woman; she is described as croaking orders, she toddles instead of walking, spills milk on herself, and is almost shat on by her parrot (40–41).

To have a relationship with a white woman is seen by the characters as diluting African culture. The greatest sin Obi could have committed was to marry a white woman, and his one saving grace act in the eyes of the community is that he did not. When he was leaving, an elder speaking at his going-away party had warned him:

> I have heard of young men from other towns who went to the whiteman's country, but instead of facing their studies, they went after the sweet things of the flesh. Some of them even married white women. . . . A man who does that is lost to his people. (12)

And when he returns to Umuofia, a character says "they should all thank God that Obi had not brought home a white wife" (61). In this sense, where African women are the guardians of African culture, white women become the threat. In the end, African and white women remain marginalized: African women as bastions of African culture, as keepers of culture are protected from impurity through patriarchy, and white women, as threats, are kept at a distance through that same patriarchy.

In *We Need New Names*, white women are not necessarily seen as threats to African culture. Where the novel allows for black women to be flawed but full and heroic characters, white women are caricatured and nameless. The first white woman we meet is the one taking photos of Darling and her friends. White women are NGO workers, Peace Corps volunteers, fat brides marrying African immigrant males in the United States, and CNN-watching liberals. In both Jordan's and Achebe's novels, white women augment patriarchy either through silence or through their presence. In *We Need New Names* white women are ineffectual agents of an exploitative globalization and largely inconsequential.

There is a quick point to make here. In *The Wrath of Ancestors* and *No Longer at Ease*, sex doesn't happen on stage, on the page. Women become pregnant offstage, only returning to give birth or to have an abortion (that itself takes place offstage). In *We Need New Names* there is a graphicness that would have been unimaginable in the novels of synthesis and decolonization. Chipo narrates to Darling how her grandfather raped her. Darling in the United States spends a lot of time watching Internet pornography together with her friends, with some of the sex acts described in great detail. Understood within the lens of patriarchy, African women in their purity could not be seen having sex, much less sexual violence being perpetrated against them, especially by African men. But in Darling's world, incestuous rapes and pornography happen.

## DIFFERENCES IN AESTHETICS: TRANSLATION, AFRICANIZATION, AND STRATEGIES OF NARRATION

There is marked difference between the intertexuality of the decolonizing novel and that of *We Need New Names*. In Bulawayo's novel, the intertexuality is embedded in the narration: for example, the woman "dangling in a tree like a strange fruit" (18). When they are playing country games, no one wants to be Congo, Somalia, or other countries that are described as "places of hunger" (Marechera's *House of Hunger*, 51), where things are falling apart (Achebe, 51), and "there is no night so long that doesn't end with dawn" (Ngugi's *Matigari*). But there is no discernible intertexuality with the early South African writing, which raises the question: What kind of a literary tradition remains blind and deaf to the literature that comes before it? And what does it mean to have a literary tradition that is resting on the wrong foundation? Looking at Bulawayo's seamlessly paying homage to the decolonization literature, we can assume that early South African writing could also have been a reference point, thus making her novel more grounded in her literary tradition. But without being aware of her full literary tradition, her starting point is the Makerere generation.

The questions also apply to *No Longer at Ease*. In England, Obi does not study law as his people expected him to. Instead, he majors in English, and therefore his literary points of reference lean toward the English literary canon. The interview with the Chairman takes a literary bent and they end up showcasing their knowledge of Graham Greene, W. H. Auden (Anglo-American), and Charles Dickens (45–46). And his favorite poet is A. E. Housman (172), whom he revisits whenever things go awry. The point is not that he loves European literature; it is that it becomes his reference point. Tejumola

Olaniyan in his essay, "The Paddle That Speaks English: Africa, NGOs, and the Archaeology of an Unease," argues that what English literature does is give Obi a "discursive formation" that

> provides him with his easiest, most accessible, and most comfortable frames of reference and interpretation. "What an Augean stable!" he muttered in exclamation to the pervasive corruption he sees around him. And all through the text, there are references to Charles Dickens, W. H. Auden, T. S. Eliot, Evelyn Waugh, and Graham Greene. These provide the dominant metaphors by which Obi lives and reads the world. We would be hard pressed to find one clear instance in the text in which Obi references Igbo imaginative expression as template of a moral or political lesson. There are a few instances, but it is often unclear whether they are the narrator's or Obi's thoughts. (53)

Not only is there a lack of references to "Igbo imaginative expression," but also, besides a quick mention of Tutuola, there are no references to African literature, except the obvious link to *Things Fall Apart*. For Obi, then, African literature begins with Tutuola as opposed to, let's say, Mofolo's *Chaka*. There is absolutely no consciousness of the rich literary tradition in South Africa. Because the decolonizing writers themselves followed the "oral—literary interface," the intertexuality that exists in their novels is between their works and orature, as opposed to earlier African writing.

In *The Wrath of Ancestors* the intertexuality is with orature. Jordan uses not just proverbs but also praise songs and poems and stories. When *No Longer at Ease* and *The Wrath of the Ancestors* are read side by side as one thinks about translation theories, it becomes clear that language in *No Longer at Ease* reads like a translated work, and that the best way to understand the language use in the decolonization novel is to use translation theory. When we read the literature of decolonization outside the translated early African literature, we can talk about how Achebe, Ngugi, and others have Africanized English. Read within the early South African literature, what the writers were doing when thinking about Africanization became acts of translation. As part of his translation strategy, A. C. Jordan leaves some words in isiXhosa, for example, *thikolosh*. In *No Longer at Ease*, Achebe leaves some words in their original Igbo—for example, *chi, osu*. Jordan, in order to remind the reader that the book is translated, literalizes the translation. Characters are presented as "fattening their statements" (215), while others tell the truth by "cutting their gizzards open" (149), or become stoic by "hardening their livers" (45). In *We*

*Need New Names*, Bulawayo employs some of the translation strategies—we assume the character is narrating in Ndebele because English words are italicized. But she also uses the Achebe aesthetic and Africanizes her English by translating directly.

Thinking about the form of the three novels, the novel of synthesis and the decolonization novel are linear, even where flashbacks are employed. In the *Wrath of the Ancestors* the story is linear; it begins with Zwelinzima and friends in a teacher's training college and ends with Zwelinzima's death. Thomas Mofolo's *Traveller to the East* is linear as well. And while *No Longer at Ease* employs a long flashback and is bracketed by Obi's court trial, there is an obvious linearity that emerges as it moves from an innocent Obi to a corrupted Obi. *We Need New Names*, on the other hand, is narrated in fragments and digressions in a way that reflects the inchoate amalgamation that is Zimbabwe and its diaspora. If the colonial world could be contained in the linear but flashback-employing novel, the globalized world today calls for different narrative strategies—diaries, blogs, fragments, digressions—all in one novel.

## COSTS AND OPPORTUNITIES

The world of *The Wrath of Ancestors* is bifurcated, on the one side you have African culture, and on the other, white culture—and, even as the book suggests a cultural synthesis, it is not for the two worlds to merge but rather to learn from each other. The world of *No Longer at Ease* is more complicated— Obi is a returnee from England to a decolonizing Nigeria where power is shifting from white and colonial hands to divided and corrupt black hands. But the world is still black and white.

But, as we have seen, the world of *We Need New Names* is vastly more complex—you have a growing Chinese presence in Zimbabwe, white Zimbabweans in gated communities, and issues of class between poor and rich, powerful black Zimbabweans. In the literature of decolonization, the contradictions of neocolonialism have not yet ripened, while post-Makerere literature draws its oxygen from the shattered and betrayed dreams in the earlier literature. In the literature of decolonization, Britain and other nations in Europe are the main countries that African characters travel to with the intention of coming back. The post-Makerere characters, in contrast, immigrate to the United States, where life is further complicated by questions of race, class and their relationship to an Africa they will never return to.

But the real question here is: Can we really say that we are students and scholars of African literature if we start the literary clock with the Makerere generation of writers? That is, with the literature of decolonization while not accounting for the earlier literature of synthesis? While not taking into account the aesthetics and politics of early South African writing? And that raises another question: What other literary African writing is missing in the production of African literary criticism? When did the African diaspora start and when stop producing African-American literature that was not African?

For example, the anthology *Two Centuries of African English* (edited by Lalage Brown), starts with the premise that the writings now called slave narratives were part of an African literary canon. The writing included covers a wide span of time and space. It has letters written by Ignatius Sancho in 1769 while he was living in Richmond, Virginia; Sancho was then a freed slave but he had been born on a slave ship. It includes excerpts from Olaudah Equiano's *Experience of Slavery* (1789), about his life in Nigeria before being captured and sold into slavery, and polemical pieces by the likes of Ezekiel Mphahlele (1962) and Ali Mazrui (1969). Brown's criteria for inclusion was the degree to which one identified as African (3), while excluding persons of African descent who have become part of other cultures and societies, because they represent other traditions (3). Brown's premise is fascinating in that it includes writings not usually associated with African writing, thereby raising the question: Why is it that we don't read early slave narratives as part of African literature? Seeing the narratives as part of African literature does not make them any less foundational in African American literature, neither does it make African literature any less African.

While Achebe here was not making the argument that the book be read as African literature, and was instead using Equiano to show that Africans can master English, he observed that

> Equiano was an Ibo (I believe from the village of Iseke in the Orlu division of Eastern Nigeria). He was sold as a slave at a very early age and transported to America. Later he bought his freedom and lived in England. In 1789 he published his life story, a beautifully written document which, among other things, set down for the Europe of his time something of the life and habit of his people in Africa, in an attempt to counteract the lies and slander invented by some Europeans to justify the slave trade. (29)

But more directly, Achebe had asked the historian Paul Edwards to abridge the narrative for publication. It was published in 1967 by the AWS under the title, *Equiano's Travels: His Autobiography; The Interesting Narrative of the Life of Olaudah Equiano or Gustavus Vassa the African.* In other words, for Achebe as the editor of the AWS, Equiano's narrative was part of the African literary tradition.

The narrative adds another dimension to early and ongoing conversations between Africans and African Americans. It sets an excellent foundation for Africans to enter into African American literature, and vice versa. And it gives a solid basis with which to think about contemporary works by African writers that are rooted in Africa and the United States, and whose plots deal with African and African American relationships via whiteness, such as Chimamanda Adichie's *Americanah* and NoViolet Bulawayo's *We Need New Names.* In the preface to the 2006 Waveland edition of Equiano's narrative, S. E. Ogude read it within an African literary tradition, or as creating a moment for Africans and African Americans to be in conversation about memory and history. Of Equiano, he wrote that "he was proud of his culture and conscious of his roots, yet he was steeped in other people's way of life and religion," making him the "first modern African" (viii). As an example, imagine reading Equiano, Sol Plaatje, Bessie Head, Gillian Slovo, Binyavaga Wainaina, and Okey Ndibe as part of African memoir writing, or imagine reading Equiano alongside the African travel memoirs by Richard Wright and Maya Angelou.

The argument can be extended to early Afro-Arab and Afro-Latino writing as well. Janheinz Jahn in *Neo-African Literature: A History of Black Writing,* for example, includes Antar, a foundational poet for Arabic literature, the son of a black female slave writing in the chivalric Bedouin tradition around 600 AD in Saudi Arabia (26), and Juan Latino, born in Guinea in 1516 before being enslaved in Spain at the age of 12 (31).

If the former British empire can, through its creation of commonwealth literature and prizes, claim literatures coming from former colonies, why can't African countries also claim the literature coming from former empires that directly impacted the trajectory of African aesthetics, if only to understand that which in part forms it? And claim literatures by enslaved Africans for whom Africa remained a large part of their identity?

In short, rather than arguing about the identity of African literature along content, race, and geography, the category should be opened to allow not just for African diaspora or literatures coming from the black Atlantic, but for a nonhierarchical African commonwealth literature or literatures of Africa.

# Manufacturing the African Literary Canon

## Costs and Opportunities

Our involvement in African writing introduced me to a new aspect of publishing—the author in prison. At one time or another our African authors have become political prisoners. . . . In fact at one time, our weekly in-house circular which lists forthcoming visits by authors carried a column headed 'Authors in Prison' which we updated each month.

• • •

When I returned to London, I was convinced that the ordinary publishing trade could be fully adequate for needs of Africans at this stage in their development. I decided to give it a try.
—Alan Hill, *In Pursuit of Publishing*

When the top 100 African books were announced in 2002 in Ghana to celebrate half a century of decolonization, jurors led by literary critic Njabulo Ndebele were making a bold statement—the African literary canon had arrived and it was here to stay. In their preamble to the call for nominations the jurors stated among other things that the prize was "to celebrate the achievements of African writers over the last century." They called for books written by Africans and produced in the 20th century and made the case that

[o]ver the last hundred years African writers have written of their lives, experiences, culture, history and myth; they have written in diverse forms, styles and in many languages. They have been published widely on the African continent, in Europe, the Americas and Asia. They have written in English, French, Portuguese, Arabic, Swahili, and in many other indigenous languages. And they have written with extraordinary originality, flair and great integrity. Nonetheless their work as a corpus deriving from the African continent remains largely unknown and uncelebrated. (*Africa's 100 Best Books of the 20th Century*)

In the same way that early South African writing is recognized and then glossed over, cast into the subcategory of the "oral-literate interface," writing outside the Makerere consensus of the political novel in English is recognized and just as quickly dismissed. The jurors name three European languages and only two African languages—Kiswahili and Arabic. And the rest of African languages—some, such as Yoruba or Igbo, with millions of speakers—are broadly cast as indigenous. According to the Oxford English Dictionary,[1] the meaning of indigenous is "Born or produced naturally in a land or region; native or belonging naturally to (the soil, region, etc.)" and is "used primarily of aboriginal inhabitants or natural products." Aboriginal means "First or earliest as recorded by history; present from the beginning; primitive. Of peoples, plants, and animals: inhabiting or existing in a land from earliest times; strictly native, indigenous." In popular usage, however, just like in the usage of native or vernacular languages, the term confers a junior status— there are the global languages such as English and French, and there are the indigenous languages from ancient times, ethnic and close to the soil, as opposed to European languages that are dynamic and global. A local writer writes in an African language while an international writer is one who writes to a national and international cosmopolitan audience.

It was not accurate to cast all writers as having produced work that "as a cor- pus deriving from the African continent remains largely unknown and uncel- ebrated." By then Wole Soyinka had won the Nobel Prize for Literature, and authors like Achebe, Ngugi, Nawal El Saadawi, and Ama Ata Aidoo had won Pan-African, Western, and international acclaim. In any case to whom are these writers unknown? Mofolo's *Traveller to the East* was a literary classic among the Basotho and the Kiswahili poet Shaaban Robert was a legend with his poem "Titi la Mama," read in the original Kiswahili and translated copiously.

All in all it feels that the preamble to the list was calibrated to appeal to the Western reader. The jurors asked readers to see the list "as a basis for having African writers in your own cities and countries interviewed, or given a plat- form to speak and to debate their own work" and to see it, "as an excuse to buy or loan books and to extend the breadth of your knowledge and understand- ing of the great wealth of fiction and nonfiction written by Africans about their lives and societies" (*Africa's 100 Best Books of the 20th Century*). Had the list been for African consumption, there would have been a more nuanced approach to the term African, urging readers to think beyond national bor- ders. And even then, most Africans have been reading some of these authors as set books, from primary through university.

As if hearkening back to the debates from the 1962 Makerere Conference, they also addressed the question of who is an African writer and by extension the strictures by which a book may qualify as African literature:

> After extensive discussion and debate the ZIBF [Zimbabwe International Book Fair] has, for the purpose of this project, identified an African as: "someone either born in Africa or who became a citizen of an African country." This definition incorporates those African writers who have moved from their countries of birth to other continents. The issue of authors who are not by this definition deemed African but who consider themselves to be, or of those who have made a notable contribution to African scholarship and literature, will be addressed on their merit should their books be nominated. (*Africa's 100 Best Books of the 20th Century*)

Using this definition precludes writers such as Tope Folarin[2] (born in the United States to Nigerian parents) who have very strong ties to the continent even though their passports are from non-African countries. And while they might or might not consider themselves African writers, their novels can be seen as part of African diasporic literature, if not outright African literature. In other words, writers and their passports cannot decide what their books are—that is the function of literary criticism. Or rather, while writers might make an argument for how their books are to be read, it is the function of literary criticism to be the arbitrators of where their works fall within the African literary tradition.[3]

In the end, the nomination preamble and criteria tilted toward the Makerere writers, writing in English and French, and a Western readership. Slave narratives and writing in African languages, with very few exceptions, were bracketed out. Of the 70 books listed in the creative category, less than 10 were originally written in an African language. And of the scholarship/nonfiction titles, all are in English or French. Imagine a European literary canon and criticism where 90 percent of the books were written in non-European languages.

The jurors could not have foreseen just how rapidly the African literary landscape would change over the next few years. In 2002, when the canon was being built, or named, the explosion that would challenge its very existence had not yet come, but the rumblings were there. Leila Aboulela won the inaugural Caine Prize for African Writing in 2000, followed by Helon Habila (2001), Binyavanga Wainaina (2002), and Yvonne Adhiambo Owuor

(2003). In 2002 there was no Adichie or Bulawayo, *Purple Hibiscus* was to come out the following year in 2004, *Half of a Yellow Sun* in 2006, and *We Need New Names* in 2013. In a few years there would be detective and crime fiction coming from writers such as Kwei Quartey, Angela Makholwa, and myself, against the backdrop of white South African crime writers. Nnedi Okorafor's sci-fi *Who Fears Death* and Kiiru Taye's romance novels with Mill and Boon–inspired titles like *Men of Valor*, *Keeping Secrets*, and *Riding Rebel* were forthcoming.

In place of *Transition*, now thriving quietly at Harvard after Henry Louis Gates acquired it in 1991, journals like *Kwani?* and *Chimurenga* came to represent the dreams and aspirations of the post-Makerere generation. Urban in content and insurgent, these two journals are more like literary extensions of the earlier South African *Drum* magazine that featured the likes of Can Themba, Lewis Nkosi, and Nat Nakasa—young, cynical, polemical, disdainful of organized politics, but armed with incisive societal analysis. *Jalada*, a journal formed in 2014, would go on to make literary history by translating a short story by Ngugi into over 70 languages.

This is the problem of constituting a canon as a fortress against Western paternalism while at the same time eyeing the Western market: literary events overtake it very fast. Once set on the ahistorical rails of the Makerere tradition, it was going to be very difficult for literary criticism to anticipate and be open to the coming changes. The circling of wagons around the political novel in English did not just cut off early South African writing from the literary tradition, it also defended the Makerere literature from other popular forms of the novel—that is, science, crime, detective, and romance fictions.

The missionary presses produced a literature that placed a high premium on synthesis. British publishers, with the active participation of colonially educated Africans, produced an aesthetic that largely favored political realist writing. Post-Makerere writers and African publishers, in defining themselves against the Makerere literary tradition, are mainstreaming emerging forms of detective, science, and romantic fictions.

## THE AFRICAN POLITICAL NOVEL

When Taiye Selasi in her Berlin Lecture called for the abolition of the term "African Literature," she was eliding over two central realities. First, the category of African literature was a creation of Western critics that they then imposed on writers from Africa. Africans actively and consciously courted it as part and parcel of cultural and intellectual decolonization. Second, while African literature was not necessarily seen as a rejection of European literature, it was understood that while European literature was the center during colonialism, African literature would become the starting point for postcolonial African students embarking on literary journeys whether as writers or critics, all within a Pan-African literary identity that was decidedly political in nature.

In the acknowledgments of the AWS book, *Two Centuries of African English: A Survey and Anthology of Non-Fictional English Prose by African Writers since 1769*, Lalage Brown, the editor, appended a note with the heading, "Note: Literature And Politics," that reads:

> Not all modern authors included in this anthology are necessarily in good political standing in their own countries. It should therefore be made plain that this is a book concerned with modes and styles of literature and that all the extracts are used to prove one point: that African authors have produced good and interesting writing in English prose. Whether or not all those who write interestingly have sound political judgment is a question outside the scope of this book. (xii)

To my mind, it is unusual to have such a caveat, and it raises the question of what reader is being addressed. Is it the censorship board in South Africa, because the anthology includes those exiled by the apartheid government like Mphahlele? Or the Kenyan authorities since, by the time the book was published in 1973, Tom Mboya had already been assassinated, as would J. M. Kariuki two years later by the Jomo Kenyatta government? Or does the note betray the author's own feelings about the political nature of African writing? Regardless of its peculiarity, the note does capture the political nature of African writing.

The Makerere novel, by being born from an imagination formed by colonialism and anticolonial struggles, was simply political because it worked on Manichean ever-present contradictions. These African writers had a clear duty to expose those contradictions through their art. And this is what their publishers expected of them. James Currey, for example, in *Africa Writes Back* explained, "The South African books chosen for the African Writers Series reflected first and foremost the realities of life suffered by people oppressed by the laws of color by writers" who "had to have been born in Africa" (189).

Wole Soyinka, in a 1967 essay, "The Writer in the African State," argued that African writers had undergone three stages. The first, during decolonization, required that the writers contribute to the nationalist cause toward independence, meaning that they had to "postpone that unique reflection on experience and events which is what makes a writer and constitute himself into a part of that machinery that will actually shape events" (11). In the second stage, the writers now became part of nation building and put "energies to enshrining victory, to re-affirming his identification with the aspirations of nationalism and the stabilisation of society" (12). And in the third stage the writers found themselves in a state of "disillusionment," leading to Soyinka calling for "an honest examination of what has been the failure of the African writer, as a writer" (12). He concluded his essay by asking writers to reengage with the material reality of their societies:

> Where the writer in his own society can no longer function as conscience he must recognise that his choice lies between denying himself totally or withdrawing to the position of chronicler and post-mortem surgeon. But there can be no further distractions with universal concerns whose balm is spread on abstract wounds, not on the gaping jaws of black inhumanity. A concern with culture strengthens society, but not a concern with mythology. (13)

Soyinka was decrying Negritude and the concept of a return to a mythological past, "the myth of irrational nobility" and "racial essence," but it is clear that he recognized the existence of the African writer who, then, for better or worse, had a duty to society. Indeed, while African writers in the 1960s debated what constitutes African literature, that they had a duty to society was never really in question.

Ngugi, a Makerere University alumnus, was still a student at the time of the 1962 conference. In 2013, 51 years later, he returned to give a keynote address in which he reminisced about the conference, the role it had played in African literature and what Achebe (who had just died) and the other writers had come to mean:

> These writers would later give us what's the nearest thing to a genuine Pan African intellectual article: the book, African literature. When Achebe passed on recently he was mourned all over the continent. His novel, *Things Fall Apart*, the text most discussed at the conference alongside that of Dennis Brutus of South Africa, is read in all Africa. The work of others like Okot

p'Bitek and Wole Soyinka, and that of the generations that have followed, Dangarembga, Ngozi Adichie and Doreen Baingana are equally well received as belonging to all Africa. Thus if Makerere was the site and symbol of an East African intellectual community, it also marked the birth of literary Pan-Africanism. ("Makerere Dreams," 5–6)

Along the same lines, even though Simon Gikandi, in his essay "Chinua Achebe and the Invention of African Culture," first lamented "about the institutionalization of *Things Fall Apart* and the wisdom of using it as supplement for African culture or the authorized point of entry into Igbo, Nigerian, or African landscapes," he also recognized it for its Pan-African historical moment:

> It is not an exaggeration to say that my life was never to be the same again. For reading *Things Fall Apart* brought me to the sudden realization that fiction was not merely about a set of texts which one studied for the Cambridge Overseas exam which, for my generation, had been renamed the East African Certificate of Education; on the contrary, literature was about real and familiar worlds, of culture and human experience, of politics and economics, now re-routed through a language and structure that seemed at odds with the history or geography books we were reading at the time. (*Maps of Englishness*, 4)

He added that "there is consensus that *Things Fall Apart* was important for the marking and making of that exciting first decade of decolonization" (4). And with an emerging Pan-African literature, it was only a matter of time before the role of English literature (though not the English language) in African education was questioned.

In a 1968 call titled "On the Abolition of the English Department," three professors at the University of Nairobi, Ngugi Wa Thiong'o, Henry Owour-Anyumba, and Taban Lo Liyong, argued that in the teaching of literature was a "basic assumption that the English tradition and the emergence of the modern West is the central root of our consciousness and cultural heritage" in which "Africa becomes an extension of the West." "Why can't African literature be at the center so that we can view other cultures in relationship to it?" they asked. They called for the abolition of the English Department and in its place a department of African literature and languages. They were clear that they were not "rejecting other cultural streams, especially the western stream" ("Abolition," 439). The ideal curriculum would constitute the oral tradition, Swahili literature (with Arabic and Asian literatures), a selected course in European literature, and modern African literature, and knowledge of Swahili, English, and French would be a must (440). They concluded that

> with Africa at the center of things, not existing as an appendix or a satellite of other countries and literatures, things must be seen from the African perspective. The dominant object in that perspective is African literature, the major branch of African culture. Its roots go back to past African literatures, European literatures, and Asian literatures. These can be studied meaningfully in a Department of African Literature and Languages in an African University. (441)

Their goal was to change the curriculum from a British-based one to one that reflected world literature with African literature at the center. For Amoko Apollo Obonyo in *Postcolonialism in the Wake of the Nairobi Revolution: Ngugi Wa Thiong'o and the Idea of African Literature*, the document was contradictory. For him, "To the extent that the movement sought to uncouple the study of literature in English from the nationalist history of England, it represented a radical contestation of the ideology of English literature to date." And, "the movement embodied powerfully contradictory impulses, at once rejecting and reproducing the cultural nationalist fallacies of colonial discourse" (4–5). But in my reading of the document, its authors were very careful to say their revolution was not reductionist and essentialist—European literature and languages were going to be part of the curriculum. The contradiction was that in calling for the Department of African Literature and Languages, they did not mean African literature written in African languages. Rather, they meant linguistics. That is, African languages should be taught within the department. The only African language literature mentioned was Kiswahili (440).

Early South African writing in African languages, in translation or written originally in English, were not mentioned at all. What it did call for is a study of orature to "supplement (not replace) courses in Modern African Literature" (441). This document that was going to change literature departments throughout the postcolonial world in the end cemented the myth that before the Makerere writers there was only orature. And even though the call for orature meant there was a place for African languages, the caveat of supplementing showed that they would play a junior role. But still the document showed that the Makerere writers right from the beginning understood their written work as contributing to political and cultural decolonization. And when decolonization turned into a mess of neocolonial authoritarian military and civilian regimes, they saw their work as contributing to egalitarian and democratic societies. And they saw themselves as African writers contributing to African literature.

Frantz Fanon in *The Wretched of the Earth* outlines several stages that the African intellectual would have to go through in order to become useful in the anticolonial struggle. The first stage was complete identification with colonial culture (222). The second stage finds the intellectual trying "to remember what he is" (222). In the second stage, the dissociation starts and the intellectual "sets up high value on the customs, traditions, and the appearances of his people; but his inevitable painful experience only seems to be a banal search for exoticism. The sari becomes sacred, and shoes that come from Paris or Italy are left in favor of pampooties" (221). In the last stage "which is called the fighting phase, the native after having tried to lose himself in the people and with the people, will on the contrary shake the people" (222).

The novel, and novelists, in the fighting stage had to do the work of decolonization by contributing to national consciousness and by carrying dynamic African culture. No matter where one stood on the question of the writer as a revolutionary versus the writer offering a mirror to society, it was a given that literature as well as the writer had a duty to "shake the people." In his essay "The Novelist as Teacher," Chinua Achebe argues that for him, his role as a writer is to "help my society regain belief in itself and put away the complexes of the years of denigration and self-abasement" (105). A little later, he argues that the writer "cannot expect to be excused from the task of re-education and regeneration that must be done" and then concludes that:

> I would be satisfied if my novels (especially the ones I have set in the past) did no more than teach my readers that their past—with all its imperfections— was not one long night of savagery from which the first Europeans acting on God's behalf delivered them. (105)

In other words, for Achebe, rolling back the myths used to justify colonialism was an integral part of the African writer's mission. The writer in short had a duty to speak out against the sort of internalized racism and belief in cultural inferiority that Africans had inherited from colonialism. In *Writing against Neocolonialism*, Ngugi Wa Thiong'o argues that African writers had gone through "the age of the anti-colonial struggle; the age of independence; and the age of neocolonialism." The African writer was born on the crest of this anti-colonial struggle and world-wide revolutionary ferment. The anti-imperialist energy and optimism of the masses found its way into the writing of the period. . . . It was Africa explaining itself, speaking for itself, and interpreting its past. It was Africa rejecting its past as drawn by the artists of imperialism. The writer even flaunted his right to use the language of the former colonial master anyway he liked. No apologies. No begging. The Caliban of the world had been given European languages and he was going to use them even to subvert the master. (158)

In this context, a writer like Mofolo and his savage African protagonist seeking European enlightenment in the *Traveller to the East*, was not a political writer. *Mhudi* and *Wrath of Ancestors* were not written with the ideologies of the third stage, the fighting stage. With their calls for synthesis, they would have been somewhere between the 1st and 2nd stages—caught between identifying with African and European cultures. In short, for the Makerere writers early South Africans would have seemed blind to the political contradictions sharpening around them.

## THE LOVEDALE AESTHETIC, MHUDI, AND AFRICAN LITERARY CRITICISM

Oyekan Owomoyela, in his essay "The Literature of Empire: Africa," credits Lovedale Press with establishing isiXhosa literature, saying that it "owes its birth to the Lovedale Press; one of the earliest products of the Lovedale mission school, Tiyo Soga, translated John Bunyan's *The Pilgrim's Progress* into Xhosa as U-hambo lom-hambi (1868), and also played a central role in the translation of the Bible into the same language" (7). With Lovedale largely having a monopoly, there was pressure to write books sympathetic to the Christianizing mission and sometimes outright censorship, as Jeffrey Peires shows in his essay "Lovedale Press: Literature for the Bantu Revisited." And that pressure might explain why, in *Traveller to the East*, Mofolo created an Africa straight out of the myth of the noble savage. In *Traveller to the East*, a Penguin Modern Classic that is out of print, one can see the missionary fingerprints all over the book. Fekisi, the protagonist, moves from African savage darkness to Christian enlightenment. The book opens: "In the black darkness, very black in the times when the tribes were still eating each other like wild beasts, there lived a man called Fekisi" (1).

In part this might explain the near complete lack of awareness of *Traveller to the East* in the African literary tradition. For the revolutionary Makerere writers writing in a time of decolonization, Fekisi, in his journey toward Christian enlightenment, would have appeared a caricature, a confirmation of internalized racism. It would have appeared antithetical to the struggle for political, economic and cultural independence. It was not a literature one could take seriously enough to be studied as an integral part of the African literary tradition.

Phaswane Mpe, the late writer and scholar, in a 1999 essay, "The Role of the Heinemann African Writers Series," gave a number of reasons why the Makerere writers eclipsed early South African writers. Mpe argued that "[t]he fact that *Chaka* and *The Wrath of the Ancestors* were initially published in African languages meant that they were immediately accessible only to those who could read Sesotho and Xhosa" (106). At the same time Mpe cited the censorship and editorial interventions that led to the books losing their aesthetic appeal, meaning that "critics who could have popularized the novel, who found it interesting at least, remained rather patronizing" (106). For Mpe the bottom line was that "these writers were victims of their own publishing history, of either writing in African languages and/or publishing in their home countries, without sufficient exposure to worldwide readership" (106). While he went further than most literary scholars in acknowledging early South African writing as part and parcel of the literary tradition, his argument was flawed in a number of ways. For one, the novels had been translated into English. Aesthetic appeal and critical attention are two different things—aesthetic appeal might help with the book becoming popular, but it is critical attention that builds a literary tradition. Imagine if English critics had dismissed William Defoe's *Robinson Crusoe* and *Moll Flanders*—the two novels that are considered as giving a foundation to the English novel—as structurally flawed with fluctuating aesthetic appeal.

Isabel Hofmeyr, in *The Portable Bunyan*, while looking at the relationship between Bunyan's *The Pilgrim's Progress* and Mofolo's *Traveller to the East*, notes the book's absence from serious critical readings. She notes that for some critics Mofolo was "a victim of false consciousness, uneasily pinioned between 'two cultures': 'Africa' and the West'" (166). But rather than accept a reading of African/European or Western/indigenous, she sees him as trying to "author a cluster of identities centered on being a commoner, a Sotho, a male, an African, and a Protestant" (167). And there are ways in which the novel undermines colonialism by having Fekisi find a utopia where "there are no police, no taxes" and God is the chief of a nation that "lives in truth" (83). It can be read as a subversive text, and that might in part explain its popularity among the Sotho people.

The point is that each generation of critics does not choose what comes before them—they certainly do choose what to canonize, what to consider major literature. But they cannot expunge books from a literary tradition because of political content. Political content does not absolve literary critics and writers from the duty of being aware and accounting for their literary traditions. Regardless of political content, these early novels should be read with great scholarly care in relation to the literary tradition. Yet, like many other critics, Keith Booker, in his book *The African Novel in English: An Introduction*, dismisses all the early South African writers as producing "nothing more than religious tracts" save for Mofolo's *Chaka* (48), which he regards as having literary merit. Having dismissed all written literature in South Africa and by extension African languages, and writing only about the novel in English, *Chaka* does not merit his attention. Even though he recognizes Daniel Kunene's 1981 translation of *Chaka* as making an important intervention, after a few words he quickly moves on to Peter Abrahams, *Song of the City* (Dorothy Crisp & Co, London, 1943), and *Mine Boy* (Dorothy Crisp & Co, London, 1946). *Mine Boy*, a more politically conscious book in which racial injustice and exploitation are tackled, provided a more convenient starting point.

Indeed, as if to cement over the erasure of all the written literature before it, *Mine Boy* was marketed by Heinemann as the "first modern novel of Black South Africa" in its 1989 edition. But *Mine Boy* was not the first modern novel by a black South African written in English. Lovedale Press first published *Mhudi*, written by Sol Plaatje, in 1930 to become the first novel by a black African in English. Heinemann did republish *Mhudi* in 1978, which makes one wonder why two books, one originally published in 1930 and the other in 1946, a mere 16 years apart, do not belong in the same age.

Having fallen into the before *Things Fall Apart* there was orature understanding of African literature, I had not read early South African literature until 2012, two decades or so into my schooling. I did not start teaching early South African literature in my intro to African literature courses until 2014. Neglected, most of the early writing novels are out of print. The only one I could find easily was *Mhudi*, which I taught alongside *No Longer at Ease*, *We Need New Names*, and *Who Fears Death*. And in many ways *Mhudi* anticipates the literature of decolonization. It is set in the 1830s at a time of war between the Baralong and the Ndebele; *Mhudi* is a love story between Ra-Thanga and Mhudi and in another sense a historical epic narrated by their son, Half-a-Crown. The Ndebele are led by King Mzilikazi who is portrayed in the novel as being vicious though a closer reading reveals that his ruthless army is avenging ruthless crimes perpetrated by the Baralongs. At the same time the Boers are slowly encroaching on the cultural, political, and economic lives of the Africans. The Baralong decide to collaborate with the Boers and they defeat Mzilikazi who then carves a path from South Africa to Zimbabwe.

*Mhudi* is a novel of an uneasy synthesis. It ends with a cautious hope the Boers and Africans, after having waged war together and in spite of the looming signs of betrayal through the racism exhibited the Boers, can still learn to live, if not as friends, at least in alliance. The last image is of the protagonists riding off into the sunset with a now fixed wagon that was gifted to them by the Boers with a broken wheel:

> The old waggon meandered along and the racket of the waggon wheels on the hard road made a fierce yet not very disagreeable assault on the ears.
>
> "Tell me," said Mhudi, raising her voice as the waggon rattled along, "why were you so angry with me when I found you at the front? Promise me," she went on, "you will not again go away and leave me. Will you?"
>
> "Never again," replied Ra-Thanga, raising his voice above the creak-crack, creak, crack of the old waggon wheels. "I have had my revenge and ought to be satisfied. From henceforth I shall have no ears for the call of war or the chase; my ears shall be open only to one call—the call of your voice." (193)

It is hard not to read the wagon like a character at this point. A gift they had to repair, it is now theirs through their labor. But not quite: it stands between them, interfering so that to hear each other they have to speak over its noise. It makes a somewhat disagreeable assault on their ears. It cannot be a pleasant assault. The wagon works and they are using it, but it keeps reminding them of war, and even hints that their alliance with the Boers will break, and they will have to go to war.

In fact, I read this and hear echoes of Mzilikazi's warning. After his defeat he says, "Let them rejoice; they need all the laughter they can have today for when their deliverers begin to dose them with the same bitter medicine they prepared for me; when the Kiwas rob them of their cattle, their children and their lands, they will weep their eyes out of their sockets and get left with only their empty throats to squeal in vain for mercy" (179). It is as if the wagon is telling Mhudi, the reader, and Ra-Thanga himself that his promise to not go to war ever again is false. Mzilikazi was right. "My ears shall be open to only one call—the call of your voice," and yet he is already paying attention to the creak-crack call of the wagon. It is not a novel of synthesis in that all that ends well stays well; they can make the synthesis work, but it will not easy.[4]

NoViolet Bulawayo, born and partially raised in Zimbabwe, is a product of this war, as is the whole of Zimbabwe. Yet in her novel, we come across Mzilikazi when she is writing about Mzilikazi Road. The literary history, her literary heritage, has been leveled to a street. And the street, itself a symbol of the divide between the rich and the poor, where dogs and human beings can become road kill underneath the wheels of a Hummer, or Chinese imported buses, cannot recall the novel, *Mhudi*. Mzilikazi in *We Need New Names* does not recall the literary history of *Mhudi*—it recalls the betrayal of the 1980s decolonization.

Literary scholars had a responsibility to take into account early African writing for no other reason than it existed, instead of dismissing it as precursors to the modern African novel. But more than that, there were real questions to be asked. Can a failed synthesis in early South African writing lead to hybridity in the literature of decolonization? Under the guise of agreeing with the noble savage myth, yet writing for a people who know they were not, could Mofolo be subverting colonial racism as in mimicry with a wink to the audience? And what of the writing in Africa do these books reveal when analyzed within an African literary tradition that allows them to be in conversation with Makerere and post-Makerere writers? But they did not ask these questions. That *Mhudi* has no place in the African literary tradition points to the tragic state of an African literary criticism that begins the clock in the wrong literary era.

African literary criticism that, for example, situates Tsitsi Dangarembga's *Nervous Conditions*, or Bulawayo's *We Need New Names*, or Petina Gappah's *The Book of Memory* only within the *Makerere tradition* is resting on a false foundation. Take the example of Polo Belina Moji's essay, "New Names, Translational Subjectivities: (Dis)location and (Re)naming in NoViolet Bulawayo's 'We Need New Names,'" where she is looking at naming:

> Referentiality gives meaning to names such as Chimurenga Street—which evokes Zimbabwe's nationalist struggle for independence—or Mzilikazi

Road, with reference to the founding father of the Ndebele nation, King Mzi-likazi. The Ndebele are the ethnic majority in the author's native city of Bula-wayo. These names can be read as signifiers that inscribe the novel as a certain history of the Zimbabwean nation, given the post-independence dominance of the Shona majority and the political marginalization of the Ndebele ethnic group. (184)

If Polo Belina Moji, like myself, is an intellectual child of the postcolonial Afri-can literary criticism, and went to high schools where the Makerere writers were introduced as the fathers and mothers of the African novel, *Mhudi* and early South African writing would have remained just that: something outside the African literary tradition. She invokes Mzilikazi only within a Zimbabwean context; she does not walk him back through his wars of conquest in 1800s South Africa. Even as her analysis begs for it, she does not recall the Mzilikazi in *Mhudi* because the book exists outside the African literary tradition.

## THE ROLE OF PUBLISHERS: FROM EDUCATIONAL TO INDEPENDENT PUBLISHING

The Makerere consensus would not have survived and thrived without ac-tive participation by British publishers in the metaphysical empire. They too were invested in propagating the myth of African literature beginning with their intervention. For example, James Currey in *Africa Writes Back* titled the opening chapter "The Establishment of African Literature" with the subtitle "The Starting Line." And he begins the chapter by quoting an Achebe 1998 Harvard Lecture in which Achebe celebrates the African Writers Series. In fact it is Achebe who uses the words *starting line* in a lecture that takes the myth of the beginning of African literature for a fact:

> The launching of the Heinemann's African Writers Series was like the um-pire's signal for which African writers had been waiting on the starting line. In one short generation an immense library of writing had sprung into being from all over the continent and, for the first time in history, Africa's future generations of readers and writers—youngsters in schools and colleges— began to read, not only David Copperfield and other English classics that I and my generation has read, but also works by their own writers about their own people. (1)

So here is the publisher using the writer, and the writer using the publisher to justify an African literary clock that starts with the AWS. In the same opening page, after using the Achebe speech to show the AWS as the start of African literature, Currey goes on to justify the use of English: "English was the lubricant of the English-speaking world. It was not only how authority was imposed but it was also the way in which the subject peoples reacted to that imposition of power. Writers in India, the Caribbean and Africa came to take advantage of the language they shared, but they had to have publishing opportunities" (2). It is the sentence "English was the lubricant of the English world" that is the most arresting because it starts with the fact of an English speaking world, not a world in which thousands of other languages, literatures, and writers in those languages existed. The British publisher of African fiction was so thoroughly educated in the myth of the English metaphysical empire that even those pronouncements that would otherwise be seen as presenting two opposed truths pass for a fact—English is the language of the English speaking world.

The decision by Heinemann to publish the African novels through its Educational Books imprints was a practical one. The colonial cultural machinery had not been interested in cultivating African literary culture or reading for pleasure. Publishing was for educational books. It was easier for Hill to push books written by African writers through the educational publishing model. And this meant publishing African literary books with the idea that they would in turn become set books in Kenyan primary and high schools. For Hill, Heinemann Educational Books was the only firm with "the faith—the passion almost—and the will to do the job," and the "necessary business set-up to sell the books" in a continent where the "book trade . . . was almost entirely educational" (Currey, *Africa Writes Back*, 6). The idea was that the books that sold well would support newer and even experimental works.

But it did not work that way. The model for the hard fought for but lucrative educational books market took over. There was no market-driven incentive effort to develop a general readership because the goal was to have novels become exam set books. It was not without anguish. Henry Chakava, who bought out Heinemann to launch East African Educational Publishers (EAEP) in 1992, could see the contradiction. In "Selling Books in Africa: A Publisher's Reflections," a 1997 column written for a Nigerian newspaper in 1997, he worked through the questions of a profit-driven set book market versus a general paperback-buying readership:

> When I launched Spear Books in 1974, in response to worries from some of our readers and writers that the AWS was far too didactic, crafted to capture the schoolbook market as prescribed texts, the series did not, at first, get the support of my principals in London. It was aimed to attract the low-brow reader leisure time, as opposed to going to a movie or a football match, watching TV or chatting with a neighbour. The language was controlled and the length was fixed between eighty to ninety-six pages, in the belief that the African reader was young and had a short concentration span. (160)

This was in 1974 Kenya, but extend it to decolonizing Africa where repression is growing. The Biafran war in Nigeria that claimed poet Chris Okigbo had ended in 1970. Like the Spanish Civil War the side that was to lose had attracted writers and intellectuals including Chinua Achebe, who at some point was the ambassador for Biafra. As the literary writers faced increasing pressure from their respective governments, it was the popular fiction writers who kept history and day-to-day, often urban, struggles alive. For example, Mwangi Ruheni's novels *What a Life* and *What a Husband* were satirical stories about surviving Nairobi and navigating marriage, but they were also a commentary on neocolonial Kenya—the state of the economy, joblessness and landlessness, and the betrayal of the goals set by the Kenya Land and Freedom Army.

The criteria of the Spear Books paperback series for books, as Chakava explained, was narrow, and in essence he established the very hierarchy he sort to erase. Luckily the reading public went beyond his desired audience of short-attention-spanned young Africans. John Kariamiti's *My Life in Crime*, a barely fictionalized memoir of a reformed bank robber, was one such book. Chakava noted that "[o]f more than forty titles in print, the most popular Spear Book—My Life in Crime . . . has sold in excess of 100,000 copies."

Chakava, a visionary of African publishing in his own right, has paid a high price. It was EAEP that published Ngugi's first novel in Gikuyu, *Caitaini Mutharabaini (Devil on the Cross)* in 1980. This was a courageous move. Ngugi had just been released from detention where he had written the novel on toilet paper. As Ngugi was to narrate in *Coming of Age: Strides in African Publishing*, a collection of essays celebrating Chakava's 70th birthday, a few weeks before the novel's publication Chakava started receiving death threats. Then:

> A week before publication assassins waited for him at the gate of his house in Lavington. They tried to drag him into the boot of the car. An approach-

ing motorist foiled the plot. One of the attackers thought of finishing the job on the spot, or make irrevocable damage and aimed a machete at Chakava's head . . . , [he] just about managed to move it simultaneously raising his hand as a shield. The assassin cut off Chakava's finger. Then they fled the scene. The finger had to be re-attached. (17)

Chakava did not pull the book from publication even though Heinemann London wanted him to for his safety and Ngugi had reassured him he would be okay with the decision. But the model, in spite of the popular fiction imprint and African languages publishing, has remained educational publishing. In a 2015 interview aptly titled "We'll Stick to Creative Works, but Textbooks Bring in Cash," Kiarie Kamau, the chief executive officer at East African Educational Publishers, said:

The demand for a generous return on investment is there. The competition is stiff, and one must keep raising the bar in terms of strategy to perform better and better. . . . What I mean is that there is that book that reads so well, has a strong message, and has an almost eternal shelf life. But it just doesn't sell in huge quantities. What the shareholder wants to hear about is the percentage of dividend that has been declared, and that's only possible if you have a mass market product, bringing home a generous turnover. Often, that's a textbook.[5]

Like any other business, publishing has to be profitable in order to be viable. But when the managing director starts calling novels products, it is clear that the institutional orientation is toward the profitable—to stick with what has always been working, with general readership books being secondary.

Because the educational system is in English, books written in English get priority. Walter Bgoya, the publisher at the Tanzania-based Mkuki na Nyota Press, in a 2013 essay, "Publishing in Africa from Independence to the Present Day," gave the example of a bilingual textbook that Mkuki na Nyota submitted to the Committee of the Ministry of Education:

Mkuki na Nyota Publishers submitted the first of four bilingual Swahili/English textbooks, covering the equivalent of the O-level chemistry syllabus, to the Educational Materials Approval Committee of the Ministry of Education for evaluation. Although the material in both languages adequately covered the chemistry syllabus for Form 1, it was rejected solely because it was bilingual. The publisher was informed that approval would be given if the Swahili pages were removed. (28)

Only colonial education and its vestiges can explain why the committee would reject such a painstaking and creative solution. The high premium is on English. African languages are not only unequal but also not worthy of being taught. An opportunity to grow Kiswahili chemistry vocabulary was lost.

In 2002, at the time of the release of the top 100 African books, educational publishing was the norm. In Eastern Africa, EAEP, Oxford, and others were the main publishers vying for the lucrative set book market. Bgoya in the same essay writes of a survey that found that an "up to 95% of books published in Africa were educational, as compared to the broad ratio in the north of 60:40 textbooks to non-textbooks" (28). The metaphysical empire has to have a material base.

However, post-Makerere publishers are trying to create a readership and book market outside of the textbooks market. For example, *Kwani?* publishes its own series of books like the memoir by Eva Kasaya, *Tale of Kasaya*, chronicling her life as a maid in postindependence and postdictatorship Kenya. *Kwani?* also published Adichie's *Americanah* and Yvonne Owuor's *Dust* for the East African market.

But Kwani remains more of a journal than a publishing house. And without a revenue base of its own, it relies on international donors and therefore cannot develop a full list of novels for a general readership. Going back to the journal *Transition* and its being funded by the CIA front, the Congress for Cultural Freedom, the danger of donor-driven cultural production is obvious. But even when there are no insidious motives, donor priorities shift. Bgoya, in the same essay, argued that donor-funded publishing initiatives such as African Publishers Network died out as soon as donor funding dried up. Out of the many donor-funded publishing initiatives, only the Council for the Development of Social Science Research in Africa and the African Books Collective remain standing (5). In other words, national cultural initiatives such as Kwani have no longevity unless they generate their own revenue streams.

Cassava Republic Press is better poised to take on the educational books monopoly in Nigeria, thus setting an example for other publishers to follow. Bibi Bakare-Yusuf explains that the one of the objectives of Cassava Publishing is to create a general readership, or rather, whereas the goal of EAEP is to enter a novel into the set book market, for Cassava it is to find, sustain, and grow a general readership:

> As Cassava Republic, for instance, we don't have to wait for our books to be part of the curriculum before people hear or read them. We are simply creating African publishing brands whose curatorial skills readers trust, feel confident about and will remember for years to come. As a result of the confidence in our brand, educational institutions are approaching us to submit our books for assessment rather than us chasing them. (Wanner, 60)

In other words, for Cassava the movement is to first form a general readership base from which then it can engage with the educational books market. And in a reverse of the traditional model of publishing where the move is from the West to the East, Cassava Republic House opened an office in London. Cassava has gone to Europe to open up the market for African books. In a 2016 press release, Bakare-Yusuf, the publisher, announced:

> It is exciting to be launching Cassava Republic Press in the UK both as an intervention and as an opportunity to introduce the diversity of writings coming out of the continent. What we are doing is unprecedented: an African publishing house establishing a base in the UK after nearly 10 years in Africa rather than the reverse. This is the birthing of African publishing onto the world stage.[6]

Cassava has a romance imprint that, as I mentioned in the introduction, in February 2015 released a romance short story anthology by post-Makerere writers such as Binyavanga Wainaina. The stories, originally written in French or English, were translated into the mother tongues spoken by the writers. The originals and translations were then read by other writers and critics including myself, and the PDF and audio files made available for download at the Cassava website. Here the print paper publishing and digital worlds met to further push the boundaries of African literature into the world of love and erotica stories.

In the same interview Bakare-Yusuf explained that one of the underlying goals is to shift the focus from African issues to African aesthetics—to the love of story, of place, and of nuance. "We are looking for unusual or unconventional narratives that challenge stereotypes or are purely experimental in style. We focus on strong stories and characters rather than issues." In other words, Cassava is trying to move away from what Chakava considered didactic writing. It is a false dichotomy that African writers and critics have burdened themselves with. Conrad's *The Secret Agent* and *Heart of Darkness*, Dostoevsky's *Crime and Punishment*, Leo Tolstoy's *War and Peace*—all novels that we read as classics—have long political digressions. Part of the problem is an acceptance of the European literary canon as the ultimate standard. And in trying to produce an African literary canon, even one that defies the realist novel in English as the standard, the danger of colonially inherited aesthetics can cloud the reading of the African political novel.

But rebelling against the Makerere aesthetic, or at least recognizing its limitations, has allowed Cassava to start crime, romance, and children's books imprints as a way to cultivate a general readership without the hierarchy of the literary over the popular that one finds with educational set books publishers. In 2013 my detective novel, *Nairobi Heat*, originally published by Penguin SA in 2007 and Melville House in 2011, was the first book published by their crime imprint.

## POPULAR FICTION AND THE AFRICAN LITERARY TRADITION: WRITING *NAIROBI HEAT*

I fell into detective fiction by accident. Much like a found poem, *Nairobi Heat* is a found novel—at least the bare bones of the story that my imagination in turn fleshed out. While doing my PhD coursework at the University of Wisconsin at Madison, I lived very close to the football stadium where tailgating started as early as 8:00 a.m. I was not surprised when, on getting home after a late night elsewhere (there is a reason UW-Madison tops party school lists), I found a white female student dressed in a cheerleader outfit passed out by the door to my second floor apartment. I did not know her so I called 911, explained the situation, and shortly afterward an ambulance accompanied by an African American policeman arrived. She was barely conscious, and as the policeman tried to get her details through her getting sick, it suddenly hit me. Here I was an African student, an African American policeman, and a barely conscious white woman. In the novel, Ishmael Fofona is an African American working to solve the murder of a white woman in racially polarized Madison, Wisconsin. His suspect is a Rwandan who became a hero during the 1994 genocide by saving thousands of lives. He lived in Nairobi before coming to UW to teach courses on human rights.

Of course, much like a poet is predisposed to a see a stop sign as a metaphor of one thing or another where for other drivers it's utilitarian, I was predisposed to finding *Nairobi Heat* in what would otherwise have been an anecdote to narrate at parties. For one, as a scholar and reader I have found the divide between the literary and the popular to be a false opposition. African writers and literary critics, it seems to me, inherited from the British literary tradition through colonial education the English language and aesthetic standards. But the reality for my generation, which grew up at the height of the neocolonial dictatorships with all its serious punishable ridiculousness (for example, it was illegal to dream and talk about the president's death and you needed a permit to gather more than five people), was that we read the literary alongside the popular—James Hadley Chase, Frederick Forsyth, and Robert Ludlum. But we also devoured popular fiction by African writers like David Maillu, Meja Mwangi, Mwangi Ruheni, and John Kariamiti.

While their writing is diverse—for example, Kariamiti's *My Life in Crime* is a semiautobiographical account of his days as a bank robber, while Maillu specialized in borderline pornography—their books also contained social commentary: joblessness, alcoholism, hopelessness, patriarchy, history of the Mau Mau, and so on. They were entertaining to read, but considering the Kenya of the 1980s, where the literary writers like my father, Ngugi Wa Thiong'o, were in exile or in detention, it was the popular writers who kept us reading and thinking about neocolonial Kenya.

For Kenyan writers of my generation, it is impossible to think of an African literary tradition that does not include the popular fiction writers. And it's why the African literary criticism that follows the Achebe to Adichie beeline feels false and pretentious—we want literary criticism that will follow us into the gutter where, alongside William Shakespeare, Mikhail Lermontov, Bhabani Bhattacharya, Achebe, and Ngugi, we read the Maillus and Ruhenis.

I was also influenced by Walter Mosley's Easy Rawlins mystery series, especially the novel and movie *Devil in a Blue Dress*. I cannot think of his antihero, Mouse, without smiling. I might as well have been describing him when O, my antihero in *Nairobi Heat*, tells Ishmael, "we are bad people who do good things." In addition to telling an entertaining story Mosley is able to organically bring out issues of race and class within the entertaining form of the detective novel. Through reading him I realized that setting and plot have everything to do with it if you want the issues to emerge organically.

When Ishmael makes his way to Nairobi as an African American he has to confront issues of his own identity. I also introduce issues of gender and violence through Muddy, the femme fatale who survived the geno-cide and joined the Rwandan Patriotic Front. She tries to escape her violent past through the spoken word, but she is also addicted to violence. And the Nairobi urban setting means that issues of class are organically intrinsic to the form.

I was born in Evanston, Illinois, but spent the first 19 years of my life in Kenya before coming back to the United States for my bachelor's degree. At the time I was writing *Nairobi Heat* I had been in the United States for over half my life and the questions around the tensions between being African American and African had been growing. I was therefore intellectually and imaginatively already predisposed to recognize that the meeting in that puke-stained stairway fumigated with alcohol breath could lead to a story. After the policeman and the young woman had left, I called a fellow writer friend of mine and told him I had found a story to enter into a competition. When I started writing the story it turned into the novel *Nairobi Heat*, which I dedicated to David Maillu and Meja Mwangi.

Given how seriously writers like Mosley (who also writes literary fiction) or Sara Paretsky (who does for women what Mosley does for black people) take the form—and the sheer brilliance with which they take this form, which previously carried the masculine wish lists of white male writers like Raymond Chandler, and make it do work for those left out of the stories—it is a shame that literary criticism still sees popular fiction as something other than literary. In fact, looking at the world literature debates taking place today, the absence of popular fiction is glaringly absent. And yet, as evidenced by my generation's reading list, we are equal parts popular and literary fiction.

Pascale Casanova argues that to be recognized as a world writer one has to be published in Paris or New York, the stock exchanges of books.[7] Aamir Mufti, on the other hand, mounts a critique of world literature, making the connection between world literature and orientalism: it was through the encounter with Asia (India in particular), and then a recasting of that encounter through orientalism that made world literature possible, and that world literature belonged to the other before it was appropriated and then given back to the global South as world literature.[8] But, in both, the absence of popular fiction is glaringly absent. I for one would like to see the world lit soothsayers and detractors alike make the argument that Stieg Larson's Millennium trilogy, or Mosley's *Devil in a Blue Dress*, are not world literature. And then explain to me why Joseph Conrad's *The Secret Agent* makes the cut while it can be read as a political thriller.

I can say for myself that I was not thinking about world literature or global markets and being recognized at home after being stamped fit for African consumption in Paris or New York—I was writing a story for Africans and African Americans. While the novel went on to reach readers outside my intended audience, I cannot say I was writing for everybody. Crime and detective fiction, perhaps more than any other genre, will reach beyond the writer's intended audience—the form even when used differently is universally recognizable, with its bad, and good, guys, femme fatales, violence, and so on. *Nairobi Heat* and the sequel, *Black Star Nairobi*, have been popular with readers who do not necessary read African literary fiction. In Germany, where both novels have been translated into German, the novel has done well with aficionados of crime fiction as opposed to African literature. For these readers, detective fiction might very well work like a gateway drug and start them on other African works of literature.

But just because I was not thinking about global markets and literature does not mean I was not caught up in them. In 2005 or thereabouts, I had finished writing a more literary novel that was to come out in 2015 as *Mrs. Shaw* (Swallow Press). I needed a literary agent and promptly contacted Binyavanga—he had been reading and editing an excerpt of the novel for Kwani and he had then introduced me to David Godwin, a super literary agent then best known for Arundhati Roy's *God of Small Things*. David loved *Mrs. Shaw* but could not get it placed. A short story culled from the novel was nominated for the Caine Prize in 2005 and later the manuscript was shortlisted for the first and last Penguin–South Africa Prize for African writing in 2009. But none of it helped *Mrs. Shaw*, and so when I was done with *Nairobi Heat* I sent it to David who then shopped it around until it eventually found a home with Penguin, South Africa in 2007.

At the same time the world of detective and crime fiction was changing—Stieg Larsson's "Millennium trilogy"[9] had just exploded into the international scene following success in Sweden and there was a huge interest in international crime. Melville Publishing House, an independent publisher based in New York, started an international crime series and bought *Nairobi Heat* rights from Penguin, SA in 2011. It was not until 2013 that *Nairobi Heat* was finally available in Kenya through East African Educational Publishers and a little later from Nigeria's Cassava Publishing. Casanova makes it sound like publishing and literary cultures are uneven because that is the way it is now—that is, she commits the old fallacy of thinking the way the world is, is the way it ought to be, and hence reads world literature as immutable. But the reasons to me are much simpler. Colonialism first turned African writers looking to the West aesthetically. But it also did a number on African publishing by making educational publishing the model. This in turn has meant that African publishers generally have to get their books assigned in classrooms as set books if they are to thrive. The end result is that fiction publishing takes the back seat while poetry is thrown somewhere in the trunk. Or to put it differently, world literature as imagined by Casanova runs on the unequal rails of colonialism, neocolonialism, and globalization. Change the material conditions and you change world literature. In a way educational publishing has ossified. The novels they produce are poorly designed, poorly edited, and poorly marketed—after all, why put money into an appendage when the real money comes from textbook sales?

This is why the growth of independent publishing will be critical to the growth of African fiction beyond the few names in circulation in world lit debates—that is, well-edited and presented books designed for the African and global markets. And that is why the independent Nigerian publishing house, Cassava Republic Press, was warmly greeted by younger African writers. I only have to compare Cassava's *Nairobi Heat* to that of EAEP, both of which were published in 2013. There is no way of saying this gently—EAEP's cover looks cheap. It's a picture of Nairobi possibly taken in the 1970s with the scorching sun in the background—it might as well have been published in the 1970s. There is a scantily dressed woman stenciled into the A in Heat whereas the Kenyatta Conference Center (a famous building) is stenciled into the "I" in Nairobi. Judging the book by its cover, no other publisher in another market would want to buy it from EAEP. Cassava's has faded Nairobi traffic and the city into the background. Both Nairobi and Heat are in lowercase with what appears to be radio waves pulsating in the background. Cassava shrunk the novel into 123 pages to make it portable. EAEP is at 212 and, while smaller in size, it is much thicker. Cassava's version can compete internationally. EAEP's cannot.

The larger problem for writers like myself working in and outside the canon is that the African literary tradition as constituted rests on a false foundation. But it is not just the cutting away of, say, early Arabic, Amharic, Kiswahili, and South African literary roots. It is also a forcing of African literature into European aesthetic standards—a privileging of the African novel in English while banishing popular forms from the African literary tradition. African crime fiction, Hausa women's literature, science fiction, romance fiction—in other words, the reading that make our daily bread are left outside the literary canon. And the point, as I said earlier, is not to read African popular fiction as a separate category but as part of African literature, within an African literary tradition. Then it becomes possible to ask the question: What is the African detective fiction doing differently than the realist novel?

In a 2008 symposium, "Beyond Murder by Magic," held by the Jahnheinz Jahn Foundation at the Johannes Gutenberg University, one of the questions discussed was "What makes African crime fiction 'African'?" While avoiding the pitfalls of the Makerere discussions around what is African literature, the participants instead worked with the question of "the interface of African literature and crime fiction."[10] What they found was that what they have in a common "is their emphasis on the 'double' function of literature. Many African authors have a strong sense of responsibility towards society, which, independent of genre they choose, is reflected in their creative writing. Likewise, crime fiction exerts such a pull on contemporary African writers" (11). But can't that be said of all writers and literature? Or, if not of all writers, all literature to the extent that the imagination, even in science fiction or magical realism, ultimately draws from society? The question, rather, ought to be how does African crime fiction differ from the African realist novel in terms of themes and aesthetics?

Looking at the treatment of the politics of violence primarily in crime fiction and realist fiction, the differences in themes and aesthetics emerge around agency, social change, and translatability into political action. For Frantz Fanon, violent resistance to colonial rule was an integral expression of the colonized's agency. He argued that "decolonization is always a violent phenomenon" and that "at the level of individuals, violence is a cleansing force. It frees the native from his inferiority and from his despair and inaction; it makes him fearless and restores his self-respect" (94). In the realist African novel, violence is treated within a larger social and political context. In Ngugi Wa Thiong'o's *A Grain of Wheat* and *Matigari* the violent resistance to colonialism and a neocolonial dictatorship is political. Or in *Things Fall Apart* the violence, no matter how futile and individualized, is within a colonial context. In this sense violence is institutionalized and follows the Manichean colonial world of colonizer and colonized. In *Things Fall Apart* Okonkwo's individual acts of violence can be said to offer a critique of individual violence, but it is also very clear that it is happening within a growing, encroaching, and violent colonialism.

In contrast to *Things Fall Apart*, where the violence speaks to and transforms the whole society, the violence in detective fiction affects individuals with no revolutionary consequences. Kwei Quartey's *Wife of the Gods* features a marijuana-smoking police inspector by the name of Darko Dawson. Darko is investigating the murder of Gladys Mensah, a medical student, who is helping in the educational campaign against HIV/AIDS. He is also investigating a second case—the disappearance of his mother. *Wife of the Gods* covers the same thematic terrain covered by African realist novels. His suspect is a Fafali Acheampong, a priest in the village of Bedome who practices the Trokosi system—this is where families give up young girls and women to the priest to atone for their sins. On the face of it, *Wife of the Gods* covers a similar terrain as that of the Makerere generation: there are questions of gender and violence teased out through the Trokosi system, African versus Western culture, the divide of city and country, police violence, corruption, and poverty. But the novel is not a meditation on the larger issues; instead, they become the backdrop that makes the plot possible. In *Things Fall Apart*, individual acts of violence transform the whole society. In *Wife of the Gods*, individual actions transform individual lives.

The two murders and suicide happen to individuals, and in the end the cultural, economic, and political systems remain—that is, the oppressive structures remain intact. The society has not been transformed for better or worse, but individuals have. In *Nairobi Heat*, while I work with the Rwandan genocide, racial violence in the United States, and historical and criminal violence in Kenya, the trauma is individual. This, I believe, is something demanded by the form itself—it is individuals working within the limitations of their societies. Even in times of great upheaval the detectives and criminals are working within society, working within the rules even as they break them. In other words, a detective novel cannot show revolutionary violence as an act that transforms society for the better. If for Fanon violence expresses the newly found agency of the colonized,[11] violence in crime fiction is a symptom of a sick society and a necessary but evil tool for the detective. Is it a limitation? I do not think so—it just means that the detective and literary African novels are doing different work. And crime fiction, I think, is so organic to the societies that produce it that it imaginatively links the reader, the novel, and the society. In a sense, crime fiction is more of place than the realist novel.

In *The Wife of the Gods*, Efia, one of Acheampong's five wives who has had to endure beatings and rape, eventually cuts his penis off—recalling the revenge of Firdaus in Nawal El Saadawi's *Woman at Point Zero*. In *Woman at Point Zero*, Firdaus, an oppressed woman who seeks agency through high-class prostitution, kills her pimp in an act of vengeance and is sentenced to

death. But the novel is also an indictment of patriarchy fueled by neocolonial economic marginalization. There is a larger indictment of society and
repressive politics. We get to see the intersection of women's oppression via
gender, decolonization, psychology of resistance, and religious oppression.
In Tayeb Salih's *Season of Migration to the North* Mustafa engineers the self-
destruction and suicide of white women to avenge colonialism. Mustafa's
actions are understood within the alienation that came with colonialism.
Here, all three novels are indicting women's oppression but doing it differently. In Salih and Saadawi, the violence of revenge is stylized. In Quartey
an individual woman finally finds agency and cuts off the instrument of her
oppression, but the whole society, while indicted, is not threatened. But is
that not the way it is in real life? In a strange way detective fiction is more
realist than the realist novel.

In the last section in Fanon's *Wretched of the Earth*, he details clinical
cases—the psychological toll that violence and torture take on the tortured
and the torturer. One French police torturer traumatized by the violence he
inflicts on the Algerian nationalists comes to him for treatment—not so that
he can stop but so that he can carry on his work. Fanon narrates that the
police officer "had no intention of giving up his job as a torturer (this would
make no sense since he would have to resign) he asked me in plain language
to help torture Algerian patriots without having a guilty conscience, without
any behavioral problems, and with a total peace of mind" (198–99). This is
precisely the kind of character one meets in crime novels, but without the
190 pages or so in *The Wretched of the Earth* explaining national cultures,
colonialism and violent resistance, and the role of organic intellectuals that
preceded our meeting Fanon's patient. The crime novel I think is society in
shorthand; the realist African novel is society in longhand. They speak to
each other—after all, the characters, like the authors, would have read *Things
Fall Apart* as a set book, and David Maillu's thin *My Dear Bottle* as an insert,
hidden away from parents and teachers between the covers of the more literary novels.

There is one thing that worries me, though—the portrayal of African
cities as violent, misogynistic, hard-drinking, marijuana hubs. The U.S. *Nairobi Heat* cover has Africa shaped like a gun against a green background. A
very arresting, innovative cover, yet one that can be seen as showing Africa
as a violent place. The cover of the German translation is literal—it shows
a black man keeping warm by a charcoal burner. The U.S. version of *Black
Star Nairobi* shows Kenyatta International Conference Center with a time

bomb on top whereas the German version shows a black man screaming with fists raised, in the background, black coffins burning. And my response has been—why are we obsessed with how the West sees us? Why are judging African literature by how it's received by Western readers? What interests me most as a writer is contradiction. That is, Nairobi as a city of contradictions—where a wall separates rich estates from slums, wealth at the expense of the poor, where the poor kill each other to vote for the richest families, or fight each other for land when the ruling family owns half a million acres.

And at the same time the violence is real. I set *Black Star Nairobi* during the 2007–08 postelectoral violence in Kenya and the 2008 U.S. elections. The photo that is the cover of the German edition was taken during a pro-democracy demonstration.

In the end, for the literary critic it is not a question of whether the literary or the popular is better, and therefore deserving more attention. The task of the African literary critic, it seems to me, is to normalize the African literary tradition without regard to high or low forms of literature. The crime novel, working from a genre with its own demands, and written by writers who are dedicated to the form, is part of the African literary tradition. And as long as people are reading and talking about these works, we have a duty to study and teach them alongside the other literatures. There is no reason why, for example, an African literature survey course cannot start with early African writing, the Makerere, and post-Makerere writing, while including popular fiction.

The more borderless we allow African literature to be in terms of its literary history, languages, and genres, the richer the African literary tradition. The literature exists; it just needs critical attention. In the end, though, what lies at the heart of it all is the kind of African literature and tradition we want. Frantz Fanon in *The Wretched of the Earth* concludes by pleading with Africans to not follow Europe through imitation into the abyss of constant wars, conquest, and dehumanization, into the betrayal of humanism. He wrote, "If we want to turn Africa into a new Europe, and America into a new Europe, then let us leave the destiny of our countries to Europeans. They will know how to do it better than the most gifted among us. But if we want humanity to advance a step farther, if we want to bring it up to a different level than that which Europe has shown it, then we must invent and we must make discoveries."[12] Aesthetically we have had and still have the same choice. If England has canonized its literature at the expense of popular literature, and standardized English into one singular force as opposed to one rich with dialects and provincialism, and separated the peasant poets from the elite poets—why should we follow that same tired trajectory? Why not follow Fanon's plea and let the form and content of African literatures be many things? Why not listen to Achebe when, in the essay "Thoughts on the African Novel," he writes, "What I am saying really boils down to a simple plea for the African novel. *Don't fence me in.*"[13]

## CHAPTER 5

# Toward a Rooted Transnational African Literature

## Politics of Image and Naming

[H]e thought there was no point in roots if you couldn't take them with you.
—Kwame Anthony Appiah, "Cosmopolitan Patriots"

In retrospect, probably the most significant achievement of the Series was to alter the world's perception of Africa and its people.
—Alan Hill, *In Pursuit of Publishing*

Africa's image as a European racist construct has been at the center of the question: What is African literature? Achebe's dismissal of Joseph Conrad as a thoroughgoing racist and the *Heart of Darkness* as a racist text with no redemptive qualities; Taiye Selasi's response to Western reading of Africa as a country where there is no African literature; Binyavanga Wainaina's popular essay, "How to Write about Africa"; and Helon Habila's coinage of the "Caine Prize Aesthetic" to deride "African poverty porn"—all are attempts at correcting white views of Africa. On the face of it, the responses are different: Achebe was responding to the image of Africa and Africans as portrayed by Conrad; Selasi to the "Africa Is a Country" view of African literature; Binyavanga to the Africa of Western media and writers; and Habila to the stereotypes being propagated by younger African writers. But they all betray an anxiety over the white gaze.

Biodun Jeyifo in "The Nature of Things: Arrested Decolonization and Critical Theory" cautions against a dichotomization or binary of either/or in African literary criticism where African literature belongs to Africans and literary criticism to Western critics. In the essay, he contends with "the clearly emergent subsumption of all criticism and scholarship on African literature into two basic, supposedly distinct camps: first, the foreign, white, European or North American critic or scholar and second, the native, black African 'counterpart'" (434). For Jeyifo, "critical discourse not only assures the survival of literature, it also determines the condition in which it survives and the uses to which it will be put" (433). Following Jeyifo, I argue that reading African literature against Western perception ends up undermining the African literary tradition because it silences critical discourse. That is, the closing of nationalist ranks to ward off the white gaze became a defense of the 1960s Makerere consensus of the English-only realist novel and excluded early and contemporary African writing in African languages. And image-conscious reading of African literature glosses over new rooted yet transnational directions in African literature that are being offered by diasporic young writers like Tope Folarin and NoViolet Bulawayo.

Instead of opening up critical discourse so that *Heart of Darkness* can speak to the African colonial experience, or reveal contradictions in the colonial project, Achebe's criticism shuts it down. Where we should be asking questions about the nature of the African literary tradition, Selasi's solution becomes abolishing African literature as a category—because of a popular conception in the West of Africa as a country. Contradictions within Europe, the arguments for and against the Enlightenment, slavery, the French and Haitian Revolutions, and colonialism become lost to African literary criticism. If African literature is not to be fenced in by literary criticism and Achebe's plea heeded, then we have to free it by offering globalectical, Afropolitan, global, and transnational readings. In the end I argue for rooted transnationalism as one way to read post-Makerere African literature, from writers such as NoViolet Bulawayo and Chimamanda Adichie, out of the impasse of nationalistic and paternalistic readings.

## ACHEBE, CONRAD, AND THE ENLIGHTENMENT

In "An Image of Africa: Racism in Conrad's 'Heart of Darkness,'" Achebe argued that *Heart of Darkness* was a novel that "projects the image of Africa as 'the other world,' the antithesis of Europe and therefore of civilization, a place where man's vaunted intelligence and refinement are finally mocked by triumphant bestiality" (3). He was at war with the Africa imagined by colonial ideologies traceable to Enlightenment thinking about the state of nature.[1] But his dismissal shut down critical engagement with the ideologies and contradiction around the European Enlightenment—a project that attempted to liberate Europeans from the tyranny of religion and monarchies while simultaneously enslaving and colonizing. And, more than that, it leaves us with the idea that other Europeans did not contest Enlightenment racism, slavery, and colonialism. In other words, once *Heart of Darkness* is dismissed as racist, the multiple contradictions that propelled Europeans to Africa will be handed to the reader in package marked "Racist, No Need to Open."

The central issue for Achebe was not whether or not *Heart of Darkness* was great art that deserved to be part of the British canon, but rather the novel's portrayal of Africans as people trapped in a noble and savage state of nature. And because of that portrayal, it could not be great art. For him, on moral grounds and as a matter of conscience, one

> would not call that man an artist, for example, who composes an eloquent instigation to one people to fall upon another and destroy them. No matter how striking his imagery or how beautiful his cadences fall, such a man is no more a great artist than another may be called a priest who reads the mass backwards or a physician who poisons his patients. . . . poetry surely can only be on the side of man's deliverance and not his enslavement, for the brotherhood and unity of all mankind and not for the doctrines of Hitler's master races or Conrad's rudimentary souls. (9)

Thus, for Achebe, aesthetics mattered less than moral content and what eventually counted was the extent to which a novel was in the service of humanity.[2] Achebe did acknowledge that "Conrad did not originate the image of Africa which we find in his book" and that it was "the dominant image of Africa in the Western imagination" and Conrad had merely brought the peculiar gifts of his own mind to bear on it" (13). As did Clement Abiaziem Okafor who did "a point-by-point comparison of the African image" (17) of *Heart of Darkness* and *Things Fall Apart* in his essay, "Joseph Conrad and Chinua Achebe: Two Antipodal Portraits of Africa." Okafor saw *Heart of Darkness* as Conrad's "effort to portray the pernicious effects of colonialism not only on the subjugated people but ironically on the colonial agents as well" but he was "a veritable offspring of nineteenth-century European prejudices about Africa" (15). But Okafor did not follow the Enlightenment thread, through the image of Africa, back to England. Once he and Achebe dismissed Conrad as a racist, he also closed the door to the Enlightenment. The Enlightenment is important in understanding the ideological beginnings of the metaphysical empire.

Enlightenment thinkers asserted the centrality of human reason—think of Descartes exclaiming *I think therefore I am*—but they did not extend this reason to Africans. Immanuel Kant, in his essay, "What is Enlightenment?" argued that

> Enlightenment is man's emergence from his self-imposed nonage. Nonage is the inability to use one's own understanding without another's guidance. This nonage is self-imposed if its cause lies not in lack of understanding but in indecision and lack of courage to use one's own mind without another's guidance. *Dare to know!* (*Sapere aude.*) "Have the courage to use your own understanding," is therefore the motto of the Enlightenment.

Where before the world existed as willed by God, human beings were now seen as being in charge of their destinies. And things that before had been god-ordained now had a rational basis. Inequality was not god-ordained—it was a result of how human beings had organized their societies. But Kant, in *On the Different Races of Man*, argued that blacks were naturally inferior:

> The Negroes of Africa have by nature no feeling that rises above the trifling. Mr. Hume challenges anyone to cite a single example in which a Negro has shown talents, and asserts that among the hundreds of thousands of blacks who are transported elsewhere from their countries, although many of them have even been set free, still not a single one was ever found who presented anything great in art or science or any other praiseworthy quality, even though among the whites some continually rise aloft from the lowest rabble, and through superior gifts earn respect in the world.[3]

The idea of the African as irrational, primordial, ahistorical, violent and at war, living in a state of nature, or alternatively, as childlike, emotional, friendly, a junior to whiteness hearkens back to the Enlightenment.

The interesting point is not that Enlightenment thinkers were racist—it is that some of them dissented. Arguing against David Hume's contention that other races are inferior to whites, and that civilizing Africans would make them parrots (Eze, 33), James Beattie for example made the counterclaim that civilizations come and go, that those who enslaved yesterday can be enslaved today. Using a linear progression he argued that Europe was savage 2,000 years ago, just like America and Africa today, and civilization takes time (Eze, 35). For him, those called savage did have intricate art and governance but happened to lack science because they could not write. But nevertheless, he argued, they had great orality skills. And Beattie understood that inferiority arguments in the end justified slavery, and he called for the British generosity, which "animated with the heroic passion, the love of liberty," would be extended to all (Eze, 37). In Romantic England, writers such as Samuel Taylor Coleridge and William Wordsworth were opposed to slavery. Wordsworth, for example, wrote a poem[4] in celebration of Toussaint L'Ouverture who was betrayed by Napoleon and starved to death in the dungeons of St. Helena where, ironically, Napoleon found himself just a few years later.

Louis Sala-Molins, in the *Dark Side of the Light: Slavery and the French Enlightenment*, captured the central contradictions of the Enlightenment, freedom and chains:

> The Enlightenment composes the music, fills it with the most beautiful harmonies of a grand symphony to the glory of Reason, Man, the Sovereignty of the individual, and universal philanthropy. This score is being beautifully performed until suddenly a black erupts in the middle of the concert. What at that point becomes of Man, the Sovereignty, Reason and Philanthropy? They disappear into thin air. And the beautiful music pierces your eardrums with the gratings of the sarcasm. (8)

Sala-Molin concludes, "How can the Enlightenment be interpreted? Only with the Code Noir in hand" (9). But even then, French society was not a monolithic body singularly concerned with only French liberation as per the Enlightenment ideals—it was a society itself working through the contradiction of liberation for some and enslavement for others. Tom Reiss in *The Black Count: Glory, Revolution, Betrayal, and the Real Count of Monte Cristo* captured the contradiction of revolutionary France—where a black man could become a general and command respect within French society, and marry a French white woman without opposition from society. And after much debate, revolutionary France abolished slavery. But as soon as Napoleon decided that colonies such as Haiti were too valuable, he went about abolishing rights for black people in France, attempted to reinstate slavery in Haiti, and racism returned. Then the contradiction leaned heavily against liberty for all. As Reiss records, Alexandre Dumas, whose mother was a slave in Haiti and father a French nobleman, lived a free life in France, whereas a few years later, his son, the famous novelist, also named Alexandre, would struggle to survive through French racism.[5]

If Marlowe's gaze had gone beyond the banks of the river, he would have seen an African village very much like Okonkwo's Umofia, its inhabitants engaged in the business of living before being engulfed by colonialism. Like Umofia, there would be some contradictions, especially in the treatment of women and in the struggle against colonialism, but overall it would be a dynamic culture, one on the move. By the same token, Okonkwo's gaze would have gone beyond the missionary church to find a British culture itself besieged by the contradictions of a vicious class system, one that would hold on to Enlightenment ideas of the social contract while justifying colonialism. To put it differently, *Heart of Darkness* can shed light on the psychology and economic incentives that drive the district commissioner in *Things Fall Apart* who, on returning to England, wants to write a treatise to be titled "The Pacification of the Primitive Tribes of the Lower Niger."

Why shouldn't *Heart of Darkness* be a companion novel to *Things Fall Apart*? It allows the reader to look at the contradictions inherent in the Enlightenment and colonial ideologies. And African writers have been in conversation, more often than not a tense and corrective one, with European authors and aesthetics—but a conversation nevertheless—that has influenced and informed their writing. And they have entered this conversation through writing back to European authors. For example, Achebe, while broadly responding to colonial European paternalistic understandings of Africans, specifically wrote *Things Fall Apart* in response to Joyce Cary's *Mister Johnson*, a novel in which the main character is a perpetually untroubled African clerk who helps his colonial British boss come to terms with his humanity. Or take John Coetzee's *Foe*, which rewrites Daniel Defoe's *Robinson Crusoe* through the story of Susan Barton, a woman who is a castaway around the same time as Crusoe, and wants her story told by Defoe. In many ways, Ngugi's *A Grain of Wheat* writes back to Karen Blixen's *Out of Africa*. African writers entered into this conversation precisely because they had in part been formed by the same history of colonizer and colonized. The reader of African literature, then, in order to understand the conversation, must also understand the various historical and sometimes disparate circumstances that forcefully made this conversation necessary.

Achebe ended his lecture on Conrad by telling the audience that he had hoped to end on a more optimistic and conciliatory note. However, he said, "as I thought more about the stereotype image, about its grip and pervasiveness, about the willful tenacity with which the West holds it to its heart; when I thought of your television and the cinema and newspapers, about books read in schools and out of school, of churches preaching to empty pews about the need to send help to the heathen in Africa, I realized that no easy optimism was possible" (13). In the end, for Achebe what mattered was not what Conrad the writer had through his narrator revealed about imperialism, or even the myopia of Marlowe who, in spite of having general sympathies with the Africans, still sees them as inferior; what matters is the damage *Heart of Darkness* has done to Africa's image.

The consensus emerging from the Makerere generation, as it grappled with defining African literature, was that such literature had no relevance to the African reader. One of the questions raised at the 1963 Dakar Conference was the criterion for choosing what to read along with African literature. Mphahlele reported back that for a non-African novel to be read "side by side" with African literature,

> [i]t was insisted that only such literature of the British Isles should be presented as is meaningful to the African. The African should be able to identify himself with character and setting and share the thought and feeling of a work. Much of Milton would have to go, for instance. On the other hand, an African can easily share the thought and feeling within which *Macbeth, Julius Caesar, The Merchant of Venice, King Lear, The Wife of Usher's Hell, Sir Patrick Spens* and so on move. Shakespeare's plays should not be handled before sixth form. Again, the literature syllabus, it was felt, should include English writing from North America, India and Australia, translations of non-English works as well as the literature of the British Isles and Africa. (18)

Following this argument, then, *Heart of Darkness* could not be assigned in a literature class in an African university. African students would not be able identify with the novel; being on the receiving side of Kurtz's brutal civilizing mission, they would certainly not identify with the corrosive nature of imperialism on the soul of the colonizer. By positive identification with a novel becoming the basis for studying literature, an opportunity to read colonial literature as a way into British contradictions was lost.

## POST-MAKERERE AFRICAN WRITING THROUGH AN IMAGE OF AFRICA

The younger post-Makerere writers have inherited this anxiety over image and representation from the Makerere generation of African writers, but with a twist: the battle that Achebe carried to Conrad has now become fratricidal to the extent that African writers and critics are accusing other African writers of offering the West a Conradian Africa. In a move that again mirrors Tutuola's reception by African critics, today we find criticism fueled by feelings of shame at the way Africa is portrayed in the West.

Commenting on NoViolet's short story "Hitting Budapest," which won the 2011 Caine Prize, Ikhide Ikheloa wrote that "many writers are skewing their written perspectives to fit what they imagine will sell to the West and the judges of the Caine Prize." The evidence he offered was that the Caine Prize's five shortlisted stories were about a "roaming band of urchins," "a child soldier," "an interracial marriage gone awry" and "drunken simpletons." He argued their crime was in writing stories weighed down by a "monotony of misery." It is worth noting here that Ikheloa is the rare literary critic who is not part of academia. He is a retired chief of staff-ombudsman at the Montgomery County (Maryland) Board of Education. An advocate of more African writing on the Internet, he is highly influential, reaching thousands through his blog,[6] Facebook posts (he has close to 10,000 followers),[7] and Twitter account[8] (15,000). In keeping up with and taking seriously post-Makerere writers across all forms and media, he has built an archive of literary criticism that at some point members of the African literary establishment in academia will have to pay attention to. It was no surprise that his argument against what he termed elsewhere as "poverty porn"[9] reverberated widely among post-Makerere writers and was later echoed by Helon Habila.

Reviewing NoViolet Bulawayo's *We Need New Names* ("Hitting Budapest" was the first chapter of the novel) in 2013 for the *Guardian*, Habila used the term "Caine Prize aesthetic" to describe an otherwise very complex piece of fiction. By Caine Prize aesthetic, he meant writing that fed what Achebe had called in his lecture a desire or need in "Western psychology to set Africa up as a foil to Europe, as a place of negations at once remote and vaguely familiar, in comparison with which Europe's own state of spiritual grace will be manifest" (2). Habila lamented that Bulawayo was writing as if meeting a list of demands set by an African poverty-porn committee:

> There is a palpable anxiety to cover every "African" topic; almost as if the writer had a checklist made from the morning's news on Africa. There's even a rather inexplicable chapter on how the Chinese are taking over Africa, and how, as one of the street kids puts it, the Chinese "are not even our friends."

There are ways in which African literature is expected to do the work of representing Africa—to play an ambassadorial role and counter the Conradian vision of Africa. This is not to say that there are no stereotypical views of Africa in the West. But just as Achebe closed the door to the contradiction of critiquing colonialism while silencing Africans, Habila closes the door to aesthetic and political contradictions in *We Need New Names* as Bulawayo's characters navigate life in Zimbabwe and the United States in an age of globalization. Caine Prize judges have not been immune to the criticism around how the winning stories are portraying Africa. Alison Flood in a *Guardian* essay quoted Evaristo Bernardine on the 2012 shortlist:

> These stories have an originality and facility with language that made them stand out. We've chosen a bravely provocative homosexual story set in Malawi; a Nigerian soldier fighting in the Burma campaign of the Second World War; a hardboiled noir tale involving a disembodied leg; a drunk young Kenyan who outwits his irate employers; and the tension between Senegalese siblings over migration and family responsibility. . . . What we don't have is the sort of familiar tragic stories—there is no war, no starvation, no children in really terrible situations. I don't want to disparage this sort of story, as these are things which happen on the continent and need to be written about. But I wanted to show there is a bigger picture.[10]

And in a panel at the 2013 Africa Writes Festival in London, she narrated how she had actively fought against a story that was a favorite among the judges because it was telling the story of the stereotypical Africa.[11] This feeling of shame, of wanting to protect Africa's image in the West, of wanting to provide a sanitary Africa, ignores existing and historical contradictions in order to make way for an Africa-friendly literature.

This overdefensiveness can only allow writers and critics such as Evaristo and Selasi to look at Africa through the lens of either sanitary or dirty, rather than as a place of contradictions where skyscrapers coexist with slums, where wealth and poverty create each other. It allows for a literary criticism that elides over those contradictions—the hard material and identity issues facing Africans living at home or abroad—the kind of questions and contradictions raised by *We Need New Names*. The Chinese in Africa joining the Americans and the British, the fallacy of foreign aid and NGOs, questions of language, permanent immigration and identity, switching of narrators and poetic digressions, intertexuality with the Makerere generation, and so on. *We Need New Names* is squarely rooted in Zimbabwe and the United States. Darling is an insider in the United States as much as she is an insider in Zimbabwe. In contrast to earlier novels like Tayeb Salih's *Season of the Migration to the North*, where the main character, Mustafa in London, is going to go back to Sudan, and the West becomes the theater for colonial and anticolonial conflict, *We Need News Names* is squarely an African, and at the same time a diasporic and American, novel.

Critics do not know exactly what to do with this kind of literature, which simultaneously belongs to a contested African literature category and resists the easy label of immigrant literature where characters deal with cultural assimilation and discontentment. Critics have applauded Bulawayo for capturing an authentic Africa in the Zimbabwe half and criticized her for the second half set in the United States because her characters express no gratitude to the host country for the many opportunities to improve their lot. On the sustained critical ungratefulness of Darling, Michiko Kakutani in her review titled "A Child of Two Lands" argued that the "one misstep in this otherwise stunning novel" is

> speaking of the move to America, and the bitterness so many immigrants feel, as they are forced to take menial jobs or find their hopes frustrated [because] they try to project one point of view onto the experiences of a wide and varied group of immigrants, but also because they are not always true. For instance, the remarkably talented author of this book, the novel's jacket tells us, was "born and raised in Zimbabwe," and moved to the United States, where she earned an M.F.A. from Cornell and is now a Wallace Stegner Fellow at Stanford—which sounds very much like a dream achieved.[12]

This strikes me as an unusual line of criticism—as if Bulawayo has falsified her biography in her fiction. Kakutani's title points to the instinct of wanting to read this new literature using an older lens best captured by the title of a 1965 memoir by Mugo Gatheru that she alludes to, *Child of Two Worlds: A Kikuyu's Story*.[13] The implication is that one is caught between an ancient but dignified old African world and the new developed but alienating Western world. This is the same the sentiment expressed in a review of Tepilit Ole Saitoti's *The Worlds of a Maasai Warrior: An Autobiography* by Robert Pini titled "Worlds Apart: A Maasai's Encounter with the West." Pini recommended the book:

> To the anthropologist, vanishing indigenous peoples reflect the downside of Western culture's spread. In Tepilit Ole Saitoti's engaging autobiography, the encounter between Maasai and Western cultures is played out through the eyes of a keen observer who seems to appreciate looking at life from a dual perspective. (29)

Hearkening back to the reviews that followed Tutuola's *Palm Wine Drinkard*, the anthropologist is once again invoked. For Darling, it is not a question of dual worlds, she belongs to both of them, and they are both hers. Her world is not that divided; she transitions between both of them. Darling belongs to a contemporaneous Zimbabwe and United States.

That was the general trend of the early reviews—applauding the first half set in Zimbabwe and castigating the second half set in the United States. What Kakutani reveals here is a profound discomfort with literature that defies the more comfortable trope of immigrant literature that in spite of the hardships of the immigration and assimilation still finds mitigating factors such as jobs, education, and so on. Rayyan Al-Shawaf, reviewing the novel for the *Boston Globe*, wrote:

> When, at the beginning of the novel's second half, she moves to Michigan to live with her Aunt Fostalina—first in Detroit, and then in Kalamazoo—the stage is set for a host of observations concerning her new home. But they prove disappointingly run-of-the mill: the biting cold; the smorgasbord of food available for purchase at supermarkets; Americans' ignorance of the diversity of Africa; the cultural coexistence between obesity and obsession with skinny women as a feminine ideal; commercialization of sex through pornography; and the new names immigrants give their children to "make them belong in America."[14]

Jenny Shank, reviewing the novel for the *Dallas News*, observed that

[w]hen Darling moves to America, she's suddenly there, with no building of suspense or detailing of plans that the move is imminent. Characters appear and quickly disappear. Each of these chapters is intense, moving and vivid, but it's best to enjoy them as stories, and not look for overall plot momentum. This isn't Bulawayo's fault, but that of the pesky, sales-seeking subtitle "A Novel" that marks many linked story collections.[15]

Not all the critics read the novel as a successful Zimbabwean novel and a failed American novel. Shay Howell, in a *New York Daily News* review titled "In 'We Need New Names,' NoViolet Bulawayo Sketches a Heartbreaking Portrait of Zimbabwe," wrote that

[r]elocating to "Destroyedmichygen," Darling encounters racism, America's own brand of poverty, and an endless feeling of missing Zimbabwe. Darling bears witness to universal problems of poverty, hunger, and loss, and in her relocation, Bulawayo asserts that there are Darlings in need all over the world.[16]

But even then the tendency was to universalize Darling's experiences as opposed to trying to tease out what was peculiarly an American experience from a Zimbabwean experience. And the reviews that saw equal opportunity criticism of the United States and Zimbabwe spent more time talking about the Zimbabwean half, reserving the discussion of the United States to one or two paragraphs. Even Shay Howell's title of the review calls attention to Zimbabwe only. The point, however, is that what Darling experiences is not just universal—yes, poverty is universal, but her being a poor black Ndebele Zimbabwean and a victim of Mugabe's government policies who immigrates to a racially and class charged United States makes her experiences particular and local to both places.

In *A New Generation of African Writers*, Brenda Cooper made the same mistake of universalizing and hence de-racializing African experiences of the West when she wrote that "nothing so much distinguishes the post-colonial, black migrant from the European citizen. The migrant, as much as an aspiring member of the underclass, is trapped in what Bourdieu dubs the dilemma of the 'parvenus,' the uneasy, in-between people, who have to choose between conforming to, or ostentatiously rebelling against, the mores of the upper-class to which they aspire" (5). If we take the United States to be host country, *We Need New Names* and *Americanah*, by looking at the relationship between

Africans and African Americans and race in general, challenge this universalizing of the migrant experience. A celebratory June 2014 *New York Times* essay, "New Wave of African Writers with an Internationalist Bent" by Felicia R. Lee declared that "Black literary writers with African roots (though some grew up elsewhere), mostly young cosmopolitans who write in English, are making a splash in the book world, especially in the United States." Following the wider relationships between African and African Americans and competition over resources and how whites perceive them, Lee raised the question of whether African writers are being published at the expense of African American writers to Adichie. Adichie responded to say that "In the U.S., to be a black person who is not African-American in certain circles is to be seen as quote-unquote, the good black . . . Or people will say, 'You are African so you are not angry.' Or, 'You're African so you don't have all those issues.'" Universalizing the African experience in the West ignores the complex historical and changing questions on the geography and identity of African literature and literary criticism.

## WE NEED NEW TERMS: AFROPOLITAN, GLOBALECTIC, OR ROOTED TRANSNATIONALISM?

In the 1960s the question was about limiting inclusion, as African writers and critics tried to define a literary tradition with Africa at the center. But today writers who identify as African, or as African and American, for example, are all over the world. These are writers like Teju Cole who were born in the United States, lived in Africa as children and teenagers, and then moved (back) to the United States. Or NoViolet Bulawayo, born and raised in Zimbabwe, before coming to the United States as a teenager. Or Okey Ndibe, who migrated to the United States as an adult but has now lived most of his life in the United States. As Selasi asked in her Berlin lecture, "I speak no African language and hold no African passport. But the protagonists of my novel were born in Ghana and Nigeria respectively. Does this make *Ghana Must Go* an African novel, me an African novelist?" ("African Literature Doesn't Exist," 10). What literary terms are to be used to describe this new wave of writers whose imaginations are rooted in Africa and elsewhere yet have lived most or all their lives outside the continent?

Selasi, in an earlier essay, "Bye-Bye Babar (Or What Is an Afropolitan)," coined[17] the term "Afropolitan" to describe "the newest generation of African emigrants, coming soon or collected already at a law firm/chem lab/jazz lounge near you." She defined Afropolitanism this way:

> You'll know us by our funny blend of London fashion, New York jargon, African ethics, and academic successes. Some of us are ethnic mixes, e.g. Ghanaian and Canadian, Nigerian and Swiss; others merely cultural mutts: American accent, European affect, and African ethos. Most of us are multilingual: in addition to English and a Romantic or two, we understand some indigenous tongue and speak a few urban vernaculars. There is at least one place on The African Continent to which we tie our sense of self: be it a nation-state (Ethiopia), a city (Ibadan), or an auntie's kitchen. . . . We are Afropolitans: not citizens, but Africans of the world.

In her Berlin lecture she distanced her identity from her writing, arguing that, while she has an identity, it is not to be conflated with her writing. That is, she might be an Afropolitan, but her writing is not Afropolitan. For her, "Afropolitan is a personal identity" and "fiction has no need for such things" (12). But it was too late—the term, seductive in that it captured first-generation European or American Africans in a way that had not been done before, grew a life of its own. Afropolitan magazines, fashion shows, and art shows rose out of images of a shiny Africa rising.

The term spawned debates, with some African writers like Binyavanga declaring "I am a Pan-Africanist not an Afropolitan" due to the way the term has been commoditized. In a blog essay, "Why I'm Not An Afropolitan," Emma Dabiri argued that she was at first attracted to the term because she was "looking for a language that expresses [her] position as an Irish/Nigerian woman who is deeply connected to her Nigerianness" and it "positioned [her] with others through a shared cultural and aesthetic leaning rather than a perceived racial classification." But the term soon lost its luster as she found "it reeks of sponsorship and big business with all the attendant limitations." Salah Hassan, in his African Studies Association 2013 presidential address,[18] captured both the promise of the term Afropolitan and at the same time what the term gets to sweep under the rug of privileged cosmopolitanism. That is, there are different classes of Africans living in the West, experiencing the West differently. Hassan argued:

> On the one hand, we witness a growing number of exhibitions and other events celebrating the talent of contemporary African artists, writers, musi-

cians and other creative figures living in the West or moving in and out of it. On the other hand, the press and media continue to carry (and sometimes deliberately ignore) the tragic images of African youths, men and women, who have perished trekking through the deserts of North African countries in transit to Europe, and of thousands upon thousands of others who have drowned (sometimes deliberately left to face such tragic destiny) while journeying on makeshift boats across the Mediterranean Sea to Europe. Those who have made it alive have encountered a new fortress of draconian laws in a continent that has devoted its energies and legislation to its "security"—read "curbing immigration"—as felt on a daily basis by Africans living in Europe or the USA. (4)

In this sense, the term "Afropolitan," while signaling there are Africans outside the categories of immigrant and citizen, glosses over gender, class, and sexuality.[19] It cannot be an adequate lens through which to look at new African writing. For example, Adichie's *Americanah* deals with Afropolitan-type Africans both in Nigeria and the United States where dating, identifying, and studying and working within the comforts of the middle and upper classes is expected. The arguments between Africans and African Americans in *Americanah* are fraught, but within middle- to upper-class consensus. In short, in *Americanah*, a full middle class aesthetic is in display. In contrast NoViolet Bulawayo's characters in *We Need New Names* are not Afropolitan. Indeed, they are unlike anything encountered before in African literature— ungrateful toiling porn watching baby pinching anorexic crazy politically conscious African immigrants in the West to stay, the African immigrants at the blunt end of the anti-immigrant laws that Hassan references above, but who stays without apology.

There has been one point of agreement regardless of where previous generations have stood on African literature and aesthetics debates—that is, African literature is world literature. For Selasi, it follows that if Africa is a complex and diverse continent, without ties that bind one country to another, and full of distinct cultures and languages within the different countries, the category, African literature, is meaningless in that it hides more than it illuminates. And if there is no African literature, then there can be no African writers. To call her an African novelist "is first to invent some monolithic Africa," and also confine her "characters, their color—from overstepping its bounds" and it means that there is "something important in common with all other African authors, who, together with [her] produce African literature"

(4). Invoking Goethe's call for world literature, she called for a classification of literature along content as opposed to the nationality of the writer.

In the Berlin lecture, she asked, "Wouldn't it be wonderful if we classified literature not by country but by content so that one would find categories of the love story, the city novel, the novel of the nation-state, the war novel, the bildungsroman?" (13). In essence, her essay is a call for the abolition of literary categories, usually along lines of identity and culture, in world literature.[20]

In *Globalectics: Theory and the Politics of Knowing*, Ngugi also invokes Goethe and calls for African literature to be read as both local and universal. For Goethe, Ngugi argues, there was "no such thing as a patriotic art or science: both belong, like all good things, to the whole world" (44). One needs to approach world literature though a "globalectical imagination" in order to "crack open a word, gesture, encounter, any text—it enables a simultaneous engagement with the particularity of the Blakean grain of sand and the universality in the notion of the world" (42). Where Selasi is calling for the abolition of the category African literature, Ngugi is arguing that African literature be freed to be in conversation with other literatures:

> Reading globalectically is a way of approaching any text from whatever times and places to allow its content and themes to form a free conversation with other texts of one's time and place, the better to make it yield its maximum to the human. It is to allow it to speak to our own cultural present even as we speak to it from our own cultural present. It is to read the text with the eyes of the world; it is to see the world with the eyes of the text. (60)

Put this way, African literature as a category becomes less important. An African novel then is freed to be read in relation to where it's coming from and in relation to other literatures of the world, and locally; as speaking to a place where it is being read. This way, world literature does not become a universe without local departures or even end points, where texts reveal universal lessons as if they are not formed by material histories and cultures at play. World literature becomes a meeting place for literatures from different cultures and parts of the world—without favor or hierarchy. To put it another way, as physicists point out—the center is everywhere, the center is nowhere.

The danger, though, of globalectics is that it has no limits—all texts can be globalectic. In this sense it is a lot like hybridity. As useful as hybridity was in understanding that cultural contact, no matter how violent and oppressive, is not a one-way street, that by necessity there are third spaces, eventually had no limits—everything in the end can be explained by hybridity. For Homi Bhabha, in his essay "Culture's in Between," when two cultures meet, the negotiation that ensues is

> neither assimilation nor collaboration. It makes possible the emergence of an "interstitial" agency that refuses binary representation of social antagonism. Hybrid agencies find their voice in a dialectic that does not seek cultural supremacy or sovereignty. They deploy the partial culture from which they emerge to construct visions of community, and versions of historic memory, that give narrative form to the minority positions they occupy: the outside of the inside; the part in the whole. (212)

Recalling the French colonial system of assimilation and the British system of indirect rule where local power structures were put in the service of British colonialism, Bhabha is right that assimilation and collaboration cannot lead to a hybrid state because the result is colonialism in both instances. But the alternative to assimilation and collaboration is not a resistance that seeks "sovereignty." For Bhabha there is a "third space" where both cultures cannot help but form and inform each other, where hybrid agencies constantly undermine the single narrative of superiority and inferiority:

> Strategies of hybridization reveal an estranging movement in the "authoritative" even authoritarian inscription of the cultural sign. At the point at which the precept attempts to objectify itself as a generalized knowledge or a normalizing, hegemonic practice, the hybrid strategy or discourse opens up a space of negotiation where power is unequal but articulation equivocal. (212)

However, there were some severe limitations to hybridity. Hybridity does not immediately recall contradictions in each individual culture as independent before finding the negotiated third space. The third space is privileged over various contradictions within the first and second spaces. Hybridity, unless we stretch it to a point of being unrecognizable, does not speak to the fissures of English society in and of themselves and the fissures in colonial and postindependence African countries in and of themselves, even as they create interstices.

Finally, the meaning of hybridity is elusive because it is possible to find it everywhere, thereby making it limitless. For example, Robert Young, in *Colonial Desire*, states that "there is no single, or correct, concept of hybridity; it changes as it repeats, but it also repeats as it changes" (27). For Young, hybridity is the very phenomenon it is trying to help us understand, a concept that is also the thing itself, and an answer that is also the problem. So he argues that that hybridity, in relation to challenging "the centered, dominant cultural norms with their unsettling perplexities generated out of their 'disjunctive, liminal space,'" becomes "a third term which can never in fact be third because, as a monstrous inversion, a miscreated perversion of its progenitors, it exhausts the differences between them" (23). In Young's sense, hybridity is definable only in operation; it can only be seen in operation—like a hammer that becomes a hammer only in the carpenter's hand and once back in the toolbox ceases to be a hammer. Not only then does hybridity defy a stable definition, but it is also an infinitely self-replicating and mutating amorphous concept. It becomes too amorphous of a term to be useable.

Globalectics then faces the same danger. Useful in approaching a text, in that it cautions against cultural relativists and nationalistic reading, it, however, can be everywhere at the same time. Once a concept becomes of infinite possibilities, then it becomes less useful. In thinking through post-Makerere writing, what is needed are severely limited concepts that speak to being rooted in multiple places, of belonging to more than one culture as the real condition of day to day living.

In the essay "Cosmopolitan Patriots" Appiah answers the criticism that cosmopolitanism is rootless by arguing that it can be both rooted and at the same time of the world—that, in fact, the best cosmopolitan is one who is rooted somewhere. Or, as he says of his father, a cosmopolitan also carries his roots with him. A "rooted cosmopolitan" is one who is "attached to a home of one's own, with its own cultural particularities, but taking pleasure from the presence of other, different places that are home to other, different people" (3). If we are to understand the literature coming from the post-Makerere writers it has to be through its transnational nature, which is also rooted in multiple cultures, nations, and languages.

Following Appiah, rooted transnationalism will account for particularities of national cultures and at the same time for a literary arc across two or more nations. That is, novels will be rooted in multiple particularities. In this sense, the novels are not global, they are local in two or more places at once, and yet in conversation across those localities. If you think of a colorful airline flight map, it only shows the routes and destinations, transnational or multinational travels to various capitals of the world. But it does not tell us what happens in Nairobi, or Delhi, or London after the plane lands. A look at transnationalism alone, then, accounts for the relationship between the two settings. But it does not allow us to look at what is happening in each of those settings. Rooted transnationalism demands and allows that we study the novel in relation to the places it is set, following the contradictions and particularities of, say, Nairobi and London. Rooted transnationalism then helps account for literature coming from writers who are living out Susan Sontag's simultaneity. She writes in the essay, "At the Same Time . . . (The Novelist and Moral Reasoning)," that

> [p]erhaps it is our perennial fate to be surprised by the simultaneity of events by the sheer extension of the world in time and space. That we are here, now prosperous, safe, unlikely to go to bed hungry or be blown to pieces this evening . . . while elsewhere in the world, right now . . . in Grozny, in Najaf, in the Sudan, in the Congo, in Gaza, in the favelas of Rio . . . To be a traveller—and novelists are often travellers—is to be constantly reminded of the very different world you have visited and from which you have returned "home." (16)

But African writers are living out the simultaneity. The extended awareness that Sontag calls for is their reality—those who are going hungry, being blown to pieces, facing political repression, violence, genocide and threats of genocide are immediate relatives. And the reality of life as an immigrant, especially if undocumented in the United States, for example, is also precarious, not to mention racism and working jobs that hold no future. And in times of peace, in a strange way for the immigrant, one is always visiting home. And when at home, say in Kenya, they leave to return home to the United States. The simultaneity that comes through in the literature carries the localness of what essentially become two homes; it is rooted in multiple transnational realities.

Taiye Selasi in her continuing struggle to find ways to understand her work and that of her generation now sees herself as a multilocal Afropolitan[21] in an attempt to capture the transnational nature of her writing, and the heavy investments in the various localities. But multilocal in literary terms does not quite capture the transnational, or even multinational, nature of a literature invested in multiple locales. In my case, my three novels, *Black Star Nairobi*, *Nairobi Heat*, and *Mrs. Shaw*, are rooted in Nairobi and Madison, Wisconsin. *Black Star Nairobi* and *Nairobi Heat* have at their center an African American detective, Ishmael Fofona, who is working cases that take him to the past of the Rwandan genocide and the present of the Kenya 2007 electoral violence, and present and historical racism, and electoral politics in the United States. *Mrs. Shaw* features Kalumba, an exiled political activist from a factionary Kwatee Republic, who lives out the agonies of exile and return.

NoViolet Bulawayo's *We Need New Names* is rooted in Detroit and rural Zimbabwe and, more than my own work, shows us characters that live out the simultaneity of US and Zimbabwean politics. In Adichie's *Americanah*, her characters live out the simultaneity of US, European, and Nigerian class, race, and gender politics. And right behind my generation, younger writers like Tope Folarin who were born in the United States have lived in the West all their lives but, through their African parents, are also rooted imaginatively in African countries. In this sense, our work is transnational in that it is rooted and actively aware of the contradictions of each location.

One has to be mindful that there are many ways of being transnational and rooted. As Isabel Hofmeyr argues in her essay "The Black Atlantic Meets the Indian Ocean: Forging New Paradigms of Transnationalism for the Global South," transnational like global and world literatures can easily come to center the West versus the rest:

> As the humanities and social sciences take an increasingly transnational turn, the academic marketplace has become crowded with models that seek to explain the phenomena of globalisation and translocalism. Almost without exception, this scholarship has focused on north-south modes of transnationalism. Indeed the terminology itself, like the word globalisation, through its apparent neutrality appears to imply transnational processes emanating from the West and then radiating outward. But what of transnationalism within the south itself? What of nonwestern sources of globalisation, or processes of transnationalism that happen without reference to Europe? (3)

For example, *Black Ghosts* by Ken Kamoche is set in China and tells the story of an African student navigating Chinese culture and racism. Ngugi's *Wizard of the Crow* is set in an African country, the West, and India. In other words, all sorts of triangulation and multiple triangulations exist. And the West is no longer monolithic—the transnational novel is also looking at class and racial antagonisms at work, say, in the United States. *We Need New Names* deals with questions of class, race, and the underbelly of immigration and the importance of being papered, documented. *Nairobi Heat* deals with blackness in the United States and Kenya. In this sense, conversations taking place between marginalized Africans and African Americans are not centering the

West, but rather allowing for peoples with long histories interrupted by slavery and colonialism to look at the contradictions that make their relationship possible. The danger is in centering a West of the powerful, of the privileged, while forgetting other horizontal and often subversive relationships.

In his essay, "The Globalization of the Novel and the Novelization of the Global: A Critique of World Literature," Mariano Siskind argues that there are "two different but complementary models with which to think about the relation between the novel and the discourses of globalization. The first—the globalization of the novel—works not with particular textual formations but with the historical expansion of the novel-form hand-in-hand with the colonial enterprise of Western Europe. The second model—the novelization of the global—focuses on the production of images of a globalized world as they are constructed in specific novels" (336). In the first instance, we can think of the African novel in general (e.g., *Things Fall Apart*) coming into being as a result of colonial contact. And in the second instance, and in more contemporary terms, there are African novels that by content can be understood as global or at least as defying sole national, or a singular local/national definition. *We Need New Names*—set in Zimbabwe and the United States—is global in that we see the global while Darling is in Zimbabwe and the global while she is in the United Sates. And yet it seems to me that the transnationalism helps us read the global, in fact, helps us read globalectically.

A rooted transnational literature does not have to be set in more than one nation. It can draw from global cultures sitting right at home—transnational exchanges are taking place through cellphones, Skype conversations, music, literature, and movies. And outside of cultural transnationalism, war, especially the war on terror and drone warfare, creates a different kind of transnational exchange—tragic but familiar, particular and universal. The drone pilot sitting somewhere in an office in the United States, delivering indiscriminate violence all over the world without favor, might be the most rooted cosmopolitan of us all.

In the introduction to *Minor Transnationalism*, Francoise Lionnet and Shu-mei Shih note that "More often than not, minority subjects identify themselves in opposition to a dominant discourse rather than vis-à-vis each other and minority groups. We study the center and the margin but rarely examine the relationships among different margins" (2). The problem with their premise is the acceptance of terms such as *minority*, *center*, and *periphery* as starting points even as they question them. There is nothing minor about the meeting between Africans and African Americans or, more specifically, say, the 1964 meeting between Kwame Nkrumah and Malcolm X. Or the 20th century pan-African conferences that brought together black writers and intellectuals from all over the diaspora, or the 1955 Bandung conference that brought together political leaders from the global south. The center was where they were. Yet their important intervention serves as a corrective to postcolonial studies, a field obsessed with the West versus the Global South. They show a different lens through which we can re-read power, historically and in our age of globalization. Rooted transnationalism as opposed to minor transnationalism helps us map and study the networks that have all along been driving history and literature.

Aminatta Forna, born in Scotland to a Scottish mother and Sierra Leonean father, raised in Sierra Leone and Britain, and who spent periods of her childhood in Iran,[22] best exemplifies the difficulties that literary criticism has when it comes to naming literatures being produced by writers who are rooted in more than one place. And whose imaginations are free to set their novels away from their local particularities and in places that take us far away from the categories of African literature, or African diaspora literature. She is a part of a new generation of rooted transnational writers whose biographies and the literature they produce exemplify the sheer inadequacy of categories and of conceptual reading that rely on a single particular literary theory.

The politics of decolonization in Africa, to paraphrase Fanon, did not run in a straight line. Her father, Dr. Mohamed Forna, a well-respected former finance minister, ran afoul of the increasingly corrupt and despotic Siaka Stevens government and was hanged in 1975. After his death, Forna and her mother, who had already divorced him and remarried a diplomat, ended up living in Iran, Zambia, and Thailand. Drawing from her multinational and cultural backgrounds, Forna's writing does not just challenge African and British literary canons: it defies canonization itself, because canons depend on the assumed stableness of identity, race, nation, and culture. Take her latest novel, *The Hired Man* (2013), which is set in a small rural town in Croatia. Duro Kolak, the observant and detail-oriented narrator, is male, and the action of the novel centers around the assemblage of genocide, how two cultures can coexist until one day those same differences become a border and ethnic cleansing ensues. In *The Hired Man*, the violence is intimate and personal, making the resulting trauma all the more difficult to leave behind. The novel patiently explores a difficult question: How do the victimizers, the people who have committed ethnic cleansing, as well as those who did not do enough to stop it, live on past the event?

In a 2015 essay for the *Guardian* titled "Don't Judge a Book by Its Author," Forna narrates how, after a reading at a New York bookstore, she discovered that *The Hired Man* had been placed in the African literature section. After she told the owner that the book had nothing to do with Africa, that it was about Croatia, she later discovered that it was moved to the European literature section. Forna muses, "Where should a bookshop shelve a novel set in Croatia and written in English by a Scottish Sierra Leonean author?" Her first published work, *The Devil That Danced on the Water: A Daughter's Quest* (2002), is a memoir about her family and the politics that led to her father's death—the same politics that would later fuel the 1991–2002 Sierra Leonean civil war that claimed over 50,000 lives. In her memoir, the political and the personal cannot be separated; through her eyes we witness her family and Sierra Leone being slowly driven into destruction by neocolonial history. Both *The Hired Man* and *The Devil That Danced on the Water* are fueled by violent history that, in Forna's hands, becomes a 'terrible beauty," or, following Kant, a "terrible sublime."

In *Ancestor Stones* (2006), Forna uses four voices to reveal a much-challenged but unbroken thread of patriarchy stretching from precolonial to postcolonial Africa. What is remarkable about this novel set in an unnamed African country is not just its historical breadth, but that each voice is aesthetically different. Asana's is fast-talking, as she revels in telling her story. She begins her narration this way: "Hali! What story shall I tell? The story of how it really was, or the one you want to hear?" (15). Hawa's storytelling when we first meet her is tinged with the regret of one who was never in control of her destiny: "My life was not supposed to be like this," she starts. Mariama's is descriptive and poetic: "I remember how it was when I danced with my mother" (34), and through the metaphor of dance, she weaves in her mother's story. And Serah's is introspective while at the same time assuming a distance from her own story: "My mother? I haven't thought about her in a long time. My mother left" (81). And then she goes on to tell her story in such great detail that it becomes clear her mother is constantly on her mind. Through shifting narrators and time, the women live through the violence of colonialism, world wars, the hope of decolonization and education, and the betrayal of that hope and ensuing civil war, all within the crucible of patriarchy.

In *The Memory of Love* (2010), which won her the Commonwealth Writer's Prize for Best Book, Forna captures a Sierra Leone somewhere between mourning and melancholia.[23] Elias Cole, whose betrayal of a friend has deadly consequences, knows the country that has been lost through the civil war; and through mourning, is trying to recover it. But at the same time, there is no sense of the why, given the amount of destruction in terms of life, property, and mental health. Without the why, the mourning cannot be complete. And the characters seem to be somewhere between loss and trauma (experienced or inherited), knowing and recovery.

All in all, rather than trying to place Forna within national literatures, it seems better to think of her work in terms of the themes she explores—war, violence, love, betrayal, family, and history—themes that are universal in that they cut across cultures and nations, and are at the same time particular because they happen to specific cultures and peoples. As she writes in her *Guardian* essay, "The war in Sierra Leone had been characterized by amputations. . . . The former Yugoslavia became a snipers' war. We were a nation of farmers and they were a nation of hunters. When people go to war they pick up the first thing at hand, be it a machete or a rifle." Her novels then are rooted in a place and its particularities—whether in Croatia, Sierra Leone, or England.

Forna's writing shows that once we leave behind the question what is African literature and its obsessions with colonial images of Africa and their vestiges today, it becomes possible to speak about the aesthetic and political continuities and discontinuities. It becomes possible to look back to the early South African writing, it becomes possible to trace a line within the African literary tradition that starts with the novel of synthesis, decolonization, and transnationalism. The contact through colonial violence does not create transnational literature—people meet first, then go through colonial oppression and resistance, cultural violence and resistance. Hybridity and third spaces, postcolonial spaces, all develop over time to create transnational networks. These transnational networks in turn flow and crisscross the world in all sorts of formulations, unearthing local and global contradictions. In the end, though, what matters the most is not the literary concept that a critic decides to use; each literary concept will have its blind spots. What matters the most is the generosity with which the literary critic approaches African literature. It is a paradox: to not fence in African literature, we have to open it up to its past literary history, to its present rooted transnational state, and to a future where roots are everywhere, and the center nowhere.

Writers and scholars whose intertexuality begins with the Makerere literature—to put it bluntly—do not know where they are coming from. There is the argument to make that Africa is not a country, that Pan-Africanism, like identity, is a construct. It is attractive to always start anew, to be the author in this case quite literally of your own book. The beauty of history, though, is in its longevity. It never forgets precisely because it has already happened—it is not generational, and not historical in the linear from point A to point B sense. What matters now cannot into perpetuity hide what has already happened. Early slave narratives, Timbuktu manuscripts, early Amharic writing—if it has happened, it already exists, eating away our present times. Our job as literary critics is to deepen the African literary tradition by reading early African writing within it. And to broaden it by reading literatures from the diaspora, and other forms—science, crime, and romance.

In writing this book, I have come to realize that we have a crisis of periodization and specialization. At Cornell University, I was hired as a scholar of African Anglophone literature. But in practice Anglophone functions as a code for the Makerere literature and to differentiate it from Francophone and Lusophone literatures. If we included early slave narratives in the definition of African literature, early South African writing in English, the 200 or so novels in the Heinemann African Writers Series, contemporary writing of Adichie, Habila, Bulawayo, Binyavanga, and others in my generation, upcoming writing from first-generation Africans in the West, it becomes an oxymoron to talk of experts in Anglophone African literature. What are needed are scholars who are definitely aware of the literary tradition and then specialize in different periods or authors or movements, as we do with European literature. Early African writing scholar, African language and translation scholar, Makerere writers scholar, an Achebe scholar, a literature of decolonization scholar, an Adichie and transnational African literature scholar, and so on. By insisting on experts in Anglophone literature, what we are really saying is that we want scholars who teach Makerere literature survey courses as opposed to scholars who specialize in the many movements in African literature.

I feel that when it comes to African literature, literary critics are expected to account for all of it—an expectation that we do not demand of European literary critics. In my case I work primarily on the African novel with all of my training and a good amount of scholarly work spent on the Anglophone Makerere and post-Makerere literature. While I hope and trust that scholars in theater, poetry, and film will also find this book useful, and some of the issues especially of language and identity will apply, I have not studied African poetry, theater, and film in any meaningful way beyond one or two courses. In other words, I worked on the novel because that is where my training lies. If we are to rethink how we teach and critique African literary theory and literature, we should also rethink how we periodize it and what we expect of African literature scholars.

As a way to formulate the book, I asked myself: If one were to write about the rise of the African novel in English as narrative or even a biography, what would it look like? I realized that, by necessity, one would find a brief history of the European Enlightenment, a "liberatory" project that carries with it the contradiction of formulating ideologies and categories that would create an intellectual framework for colonialism and colonial education.

One would find African writers and intellectuals in South Africa writing as colonialism mutates into apartheid, then the Makerere writers, products of a colonial education, using their writing to forge—in both senses of the word—decolonization and a national consciousness.

Moving to the post-Makerere writers, one would find first- and second-generation Africans, immigrants or citizens of the West, telling their stories that are rooted and invested in multiple homes. One would find writers moving beyond the borders of the realist novel into the genres of crime and detective, romance and science fiction.

One would find a literary tradition that exists as a question and debate—one on the move with debates around identity, language, and politics swirling around it. One would think of what a nameless narrator says to Askar in Nurrudin Farah's *Maps*: "You are a question to yourself." The end of the story would also be the beginning: What is African literature? African literature is a question to itself.

And if the question was to be asked to the Palm Wine Drinkard after tapping and sampling a hundred kegs, I think he would say that there is an English metaphysical empire in my palm wine.[24]

INTRODUCTION

1. Chinua Achebe, *Hopes and Impediments: Selected Essays* (New York: Anchor Books, Doubleday, 1989), 59–60.

2. Kwame Anthony Appiah, *In My Father's House: Africa in the Politics of Culture* (London: Methuen, 1991).

3. Achebe, *Hopes and Impediments: Selected Essays*.

4. There are mentions of possible translations online, and sightings of a translated copy, but as far as I can ascertain they have yet to be published in any meaningful sense. In any case we should be talking about competing translations as opposed to whether a single translation might exist.

5. Obiajunwa Wali, "A Reply to Critics from Obi Wali," *Transition*, no. 50 (October 1975–March 1976): 46–47.

6. See D. Goluch, "Chinua Achebe Translating, Translating Chinua Achebe: *Things Fall Apart* in Polish and the Task of Postcolonial Translation," *Cross/Cultures* 137 (2011): 197–219. See also W. Kolb, "Re-writing *Things Fall Apart* in German," *Cross/Cultures* 137 (2011): 177–196, 219.

7. He would later decolonize his name and drop the Christian name, James, and become Ngugi wa Thiong'o in 1977.

8. He would change his name to Es'kia Mphahlele to reflect his growing black consciousness in 1977, the same year as Ngugi's name change.

9. The magazine was later restarted and relocated to Harvard University in 1991.

10. Steven Naifeh, "The Myth of Oshogbo," *African Arts* 14, no. 2 (February 1981): 25–27, 85–86, 88.

11. Tony Hall, "Rajat Neogy on the CIA," special anniversary issue, "Selections from *Transition*, 1961–1976," *Transition*, no. 75/76 (1997): 312–16.

12. But as enthusiastic as he was, the young Ngugi also noted the apolitical nature of the conference. In the same write-up he observes, "Although there were at times violent and deep differences of opinion on particular issues, for instance on the question of whether there was such a thing as African writing, yet the whole conference was almost

quiet on such things as colonialism, imperialism and other isms. In this it differed from the 1956 and 1959 World Congresses of Negro Writers where political discussions clouded the atmosphere" (7).

13. See Thomas Jeffrey's "A Hundred Years of Thomas Mofolo," *English in Africa* 37, no. 2 (October 2010): 37–55.

14. In a section subtitled "A Long Tradition of Writing by Africans," Currey writes about publishing Lalage Brown's *Two Centuries of African English* that in passing also discusses the early South African literature.

15. David Coplan and Bennetta Jules-Rosette, "'Nkosi Sikelel' iAfrika': From Independent Spirit to Political Mobilization" [in French], *Cahiers d'Études Africaines* 44, nos. 173/174 (2004): 345.

16. Xolela Mangcu, "Retracing Nelson Mandela through the Lineage of Black Political Thought," *Transition*, no. 112 (2013): 101–16.

17. Ntongela Masilela, *An Outline of the New African Movement in South Africa* (Trenton, NJ: Africa World Press, 2013).

18. Jean Comaroff and John L. Comaroff, *Theory from the South, or How Euro-America Is Evolving toward Africa* (London: Routledge, 2016).

19. See Brian Willan's intellectual biography, *Sol Plaatje: South African Nationalist, 1876–1932* (London: University of California Press, 1988).

20. See Ian Watt, *The Rise of the Novel: Studies in Defoe, Richardson and Fielding* (London: Bodley Head, 2015).

21. A question that for my generation of writers and scholars remains as central as it is divisive and that I discuss in greater length in chapter 6, "Toward a Rooted Transnational African Literature: Politics of Image and Naming."

22. The poet John Pepper Clarke, writing in 1965, had also called for African literature to be recognized as a body containing different identities and cultures. He argued that he places a "high premium on difference of identity"

> because there is the need to do this so that we do not fall into the popular pastime of indiscriminately lumping together African peoples. The truth is that these differences do exist among the numerous peoples of Africa, forming for each that special cultural make-up and sensibility of which any artist anywhere must partake and be impregnated with before he can bring forth any work of meaning to his people and mankind in general. (18)

23. There is the question of an established European literary canon and the "minor" writers who have been cast to the margins, but even then European literature is not immediately understood as a singular aesthetic, produced by the same kind of authors for a functional project such as nation building or to carry and showcase a singular European culture and history.

24. Opening speech, Taiye Selasi, (GB / I): "African Literature Doesn't Exist," 4 September 2013.

25. Kwame Dawes, "Interview with Kwame Dawes, Founding Director of the Af-

rican Poetry Book Fund, 2015." National Book Foundation, http://www.nationalbook.
org/innovations_in_reading_2015_apbf_interv.html#.WU6QvOvyuvs (accessed 30
December 2015).

26. There is a satirically named popular blog called *Africa Is a Country* whose stated
mission is not to be about "about famine, Bono, or Barack Obama." http://africasacoun
try.com/

27. Mphahlele on the literary criticism limiting itself to functionality wrote that in
the conference, "One felt the tendency throughout was to place an emphasis on what one
might call the sociology of African literature rather than talk about it as literature" (16).

28. Linda Gregg, "The Art of Finding," *Poets.org*, Academy of American Poets, 23
June 2016, www.poets.org/poetsorg/text/art-finding (accessed 19 July 2017).

29. But even then, the essay. as I will argue in chapter 6, mistakes reception for the
more intrinsic and, to my mind, fundamental aspect of the question, "What is African
literature?"

30. "The Question of Language," e-mail interview, 7 April 2015.

31. *Things Fall Apart* by Chinua Achebe, review by Mercedes Mackay, *African Affairs* 57, no. 228 (July 1958): 242–43.

32. Gerald Moore, *Seven African Writers* (London: Oxford, 1962), 57.

33. Alison Flood, "Achebe Rejects Endorsement as 'Father of Modern African
Literature,'" *Guardian*, 12 November 2009, http://www.guardian.co.uk/books/2009/
nov/12/achebe-rejects-father-modern-african-literature (accessed 9 March 2012).

34. "The Jalada Conversations No. 3: Chika Unigwe," *Jalada*, 1 September 2015,
https://jaladaafrica.org/jalada-conversations/the-jalada-conversations-no-3-
chika-unigwe/ (accessed 29 January 2016).

35. Ormrod gives the three kinds of French as "the language in use in northern
France and the southern Low Countries; the parallel but separate form of that language
that had developed in England during the twelfth and thirteenth centuries, usually
known as Anglo-Norman; and the technical language used in the senior royal courts
from the thirteenth century, which derived in turn from Anglo-Norman but deployed
such a range of technical vocabulary and discourse as to make it a discernibly distinct
branch of the language known as law French" ("Use of English," 753).

36. Still, the law was not a full recognition of English. The case was to be "pleaded,
counted, defended, answered, debated, and judged in the English language; and entered
and enrolled in Latin" (Ormrod, "Use of English," 756). The plaintiff would later not have
access to the records because they would be locked up in Latin. But at least procedurally,
the plaintiff would have been participating.

37. "Happy Valentine's Day!" *Ankara Press*, 14 February 2015, https://www.ankara
press.com/blogs/news/18862039-happy-valentine-s-day (accessed 25 July 2016).

38. *Nairobi Heat* (Penguin SA, 2007, and Melville House, 2011), *Black Star Nairobi*
(Melville House, 2013), and *Mrs. Shaw* (Ohio University Press, 2015); *Hurling Words at
Consciousness* (poems, Africa World Press, 2006), *Logotherapy* (poems, University of
Nebraska Press, 2016).

39. I am not arguing there are absolutely no examples of this being done. For example, Apollo Amoko in *The Cambridge Companion to the African Novel* reads it alongside other memoirs such as Mphahlele's *Down Second Avenue* and Soyinka's *Ake* (195–208). What I am saying is that these kinds of readings are rare when they should be reflexive.

## CHAPTER 1

1. For example, in his presentation at the 1986 Second African Writers' Conference, Stockholm, Soyinka recognized the psychological aspect to the language question. He argued that "African writers themselves who are so tortured, who experience such an internal turmoil in employing colonial languages" have two choices: to write in African languages or translate as he himself has done with Fagunwa's novel in Yoruba. That sounds reasonable enough. But the anger and defensiveness to my ear are palpable when a little later he addresses African writers calling for writing in African languages: "I want it understood that are not doing anything original. They should stop parading it as if they are revolutionary vanguard of a return to traditional languages" (Soyinka 1988, 35–36). He then went on to call for a universal African language, thereby missing the point—each language is unique and no African language should grow at the expense of another. In any case most writers speak their mother tongues so it's a question of using what is already in existence. In other words, he offered an impossible solution to argue against the more practicable one—writers should write in their mother tongues. The point here is that this sort of bitter response to the language question might have been mitigated by taking into account the pain that came with the "dreadful betrayal."

2. Simon Gikandi in a 2014 PMLA "Editor's Column" also spoke to this anxiety. He wrote that "Caught between the need to imagine sovereignty and the use of a language that represented its negation, postcolonial writers wrote under the tension of linguistic anxiety" (Gikandi, "Editor's Column: Provincializing English," 9).

3. See Ngugi's *Decolonising the Mind: The Politics of Language in African Literature* (London: James Currey, 1986), 12.

4. Also see Simon Gikandi, "Editor's Column: Provincializing English," *PMLA* 129, no. 1 (January 2014): 7–17, 11.

5. The fund was "founded in 1911 to improve the living conditions of African Americans and Africans through better housing and education" by the philanthropist Anson Phelps Stokes, but in real terms the mission was to civilize and Christianize (Yellin, "The (White) Search for (Black) Order," 319).

6. Frederick D. Patterson, who in 1954 was the director of the Phelp-Stokes Fund, also noted the missionary origins of the colonial education system in his essay "Education in Nigeria":

> Practically all primary level education of the Western type is under the supervision of the Christian missions. . . . The continued extensive participation of the missions in primary education reflects the early development of education in Nigeria, where

the missions were solely responsible for initiating, financing and managing all education available to Nigerian youth. (98)

7. In his essay "The Adaptation Concept in British Colonial Education," Udo Bude discusses two commissions financed by the Phelps-Stokes Fund during the 1920s to assess the colonial educational systems in Africa. The commissions called for the adaptation of "the Western education to meet local needs" including

individual housing and living conditions; the use of local resources for agriculture and handicrafts; the organisation of leisure time. Special attention was to be given to the use of African languages as media of instruction in school and the teaching of rural or agricultural science [emphasis added]. School farm work and training in local crafts formed a key element of the reform concept. (342)

The point to note here is that African languages were expected to be part and parcel of the larger question of how to balance a European educational system against African cultures.

8. See William Cobbett, *A grammar of the English language in a series of letters. Intended for the use of schools and of young persons in general; but more especially for the use of soldiers, sailors, apprentices, and plough-boys. To which are added six lessons intended to prevent statesmen from using false grammar and from writing in an awkward manner* (London: William Cobbett [printed by Mills, Jowett, and Mills] 1831).

9. And even though Owomoyela does not explicitly state it here, there was a political dimension to the demand of full immersion—mastering the language would allow them to fight for their freedom in terms that both they and the colonizers could understand.

10. Albert Memmi, *The Colonizer and the Colonized* (New York: Orion, 1965).

11. Ajayi gives another instance where Tutuola portrays English as the language for serious matters and Yoruba as the language of play:

[I]n Italy . . . he told his interviewer that in those early days "we'd take English to read something important—or what people who could speak English thought to be very important. That influenced me to write my first book in English." (*Amos Tutuola*, x)

12. See Linda Hunter and Chaibou Elhadji Oumarou, *Aspects of the Aesthetics of Hausa Verbal Art* (Cologne: Rüdiger Köppe, 2001). Also see works by Micere Mugo on orature.

13. Even today in African Studies outreach centers in the West and in cultural centers in former British colonies, it seems to me that orature is a performance of the past.

14. See Ngugi's *Globalectics: Theory and the Politics of Knowing* (New York: Columbia University Press, 2012), 73.

15. Wordsworth saw the peasant as the holder and user of language—albeit in very condescending terms where the peasant used a purer language, timeless and efficient. So he favored the language of the "humble and rustic":

[B]ecause such men hourly communicate with the best objects from which the best part of language is originally derived; and because, from their rank in society and the sameness and narrow circle of their intercourse, being less under the influence of social vanity, they convey their feelings and notions in simple and unelaborated expressions. (393)

16. Samuel Johnson, *A Dictionary of the English Language*, 2 vols. (London: Printed by WS Johnson–Strahan for J. & P. Knapton [et al.]), 175.

17. Speaking directly to Ngugi and his stand on writing in African languages, Saro-Wiwa argued:

Because he had already made his mark as a writer in English, his works have become instant subjects of translation into English, enabling him to live by his writing. If this were not the case, he might not be so sure of his decision. I also wonder if he has thought or cares about the implications of his decision for the minority ethnic groups in Kenya and for the future of Kenya as a multi-ethnic nation or, indeed, as a nation at all. Furthermore, I have examined myself very closely to see how writing or reading in English has colonized my mind. ("Language of African Literature," 156)

18. Mphahlele's rejoinder to Wali, in Barry Reckord, Ezekiel Mphahlele, Gerald Moore, Wole Soyinka, Denis Williams, and Jan Knappert, "Polemics: The Dead End of African Literature," *Transition* (1997): 337.

19. Ngugi Wa Thiong'o, "The Achebe I Knew," *The Nation*, 26 March 2013, http://thenationonlineng.net/the-achebe-i-knew-by-ngugi-wa-thiongo/ (accessed 20 March 2017).

20. Tee Ngugi, "Anthills of the Aberdares: How Achebe Lost His Lunch," *East African*, 30 March 2013, http://www.theeastafrican.co.ke/OpEd/comment/How-Achebe-lost-his-lunch/434750-1734572-a9ibxd/index.html (accessed 20 March 2017).

21. At the same time writing in English did not make African writers any safer from their respective neocolonial dictators—Ken Saro-Wiwa was hanged by the Nigerian government for opposing Shell Oil Company exploitation and the devastation of the Ogoni people and their land. Soyinka was detained and both he and Achebe ended up in exile.

22. And tangentially we should note that the relationship among the Makerere writers, even as they argued, was largely in the end Pan-African.

23. But the point also is that the two passages cannot be compared. They are written by the same author who has a preconceived notion of what he negatively views as unconscious writing. In the same way one cannot prove that *Things Fall Apart* would have been better or worse in his mother tongue, Ibo; the passage, once Africanized, cannot be de-Africanized to show one rendering of the African worldview as better than the other.

24. Interestingly, Dorothy S. Blair, in her introduction to Asia Djebar's *Fantansia*, talks of Djebar's use of French along the same line as Marechera talks of English, though for her there is an added dimension of recovering that which was lost:

At other times, in a conscious effort to escape from the shackles of writing in the "enemy's language," she seems to be colonizing the language of the colonizers. She does violence to it, forcing it to give up its riches and defying it to hand over its hidden hoard, in compensation for the treasure looted from Algiers in 1830, and also compensate her personally for being dispossessed of her Arabic heritage. (4)

25. Dele Menji Fantula, "Interview: Wole Soyinka at 80," *What's On Africa*, 15 May 2014.

26. Ngugi Wa Thiong'o, "Recovering the Original," *World Literature Today* 78, nos. 3/4 (September–December 2004): 13–15.

27. Joyce Ashuntantang, with Okey Ndibe, Sawore Omoyele, and Oyiza Adaba, "Fifty Years after *Things Fall Apart*: Interview with Chinua Achebe," *Summit Magazine* (May–July 2008): 9–14.

28. In the interview Adichie said: "I think that what is more important in this discourse is not whether African writers should or should not write in English but how African writers, and Africans in general, are educated in Africa." (Azodo, "Interview with Chimamanda Ngozi Adichie")

29. Paulin J. Hountondji, *African Philosophy: Myth and Reality* (Bloomington: Indiana University Press, 1983, 18).

30. Chimamanda Ngozi Adichie, "What Forms the Core Of Igbo Society," *The Trent*, 25 June 2014.

31. Adaobi Tricia Nwaubani, "In Africa, the Laureate's Curse," *New York Times*, 11 December 2010.

32. In short, they are disappointed that he does not become what the narrator in Tayeb Salih's *Season of Migration to the North* calls a Black Englishman, or the caricatured idea of a been-to in *Our Sister Killjoy*. On Aidoo's Been-to, Sissie

wondered why they never told the truth of their travels at home. Not knowing that if they were to keep on being something in their eyes, then they could not tell the truth to their own selves or to anyone else. So when they eventually went back home as "been-to's," the ghosts of the humans they used to be, spoke of the wonders of being overseas, pretending their tongues craved for tasteless foods which they would have vomited to eat where they were prepared best. (90)

33. Ikhide Ikheloa, "Petina Gappah: Unreliable Witnesses and the Burden of Memory," *Ikhide*, 4 January 2016, https://xokigbo.com/2016/01/04/petina-gappah-unreliable-witnesses-and-the-burden-of-memory/ (accessed 18 March 2016).

34. *Mukoma* means "uncle" in Shona.

35. Gappah herself is interested in translation and, at the time of writing this, was involved in a project translating George Orwell's *Animal Farm* from English into Shona.

36. Jalada, "Submissions," *Jalada*, 15 April 2015, accessed 1 February 2016.

37. http://www.mutiiri.com/

CHAPTER 2

1. The other reason why Wali thinks Tutuola was excluded from the conference was "because influential critics [had] repeatedly grouped him with the Negritude school." Negritude was understood by writers and activists like Mphahlele as not only apolitical but ahistorical.

2. Dylan Thomas, "Blithe Spirits," in *Critical Perspectives on Amos Tutuola*, ed. Bernth Lindfors. (Washington: Three Continents Press, 1975), 7.

3. Lindfors, *Early West African Writers*, 21.

4. Jocelyn Oliver was a book editor at Lutterworth Press, owned by the United Society for Christian Literature, where Tutuola first sent his MS.

5. Lindfors, *Early West African Writers*, 22.

6. Ironically, had they found it to be solely the product of Tutuola's deliberate artistic imagination, *PWD* would have lost its literary merit in the eyes of Faber & Faber.

7. In the letter referenced earlier from Geoffrey Faber to Daryll Forde, Faber refers to the MS as "The Palm Wine Drinker and His Dead Palm-Wine Tapster in the Deads-Town" (Lindfors, *Blind Man and the Elephant*, 116).

8. This raises the question of whether Tutuola is a reliable chronicler of events. The original title was the *Palm Wine Drunkard*. Talking about his writing process, he said that the title is one of the first things that he creates. "Then, having completed the story, I gave it the title: The Palm Wine Drinkard" (Miao, 49).

9. Lindfors, *Blind Man and the Elephant*, 117.

10. For an alternate reading of Tutuola and agency, see Peter Kalliney's *Commonwealth of Letters* where he argues that if we do not think of "Tutuola as a representative of an oppressed minority, if we think of him as yet another author, around whom the publisher must work to establish an aura of uniqueness—the inclusion of a manuscript facsimile makes Tutuola look quite comfortable in the company of modernism's leading figures. After all, only the rarest most venerated texts produce the need to consult the archival original" (162). This reading to my mind can only work with corroborating evidence rather than as a thought experiment. This is the 1950s, with its racism, colonialism, and power imbalances between the West and still colonized but decolonizing countries. A note from the publisher, or from T. S Eliot, explaining to Tutuola that as opposed to being a "problem child" he was a deracinated and high valued member of the modernist movement would suffice.

11. See Michael Omolewa in "Educating the 'Native': A Study of the Education Adaptation Strategy in British Colonial Africa, 1910–1936."

12. In "How Bunyan Became English: Missionaries, Translation, and the Discipline of English Literature" Isabel Hofmeyr writes:

> In Africa, the book undoubtedly had most influence in those parts of the continent where English-speaking missions worked under British colonial rule. Such translations (along with the English version) made their way into school syllabuses, in which they exercised considerable influence. (109)

13. That Larrabee does not correct Tutuola's English mistakes in the interview, a standard practice, also goes to show how much his English usage had become both his signature and cause for spectacle.

14. Lindfors is quoting from an article by Mike Awoyinfa, "Amos Tutuola: Nigeria's Nobel Literature Laureate Who Never Won," *Weekend Concord*, 21 June 1997, 2.

15. See John McKusick, "John Clare and the Tyranny of Grammar," *Studies in Romanticism* 33, no. 2 (Summer 1994): 255–77.

16. Immanuel Kant, in *Essays and treatises on moral, political, and various philosophical subjects*, writes:

> The sublime moves or touches, the beautiful charms. The mien of the person, who finds himself in the full sentiment of the sublime, is serious, sometimes fixed and astonished. On the other hand announces itself the lively sentiment of the beautiful by a sparkling glory in the eye, by lineaments of smiling, and frequently by loud merriment. The sublime is of a different nature. The feeling it is sometimes accompanied with dread, or even melancholy. (6)

He concludes in part that "dreadful or terrific sublime" can be accompanied by dread or even melancholy.

17. Harold Collins, in his preface to *Amos Tutuola*, captures the myriad of issues around Tutuola:

> What should a Nigerian English language for serious fiction look like? What should be the relations between the rich oral literatures of the African tribes to the new African literature in English? How should the European novel tradition influence the developing Nigerian novel? How should the modern Nigerian novel come to terms with the African past, especially the "superstitions" and the atrocities? (vii–viii)

18. Bernth Lindfors, *in Early West African Writers*, writes about how S. O. Biobaku, a postgraduate historian in London, was asked to comment on *PWD*'s authenticity, and he confirmed that it was indeed written by a Western African (22).

19. For example, in a 1953 *New Yorker* review Anthony West wrote that Tutuola is a "natural story-teller" and his "principle strength" is "the lack of inhibition in an uncorrupted innocence" (West, "*New Yorker* Review," 17).

20. After telling his readers that Tutuola has "no connection at all with the European rational and Christian traditions," Selden Rodman concludes that "[i]t is only possible to envy Mr. Tutuola his good luck in being a castaway on a little island in time where he can be archaic without being anachronistic" ("New York Times Book Review," 18). For him, if one is writing without being unencumbered by rational thought and deliberateness, then what is being produced is unmediated, close to nature—primordial.

21. In reference to this, Bernth Lindfors writes, "The trouble with his new job was that often there was nothing at all for him to do. So to keep himself busy during office hours, he started to write down on scrap paper the stories he heard on Sundays from an old man on a palm plantation" (Lindfors, "Amos Tutuola").

22. At the University of Palermo, Italy, Tutuola was asked by Professor Gorlier, "How do you relate to Fanugwa?" And he responded: "His town is far away from my own. Even, I was very like this [gesturing] when I saw his book at the school. They brought the book to the school, I read only one page. Then I gave it back to the owner" (Tutuola, Di Miao, and Gorlier, *Tutuola at the University*, 165).

23. Eric Robinson, in response to Babasola's charge that Tutuola was merely copying from oral stories and more specifically from Fanugwa, argued that "[i]t is no detriment to Mr. Tutuola's world that he has woven well-known stories into this his own version of a spiritual pilgrimage. Many of Chaucer's fabliaux were equally well known in his own time" (Robinson, Editorial, 33). While this is no adequate defense—Chaucer was himself accused of plagiarism—it does raise an important question in terms of the extent to which writers can use or reference existing popular stories, fables, and myths in their own writing.

24. Steven Tobias, in "Amos Tutuola and the Colonial Carnival," also sees Western influence in Tutuola's writing, specifically his use of

> capitalized chapter headings such as "THE INVESTIGATOR'S WONDERFUL WORK IN THE SKULL'S FAMILY'S HOUSE" . . . also hints at a Western influence. Tutuola probably derived this practice either from reading boy's adventure books or eighteenth-century novels, or quite possibly from reading English-style newspapers. The headings, as well as much of his phrasing throughout the book, without question possess both the appearance and tone of tabloid headlines. (70)

25. Eric Larrabee writes that Tutuola asked him for books, *A Survey of Economic Education* and Aldous Huxley's *Devils of Loudun*, and "other books which contain stories like that of the P.W.D . . . which are written by either West Africans, White men or Negroes, etc." (40–41). Why is Tutuola asking him for books comparable to *PWD*? Does he consider them peers? Is it so he can learn from them? Larrabee does not stop to ask any of these questions.

26. Collins relies on "Portrait: A Life in the Bush of Ghosts" by an anonymous writer simply referred to as a Nigerian Correspondent See *Critical Perspectives on Amos Tutuola*, ed. Bernth Lindfors (Washington: Three Continents Press, 1975), 35–38.

27. In a 19 May 1953 letter to Tutuola that shows just how little Eric Larrabee (then an associate editor at *Harper's Magazine*) was conscious of the larger colonial question, he writes:

> Since returning to this country, I've also had a pleasant conversation about you with Mr. Reginald Barret, of the British Embassy in Washington, who said he had talked with you when he was in Lagos a few months ago. He seemed to me a very sympathetic and understanding man, and a good representative for Nigeria to have in the United States. (Ajayi, *Amos Tutuola*, 74)

That Larrabee does not see the irony of telling Tutuola that the ambassador of the colonial power is a good representative for the Nigerian people captures the lens through which he saw Tutuola.

28. Bernth Lindfors, "Amos Tutuola: Debts and Assets," *Cahiers d'Études Africaines* 10 (1970): 306–34.

29. See *Tutuola at the University: The Italian Voice of a Yoruba Ancestor*, by Amos Tutuola, Alessandra Di Miao, and Claudio Gorlier (Rome: Bulzoni, 2000).

## CHAPTER 3

1. See Thomas Jeffrey's "A Hundred Years of Thomas Mofolo," *English in Africa* 37, no. 2 (October 2010): 37–55.

2. Sofia Samatar, Keguro Macharia, and Aaron Bady, "What Even Is African Literature Anyway," *New Inquiry*, 9 February 2015.

3. Ngugi Wa Thiong'o, "I've Lost My Literary Sister, Kenya Has Lost a Literary Icon." *Daily Nation*, 22 March 2015, http://www.nation.co.ke/lifestyle/weekend/-Kenya-has-lost-a-literary-icon/1220-2660572-svkwwlz/index.html (accessed 25 March 2017).

4. In *Things Fall Apart* colonialism is about to wreak havoc on the Ibo people; in *No Longer at Ease* colonialism is dying and the European colonizer has to come to terms with it.

## CHAPTER 4

The epigraph quotes from Alan Hill, *In Pursuit of Publishing*, 127, 206.

1. "aboriginal, adj. and n." *OED Online* (Oxford University Press, June 2016), accessed 15 July 2016; "indigenous, adj." *OED Online* (Oxford University Press, June 2016), accessed 15 July 2016.

2. For a longer discussion on citizenry and diasporic writing, please see my essay, "Don't Tell African Authors What They Can and Can't Write About," *World Today* 69, nos. 8/9 (October 2013).

3. In other words, writers and their passports cannot decide what their books are—that is the function of literary criticism. Or, rather, while writers might make an argument for how their books are to be read, it is the function of literary criticism to be the arbitrators of where their works fall within the African literary tradition. In my case, for example, I consider myself an African writer and at times a Kenyan American writer. But I do not expect literary critics to take me at my word—after all, writing books set in Kenya and the United States, and poems drawing their imagination from Kenya, I can be read as transnational/international or global. And while I do resist the idea of being read as transnational if that reading glides over national contradictions propelling Kenyan/African and US/Western societies, it is the function of literary criticism to read my literary output through different schools of thought.

4. Jahnheinz Jahn calls early South African writing "Apprentice" or "Protest Literature" and then subdivides it into three groups: conformist, hedging, or half and half or protesting. He places Mhudi under hedging (Jahn, 98).

5. Julius Sigei, "We'll Stick to Creative Works, but Text Books Bring in Cash," *Nation*, 22 August 2015.

6. Natasha Onwuemezi, "African Publisher Cassava Republic to Launch in UK," *The Bookseller*, 24 November 2015.

7. Pascale Casanova and M. B DeBevoise, *The World Republic of Letters* (Cambridge: Harvard University Press, 2007).

8. Aamir Mufti, *Forget English! Orientalisms and World Literatures* (Cambridge: Harvard University Press, 2016).

9. http://stieglarssonofficial.tumblr.com/

10. Symposium, "Beyond Murder by Magic" (11), held by the Jahnheinz Jahn Foundation.

11. See Fanon's chapter, "Concerning Violence," in *The Wretched of the Earth*.

12. Frantz Fanon, *The Wretched of the Earth* (New York: Grove Press, 1968).

13. Chinua Achebe, *Hopes and Impediments: Selected Essays* (New York: Anchor Books, Doubleday, 1989), 67.

## CHAPTER 5

1. For Okafor, Achebe in the novel is essentially undoing Conrad's image of Africa by portraying an Ibo culture "in which there are clearly defined parameters of right conduct on both personal and communal levels" ("Joseph Conrad and Chinua Achebe," 22); a society that is not predatory in nature and therefore that can "shield the weak from the strong by re-straining the mighty" (23), and where Conrad's Africans grunted and screamed, Achebe privileged oratory skills (25), and so on.

2. Achebe goes on to argue that "[a]ll those men in Nazi Germany who lent their talent to the service of virulent racism whether in science, philosophy, or the arts have generally and rightly been condemned for their perversions. The time is long overdue for taking a hard look at the work of creative artists who apply their talents, alas often considerable as in the case of Conrad, to set people against people" (9).

3. More from Kant:

So fundamental is the difference between these two races of man, and it appears to be as great in regard to mental capacities as in colour. The religion of fetishes so widespread among them is perhaps a sort of idolatry that sinks as deeply into the trifling as appears to be possible to human nature. A bird's feather, a cow's horn, a conch shell, or any other common object, as soon as it becomes consecrated by a few words, is an object of veneration and of invocation in swearing oaths. The blacks are very vain but in the Negro's way, and so talkative that they must be driven apart from each other with thrashings. (*On the Different Races of Man*)

4. "TO TOUSSAINT L'OUVERTURE 1803," *Morning Post* (London), 2 February 1803.

5. That in 2007 the then president of France, Nicolas Sarkozy, could say, "The African peasant only knows the eternal renewal of time, rhythmed by the endless repetition of the same gestures and the same words. In this imaginary world where everything

starts over and over again, there is no place for human adventure or for the idea of progress," goes to show that the postrevolution views of black people and Africans still influence French policy. "Sarkozy's Africa Vision under Fire," *News24*, 28 July 2007, http://www.news24.com/Africa/News/Sarkozys-Africa-vision-under-fire-20070728 (accessed 25 July 2014).

6. "Ikhide," *Ikhide*. Accessed 24 May 2016.

7. https://www.facebook.com/ikhide

8. @ikhide

9. Ikhide Ikheloa, "Will Twitter Kill off African Literature?," *Xokigbo*, https://xokigbo.com/2013/01/12/will-twitter-kill-off-african-literature/ (accessed 27 May 2016).

10. Alison Flood, "'African Booker' Shortlist Offers an Alternative View of Continent," *Guardian*, 1 May 2012.

11. http://carmenmccain.com/2013/07/08/in-anticipation-of-tonights-announcement-by-the-caine-prize-for-african-writing/

12. Michiko Kakutani, "A Child of Two Lands," *New York Times*, 15 May 2013, http://www.nytimes.com/2013/05/16/books/we-need-new-names-by-noviolet-bulawayo.html (accessed 1 July 2014).

13. R. Mugo Gatheru, *Child of Two Worlds, a Kikuyu's Story* (New York: Praeger, 1964).

14. Rayyan Al-Shawaf, "Book Review: 'We Need New Names' by NoViolet Bulawayo,"*Boston Globe*, 5 June 2013, https://www.bostonglobe.com/arts/books/2013/06/05/book-review-need-new-names-noviolet-bulawayo/IA7tw3rLFakZ0zRVcP9PBP/story.html (accessed 1 July 2014).

15. Jenny Shank, Book Review of *We Need New Names*, by NoViolet Bulawayo, *Dallas News*, 31 May 2013, https://www.dallasnews.com/arts/books/2013/05/31/book-review-we-need-new-names-by-noviolet-bulawayo (accessed 14 July 2017).

16. Shay Howell, "In 'We Need New Names,' NoViolet Bulawayo Sketches a Heartbreaking Portrait of Zimbabwe," *New York Daily News*, 17 October 2013, http://www.nydailynews.com/blogs/pageviews/new-names-noviolet-bulawayo-sketches-heartbreaking-portrait-zimbabwe-blog-entry-1.1641145 (accessed 1 July 2014).

17. Taiye Selasi, "Bye-Bye Babar (Or What Is an Afropolitan)," *LIP Magazine*, 3 March 2005, http://thelip.robertsharp.co.uk/?p=76 (accessed 1 July 2014).

18. Salah Hassan, "Rethinking Cosmopolitanism: Is 'Afropolitan' the Answer?" 2013, http://www.princeclausfund.org/files/docs/5_PCF_Salah_Hassan_Reflections_120x190mm5DEC12_V2.pdf (accessed 1 July 2014).

19. In a LitHub interview, Petina Gappah captured the privilege in Afropolitan very well:

I'm not an Afropolitan. I am the daughter of a goatherd; my father didn't go to school until he was 11. I'm the first person in my family to be in the middle class. I write about the life I know, which is the transition from the township to the suburbs, and the transition from Zimbabwe to living outside. But it's not something I was born to. My son is different. My son was born into the middle class, in Geneva; he speaks a gazillion languages. And so his experience of being an "Afropolitan" might be what Taiye's talking about. ("Petina Gappah on Zimbabwe, Language, and 'Afropolitans,'" *LitHub*, 22 February 2016, http://lithub.com/petina-gappah-on-zim babwe-language-and-afropolitans/)

20. Selasi does not deny that writers have an identity. She writes, "I consider myself West African, among other cultural identities, and a writer, among other creative ones. But I am not an African writer. At no point in my writing process—in the act of actually being a writer: seated at the laptop, wherever I may be—do I experience a nationality" (13).

21. "Taiye Selasi: I'm a Multi Local Afropolitan," *YouTube*, 26 February 2014. Accessed 9 March 2015.

22. "About Aminatta Forna," *Aminatta Forna*, http://www.aminattaforna.com/about-aminatta-forna.html (accessed 23 May 2016).

23. I share Freud's thoughts on mourning and melancholia in chapter 3, under the section "Religion and Culture."

24. Dambudzo Marechera has a poem called "There Is a Dissident in My Soup."

# WORKS CITED

Abrahams, Peter. *Mine Boy*. London: Heinemann Educational Books, 1963.

Achebe, Chinua. *Arrow of God*. London: Heinemann, 1964.

Achebe, Chinua. "English and the African Writer." *Transition* 18 (1965): 27-30.

Achebe, Chinua. "English and the African Writer." Special anniversary issue, "Selections from *Transition*, 1961–1976." *Transition* 75/76 (1997): 342–49.

Achebe, Chinua. *Hopes and Impediments: Selected Essays*. New York: Doubleday, 1990.

Achebe, Chinua. "An Image of Africa: Racism in Conrad's 'Heart of Darkness.'" Special issue, "Literary Criticism." *Research in African Literatures* 9, no. 1 (Spring 1978): 1–15.

Achebe, Chinua. *No Longer at Ease*. New York: Anchor, 1994.

Achebe, Chinua. "The Novelist as Teacher." In *African Literature: An Anthology of Criticism and Theory*, edited by Tejumola Olaniyan and Ato Quayson, 103–5. Malden, MA: Blackwell, 2007.

Achebe, Chinua. *Things Fall Apart*. New York: Anchor, 1994.

Achebe, Chinua, and Abiola Irele. *Things Fall Apart: Authoritative Text, Contexts and Criticism*. New York: W.W. Norton, 2009.

Achebe, Chinua, and Bradford Morrow. "Chinua Achebe: An Interview by Bradford Morrow." *Conjunctions* 17 (1991): 7–28.

Adichie, Chimamanda Ngozi. *Americanah*. New York: Alfred A. Knopf, 2013.

Adichie, Chimamanda Ngozi. *Half of a Yellow Sun*. New York: Alfred A. Knopf, 2006.

Adichie, Chimamanda Ngozi. *Purple Hibiscus: A Novel*. Chapel Hill: Algonquin Books, 2003.

Adichie, Chimamanda, et al. "What Forms the Core of Igbo Society." *The Trent*, 1 July 2016. www.thetrentonline.com/chimamanda-adichie-forms-core-igbo-soci ety-must-read/. Accessed 19 July 2017.

Afolayan, Adebisi. "Language and Sources of Amos Tutuola." *Perspectives on African Literature* (1971): 49–63.

"Africa's 100 Best Books of the 20th Century." Columbia University Libraries. library. columbia.edu/locations/global/virtual-libraries/african_studies/books.html. Accessed 14 July 2017.

Aidoo, Ama Ata. "Interview." In *In Their Own Voices: African Women Writers Talk*, edited by Adeola James. London: Heinemann, 1990.

Aidoo, Ama Ata. *Our Sister Killjoy: Or, Reflections from a Black-eyed Squint*. London: Longman, 1994.

Ajayi, Jare. *Amos Tutuola: Factotum as a Pioneer*. Ibadan: Creative Books, 2003.

Al-Shawaf, Rayyan. "Book Review: 'We Need New Names' by NoViolet Bulawayo." *Boston Globe*, 5 June 2013. https://www.bostonglobe.com/arts/books/2013/06/05/book-review-need-new-names-noviolet-bulawayo/IA7tw3rLFakZ0zRVcP9PBP/story.html. Accessed 1 July 2014.

Amoko, Apollo Obonyo. *Postcolonialism in the Wake of the Nairobi Revolution: Ngugi Wa Thiong'o and the Idea of African Literature*. New York: Palgrave Macmillan, 2010.

Anderson, Benedict R. *Imagined Communities: Reflections on the Origin and Spread of Nationalism*. London: Verso, 1991.

Appiah, Kwame Anthony. "Cosmopolitan Patriots." *Critical Inquiry* 23, no. 3 (Spring 1997): 617–39.

Appiah, Kwame Anthony. *In My Father's House: Africa in the Politics of Culture*. London: Methuen, 1991.

Ashcroft, Bill, Gareth Griffiths, and Helen Tiffin. *The Post-colonial Studies Reader*. London: Routledge, 1995.

Ashuntantang, Joyce, with Okey Ndibe, Sawore Omoyele, and Oyiza Adaba. "Fifty Years after *Things Fall Apart*: A Chat with Chinua Achebe." *Summit Magazine* (May–July 2008): 9–14.

Attwell, David. *Rewriting Modernity: Studies in Black South African Literary History*. Athens: Ohio University Press, 2006.

Azado, Ada U. "Interview with Chimamanda Ngozi Adichie: Creative Writing and Literary Activism." *IUN*, 2008. http://www.iun.edu/~minaua/interviews/interview_chimamanda_ngozi_adichie.pdf. Accessed 30 June 2014.

Azikiwe, Ben. "Murdering Women in Nigeria." *Crisis* 7 (1930): 64–65.

Azim, Firdous. *Colonial Rise of the Novel*. London: Routledge, 2014.

Beach, Adam. "The Creation of a Classical Language in the Eighteenth Century: Standardizing English, Cultural Imperialism, and the Future of the Literary Canon." Special issue, "Ideological Turns." *Texas Studies in Literature and Language* 43, no. 2 (Summer 2001): 117–41.

Benjamin, Walter. "The Task of the Translator." 1923, reprinted in *The Translation Studies Reader*, edited by Lawrence Venuti, 15–23. London: Routledge, 2000.

Bgoya, Walter, and Mary Jay. "Publishing in Africa from Independence to the Present Day." *Research in African Literatures* 44, no. 2 (Summer 2013): 17–34.

Bhabha, Homi. "Culture's in Between (Concept of Culture)." *Art Forum* 32, no. 1 (1993): 167–70, 211–14.

Bhabha, Homi. "Of Mimicry and Man: The Ambivalence of Colonial Discourse." Special issue, "Discipleship: A Special Issue on Psychoanalysis." *October* 28 (Spring 1984): 125–33.

Blumenthal, Henry, and Renée Kahane. "Decline and Survival of Western Prestige Languages." *Language* 55, no. 1 (March 1979): 183–98.

Bondy, Francois. "James Baldwin, as Interviewed by Francois Bondy." *Transition*, no. 12 (January–February 1964): 12–19.

Booker, M. Keith. *The African Novel in English: An Introduction*. Portsmouth, NH: Heinemann, 1998.

Borkowski, David. "Class(ifying) Language: The War of the Word." *Rhetoric Review* 21, no. 4 (2002): 357–83.

Bourdieu, Pierre. *Language and Symbolic Power*. Cambridge: Polity Press, 1991.

Boyce Davies, Carole. "Some Notes on African Feminism." In *African Literature: An Anthology of Criticism and Theory*, edited by Tejumola Olaniyan and Ato Quayson. Malden, MA: Blackwell, 2007.

Bragg, Melvyn. *The Adventure of English: The Biography of a Language*. New York: Arcade, 2003.

Brooks, Jerome. "Chinua Achebe, the Art of Fiction No. 139." *Paris Review* 133 (Winter 1994). https://www.theparisreview.org/interviews/1720/chinua-achebe-the-art-of-fiction-no-139-chinua-achebe. Accessed 13 August 2014.

Brown, Lalage, ed. *Two Centuries of African English: A Survey and Anthology of Non-Fictional English Prose by African Writers since 1769*. Westport, CT: Heinemann, 1973.

Bulawayo, NoViolet. *We Need New Names*. New York: Little Brown, 2014.

Caminero-Santangelo, Byron. *African Fiction and Joseph Conrad: Reading Postcolonial Intertexuality*. Albany: State University of New York Press, 2005.

Chakava, Henry. "Selling Books in Africa: A Publisher's Reflections." *Logos* 10, no. 1 (1997): 52–54.

Chambers, J. D. "Enclosure and the Labour Supply in the Industrial Revolution." *Economic History Review* 5, no. (1953): 319–43.

Chrisman, Laura. *Postcolonial Contraventions: Cultural Readings of Race, Imperialism and Transnationalism*. Oxford: Manchester University Press, 2008.

Cobbett, William. *A grammar of the English language in a series of letters. Intended for the use of schools and of young persons in general; but more especially for the use of soldiers, sailors, apprentices, and plough-boys. To which are added six lessons intended to prevent statesmen from using false grammar and from writing in an awkward manner*. London: William Cobbett [printed by Mills, Jowett, and Mills], 1831.

Collins, Harold R. *Amos Tutuola*. New York: Twayne, 1969.

Comaroff, Jean, and John L. Comaroff. *Theory from the South, or How Euro-America Is Evolving toward Africa*. London: Routledge, 2016.

Conrad, Joseph. *Heart of Darkness*. Edited by Paul O'Prey. London: Penguin, 1989.

Cooper, Brenda. *Magical Realism in West African Fiction: Seeing with a Third Eye*. London: Routledge, 2004.

Cooper, Brenda. *A New Generation of African Writers: Migration, Material Culture and Language*. Woodbridge, Suffolk: James Currey, 2008.

Coplan, David, and Benetta Jules-Rosette. "'Nkosi Sikelel' iAfrika': From Independent Spirit to Political Mobilization" [in French]. *Cahiers d'Études Africaines* 44, nos. 173/174 (2004).

Cosentino, Donald. "In Memoriam: Amos Tutuola, 1920–1997." *African Arts* 30, no. 4, Special Issue: The Benin Centenary, Part 2 (Autumn 1997): 16–17.

Couzens, Tim, and Stephen Gray. "Printers' and Other Devils: The Texts of Sol T. Plaatje's *Mhudi*." *Research in African Literatures* 9, no. 2 (Autumn 1978): 198–215.

Crais, Clifton. "Of Men, Magic, and the Law: Popular Justice and the Political Imagination in South Africa." *Journal of Social History* (1998): 49–72.

Crocker, Joe Wilson. "Review of Hunt, *Rimini*." *Quarterly Review* 14 (January 1816): 475–81.

Crystal, David. *The Fight for English*. Oxford: Oxford University Press, 2006.

Currey, James. *Africa Writes Back: The African Writers Series and the Launch of African Literature*. Oxford: James Currey, 2008.

Dabiri, Emma. "Why I'm Not an Afropolitan." *Africa Is a Country*. 21 January 2014. http://africasacountry.com/2014/01/why-im-not-an-afropolitan/. Accessed 14 July 2017.

Dabydeen, David. "Strategies to Relieve Suffering." *Third World Quarterly* 12, no. 1 (January 1990): 223–25.

Dangarembga, Tsitsi. *Nervous Conditions*. Banbury: Ayebia Clarke, 2004.

Davis, Caroline. *Creating Postcolonial Literature: African Writers and British Publishers*. New York: Palgrave Macmillan, 2013.

Dawes, Kwame. "Interview with Kwame Dawes, Founding Director of the African Poetry Book Fund, 2015." National Book Foundation, http://www.nationalbook.org/innovations_in_reading_2015_apbf_interv.html#.WU6QvOvyuvs. Accessed 30 December 2015.

Dele, Fantula. "Interview: Wole Soyinka at 80." *What's On Africa*, The Royal African Society, 15 May 2014. http://whatsonafrica.org/interview-wole-soyinka-at-80/. Accessed 19 July 2017.

Economist. "*Things Fall Apart*: A Golden Jubilee." *Economist*, 25 October 2008. http://www.economist.com/node/12459705. Accessed 13 August 2014.

Eliot, T. S. *Selected Prose of T. S. Eliot*. Edited by Frank Kermode. New York: Harcourt Brace Jovanovich, 1975.

Emelife, Jennifer. "Jalada Mobile Festival: Q&A with Moses Kilolo." *Praxis Magazine for Arts & Literature*, 22 May 2017. https://www.praxismagonline.com/jalada-mobile-festival-qa-moses-kilolo/. Accessed 14 July 2017.

Equiano, Olaudah. *Equiano's Travels: The Interesting Narrative of the Life of Olaudah Equiano or Gustavus Vassa, the African*. Edited by Paul Edwards. Long Grove, IL: Waveland, 2006.

Eze, Emmanuel Chukwudi. *Race and the Enlightenment: A Reader*. Malden, MA: Blackwell, 2009.

Fanon, Frantz. *The Wretched of the Earth*. New York: Grove, 2004.

Farah, Nuruddin. *Maps: A Novel*. New York: Arcade, 2016.

Flood, Alison. "Achebe Rejects Endorsement as 'Father of Modern African Literature.'" *Guardian*, 12 November 2009. http://www.guardian.co.uk/books/2009/nov/12/achebe-rejects-father-modern-african-literature. Accessed 9 March 2012.

Forna, Aminatta. "About Aminatta Forna." *Aminatta Forna*. http://www.aminattaforna.com/about-aminatta-forna.html. Accessed 23 May 2016.

Forna, Aminatta. *Ancestor Stones*. New York: Atlantic Monthly, 2006.

Forna, Aminatta. *The Devil That Danced on the Water: A Daughter's Quest*. New York: Atlantic Monthly, 2002.

Forna, Aminatta. "Don't Judge a Book by Its Author." *Guardian*, 13 February 2015. https://www.theguardian.com/books/2015/feb/13/aminatta-forna-dont-judge-book-by-cover. Accessed 14 July 2017.

Forna, Aminatta. *The Hired Man*. London: Bloomsbury, 2013.

Forna, Aminatta. *The Memory of Love*. New York: Atlantic Monthly, 2010.

Fox, Robert Eliot. "Tutuola and the Commitment to Tradition." *Research in African Literatures* 29, no. 3 (Autumn 1998): 203–8.

Freud, Sigmund. 1917. "Mourning and Melancholia." In *The Standard Edition of the Complete Psychological Works of Sigmund Freud, Volume XIV (1914–1916): On the History of the Psycho-analytic Movement, Papers on Metapsychology and Other Works*, edited by James Strachey, 237–58. London: Hogarth Press, 1917.

Gappah, Petina. *The Book of Memory*. New York: Farrar, Straus and Giroux, 2016.

Gatheru, R. Mugo. *Child of Two Worlds, a Kikuyu's Story*. New York: Praeger, 1964.

Gérard, Albert. *African Language Literatures: An Introduction to the Literary History of Sub-Saharan Africa*. Harlow, Essex: Longman, 1981.

Ghosh, Amitav. "Ghosh Letter to Administrators of Commonwealth Writers Prize," 18 March 2001. Available at www.ezipangu.org/english/contents/news/forward/3/2.html. Accessed 19 July 2017.

Gikandi, Simon. "Chinua Achebe and the Invention of African Culture." Special issue, "Nationalism." *Research in African Literatures* 32, no. 3 (Autumn 2001): 3–8.

Gikandi, Simon. "Editor's Column: Provincializing English." *PMLA* 129, no. 1 (January 2014): 7–17.

Gikandi, Simon. *Maps of Englishness: Writing Identity in the Culture of Colonialism*. New York: Columbia University Press, 1996.

Giwa, Tunde. "Black Like Us—An Essay." *Chimurenga Library*, June 2008. http://chimurengalibrary.co.za/black-like-us-an-essay-by-tunde-giwa. Accessed 14 July 2016.

Glissant, Édouard. *Poetics of Relation*. Trans. Betsy Wing. Ann Arbor: University of Michigan Press, 1997.

Goluch, D. "Chinua Achebe Translating, Translating Chinua Achebe: *Things Fall Apart* in Polish and the Task of Postcolonial Translation." *Cross/Cultures* 137 (2011): 197–219.

Gordimer, Nadine. "Turning the Page: African Writers on the Threshold of the Twenty-first Century." *Transition* 56 (1992): 4–10.

Green, Michael. "Generic Instability and the National Project: History, Nation, and Form in Sol T. Plaatje's 'Mhudi.'" *Research in African Literatures* 37, no. 4 (Winter 2006): 34–47.

Greene, Sandra. "Modern 'Trokosi' and the 1807 Abolition in Ghana: Connecting Past and Present." Special issue, "Abolishing the Slave Trades: Ironies and Reverberations." *William and Mary Quarterly*, 3rd ser., 66, no. 4 (October 2009): 959–74.

Gregg, Linda. "The Art of Finding." *Poets.org*, Academy of American Poets, 23 June 2016. www.poets.org/poetsorg/text/art-finding. Accessed 19 July 2017.

Habila, Helon. "Tradition and the African Writer by 2014 Judge, Helon Habila." Caine Prize for African Writing, 11 June 2014. http://caineprize.com/blog/2015/12/1/tradition-and-the-african-writer-by-2014-judge-helon-habila. Accessed 14 July 2017.

Habila, Helon. Review of *We Need New Names* by NoViolet Bulawayo. *Guardian*, 20 June 2013. https://www.theguardian.com/books/2013/jun/20/need-new-names-bulawayo-review. Accessed 14 July 2017.

Hall, Tony. "Rajat Neogy on the CIA." Special anniversary issue, "Selections from *Transition*, 1961–1976." *Transition*, no. 75/76 (1997): 312–16.

"Happy Valentine's Day!" *Ankara Press*, 14 February 2015. https://www.ankarapress.com/blogs/news/18862039-happy-valentine-s-day. Accessed 25 July 2016.

Hassan, Salah. "Rethinking Cosmopolitanism: Is 'Afropolitan' the Answer?" 2013. http://www.princeclausfund.org/files/docs/5_PCF_Salah_Hassan_Reflections_120x190mm5DEC12_V2.pdf. Accessed 1 July 2014.

Hill, Alan. *In Pursuit of Publishing*. London: J. Murray, in association with Heinemann Educational, 1988.

Hofmeyr, Isabel. "The Black Atlantic Meets the Indian Ocean: Forging New Paradigms of Transnationalism for the Global South—Literary and Cultural Perspectives." *Social Dynamics* 33, no. 2 (2007): 3–32.

Hofmeyr, Isabel. "Dreams, Documents and 'Fetishes': African Christian Interpretations of 'The Pilgrim's Progress.'" Special issue, "Signs, Texts and Objects within African Christian History." *Journal of Religion in Africa* 32, 4 (November 2002): 440–56.

Hofmeyr, Isabel. "How Bunyan Became English: Missionaries, Translation, and the Discipline of English Literature." *Journal of British Studies* 41, no. 1 (January 2002): 84–119.

Hofmeyr, Isabel, and John Bunyan. *The Portable Bunyan: A Transnational History of The Pilgrim's Progress*. Princeton: Princeton University Press, 2004.

Holborow, Marnie. *The Politics of English: A Marxist View of Language*. London: Sage, 1999.

Hountondji, Paulin J. *African Philosophy: Myth and Reality*. Bloomington: Indiana University Press, 1983.

Howell, Shay. "In 'We Need New Names,' NoViolet Bulawayo Sketches a Heartbreaking Portrait of Zimbabwe." *New York Daily News*, 17 October 2013. http://www.nydailynews.com/blogs/pageviews/new-names-noviolet-bulawayo-sketches-heartbreaking-portrait-zimbabwe-blog-entry-1.1641145. Accessed 1 July 2014.

Hughes, Langston. *Poems from Black Africa: Ethiopia, South Rhodesia, Sierra Leone, Madagascar, Ivory Coast, Nigeria, Kenya, Gabon, Senegal, Nyasaland, Mozambique, South Africa, Congo, Ghana, Liberia*. Bloomington: Indiana University Press, 1963.

Hughes, Langston, et al. "Transition Conference Questionnaire." *Transition*, no. 5 (30 July–29 August, 1962): 11–12.

Hunter, Linda, and Chaibou Elhadji Oumarou. *Aspects of the Aesthetics of Hausa Verbal Art*. Cologne: Rüdiger Köppe, 2001.

Ikheloa, Ikhide. "Petina Gappah: Unreliable Witnesses and the Burden of Memory." *Ikhide*, 4 January 2016. https://xokigbo.com/2016/01/04/petina-gappah-unreliable-witnesses-and-the-burden-of-memory/. Accessed 18 March 2016.

Ikheola, Ikhide. "The 2011 Caine Prize: How Not to Write About Africa." *NEXT Newspaper*, May 2011. Reprinted at *Ikhide*, 4 January 2013, https://xokigbo.com/2012/03/11/the-2011-caine-prize-how-not-to-write-about-africa/. Accessed 14 July 2017.

Ikheloa, Ikhide. "Will Twitter Kill Off African Literature?" *Xokigbo*. https://xokigbo.com/2013/01/12/will-twitter-kill-off-african-literature/. Accessed 27 May 2016.

Irele, Abiola. *The African Experience in Literature and Ideology*. Bloomington: Indiana University Press, 1990.

Irele, Abiola. *The Cambridge Companion to the African Novel*. Cambridge: Cambridge University Press, 2009.

Irele, F. Abiola, and Simon Gikandi, eds. *The African Imagination: Literature in Africa and the Black Diaspora*. New York: Oxford University Press, 2001.

Irele, F. Abiola, and Simon Gikandi, eds. *The Cambridge History of African and Caribbean Literature*. Cambridge: Cambridge University Press, 2004.

Jahn, Janheinz. *Neo-African Literature: A History of Black Writing*. New York: Grove Press, 1969.

Jakobson, Roman. "On Linguistic Aspects of Translation." In *The Translation Studies Reader*, edited by Lawrence Venuti, 113–18. London: Routledge, 2000.

James, Adeola. "Interview with Ama Ata Aidoo." In *In Their Own Voices: African Woman Writers Talk*, edited by Adeola James, 8–27. London: James Currey; Portsmouth, NH: Heinemann, 1990.

Jay, Paul. *Global Matters: The Transnational Turn in Literary Studies*. Ithaca: Cornell University Press, 2010.

Jeffrey, Thomas. "A Hundred Years of Thomas Mofolo." *English in Africa* 37, no. 2 (October 2010): 37–55.

Jeyifo, Biodun. "The Nature of Things: Arrested Decolonization and Critical Theory." In *African Literature: An Anthology of Criticism and Theory*, edited by Tejumola Olaniyan and Ato Quayson, 432–43. Malden, MA: Blackwell, 2007.

Johnson, Samuel. "A dictionary of the English language: in which the words are deduced from their originals, explained in their different meanings, and Authorised by the Names of the Writers in whose works they are found. Abstracted from the folio edition, by the author, Samuel Johnson, A.M. To which are prefixed, a grammar of the

English language, and the preface to the folio edition." 11th ed. London, 1798. *Eighteenth Century Collections Online*. Gale. Cornell University. Accessed 12 July 2017.

Jordan, A. C. *Towards an African Literature: The Emergence of Literary Form in Xhosa*. Berkeley: University of California Press, 1973.

Jordan, A. C. *The Wrath of the Ancestors: A Novel*. Cape Province: Lovedale, 1980.

Kahane, Henry. "A Typology of the Prestige Language." *Language* 62, no. 3 (September 1986): 495–508.

Kakutani, Michiko. "A Child of Two Lands." *New York Times*, 15 May 2013. http://www.nytimes.com/2013/05/16/books/we-need-new-names-by-noviolet-bulawayo.html. Accessed 1 July 2014.

Kalliney, Peter. *Commonwealth of Letters: British Literary Culture and the Emergence of Postcolonial Aesthetics*. Oxford: Oxford University Press, 2013.

Kamau, Kiarie, and Kirimi Mitambo. *Coming of Age: Strides in African Publishing. Essays in Honour of Dr Henry Chakava at 70*. Nairobi: East African Educational Publishers, 2016.

Kamoche, Ken. *Black Ghosts*. Nairobi: East African Educational Publishers, 2015.

Kant, Immanuel. *Essays and treatises on moral, political, and various philosophical subjects. By Emanuel Kant, . . . from the German by the translator of The principles of critical philosophy. . . .* Vol. 2. London, 1798–99. *Eighteenth Century Collections Online*.

Kasaya, Eva. *Tale of Kasaya*. Nairobi: Kwani Trust, 2010.

Kolb, W. 2011. "Re-writing *Things Fall Apart* in German." *Cross/Cultures*, no. 137: 177–96, 219.

Korang, Kwaku. "Homage to a Modern Literary Father." Special issue, "Achebe's World: African Literature at Fifty." *Research in African Literatures* 42, no. 2 (Summer 2011).

Krings, Matthias. "A Prequel to Nollywood: South African Photo Novels and Their Pan-African Consumption in the Late 1960s." *Journal of African Cultural Studies* 22, no. 1 (2010): 75–89.

Kunene, Daniel. "*The Wrath of the Ancestors* by A. C. Jordan, Priscilla P. Jordan." *World Literature Today* 57, no. 1 (Winter 1983): 161–62.

Larrabee, Eric. "Amos Tutuola: A Problem in Translation." *Chicago Review* 10, no. 1 (Spring 1956): 40–44.

Larrabee, Eric. "Palm-Wine Drinkard Searches for a Tapster." In *Critical Perspectives on Amos Tutuola*, edited by Bernth Lindfors, 11–12. Washington, DC: Three Continents Press, 1975.

Larson, Charles R. *The Ordeal of the African Writer*. London, Zed Books, 2001.

Lee, Felicia R. "New Wave of African Writers with an Internationalist Bent." *New York Times*, 29 June 2014. https://www.nytimes.com/2014/06/30/arts/new-wave-of-african-writers-with-an-internationalist-bent.html?mcubz=2. Accessed 30 June 2014.

Lewis, Cecil T. "Primitive Verbal Fantasy." *Phylon* 16, no. 1 (1955): 117–18.

Leys, Colin. *Underdevelopment in Kenya: The Political Economy of Neo-colonialism 1964–1971*. London: Heinemann, 1975.

Lindfors, Bernth. "Amos Tutuola: Debts and Assets." *Cahiers d'Études Africaines* 10, no. 38 (1970): 306–34.

Lindfors, Bernth. *The Blind Men and the Elephant and Other Essays in Biographical Criticism*. Trenton, NJ: Africa World Press, 1999.

Lindfors, Bernth. "A Decade of Black Orpheus." *Books Abroad* 42, no. 4 (Autumn 1968): 509–16.

Lindfors, Bernth. *Early West African Writers: Amos Tutuola, Cyprian Ekwensi and Ayi Kwei Armah*. Trenton, NJ: Africa World Press, 2010.

Lindfors, Bernth, ed. *From West Africa*. Washington, DC: Three Continents Press, 1975.

Lionnet, Françoise, and Shu-mei Shih. *Minor Transnationalism*. Durham: Duke University Press, 2005.

Louis, W. Roger. *History of Oxford University Press. Vol. III: 1896 to 1970*. Corby: Oxford University Press, 2013.

Low, Gail. "The Natural Artist: Publishing Amos Tutuola's 'The Palm-Wine Drinkard' in Postwar Britain." *Research in African Literatures* 37, no. 4 (December 2006): 15–33.

Mackay, Mercedes. "*Things Fall Apart* by Chinua Achebe (Review)." *African Affairs* 57, no. 228 (July 1958): 242–43.

MacKenzie, Norman. "The Place of English in African Education." *International Review of Education / Internationale Zeitschrift für Erziehungswissenschaft / Revue Internationale de l'Education* 5, no. 2 (1959): 216–23.

Mangcu, Xolela. "Retracing Nelson Mandela through the Lineage of Black Political Thought from Walter Rubusana to Steve Biko." *Transition*, no. 112 (2013): 101–16.

Marechera, Dambudzo. *The House of Hunger*. Long Grove, IL: Waveland Press, 2013.

Marx, Karl, and Friedrich Engels. "18th Brumaire of Louis Bonaparte." In *The Marx-Engels Reader*, edited by Robert C. Tucker. New York: Norton, 1978.

Masilela, Ntongela. "The 'Black Atlantic' and African Modernity in South Africa." *Research in African Literatures* 27, no. 4 (Winter 1996): 88–96.

Masilela, Ntongela. *An Outline of the New African Movement in South Africa*. Trenton, NJ: Africa World Press, 2013.

Mbembe, Achille, and R. H. Mitsch. "Life, Sovereignty, and Terror in the Fiction of Amos Tutuola." *Research in African Literatures* 34, no. 4 (Winter 2003): 1–26.

McEathron, Scott. "Wordsworth, Lyrical Ballads, and the Problem of Peasant Poetry." *Nineteenth-Century Literature* 54, no. 1 (June 1999): 1–26.

McGann, Jerome. "Keats and the Historical Method in Literary Criticism." *MLN* 94 (December 1979): 988 1032.

Memmi, Albert. *The Colonizer and the Colonized*. New York: Orion, 1965.

Miniclier, C. C. "Spearman—Africa's Superman." *Boston Globe*, 9 August 1970.

Modisane, Bloke. "African Writers' Summit." *Transition*, no. 5 (30 July–29 August 1962): 5–6.

Mofolo, Thomas. *Traveller to the East*. London, Penguin, 2007.

Moji, Polo Belina. "New Names, Translational Subjectivities: (Dis)location and (Re)naming in NoViolet Bulawayo's 'We Need New Names.'" *Journal of African Cultural Studies,* 27, no. 2 (2015): 181–90.

Moore, Gerald. *Seven African Writers*. London: Oxford, 1962.

Morapal, Koliswa. "Shehe! Don't Go There! AC Jordan's *Ingqumbo Yeminyanya* (The Wrath of the Ancestors) in English." *Southern African Linguistics and Applied Language Studies* 26, no. 1 (2008): 69–85.

Morrow, Bradford. "An Interview: Chinua Achebe." *Conjunctions* 17 (Fall 1991). www.conjunctions.com/print/article/chinua-achebe-c17. Accessed 19 July 2017.

Mphahlele, Ezekiel. "African Literature and Universities: A Report on Two Conferences to Discuss African Literature and the University Curriculum." *Transition*, no. 10 (September 1963): 16–18.

Mpe, Phaswane. "The Role of the Heinemann African Writers Series in the Development and Promotion of African Literature." *African Studies* 58, no. 1 (1999): 105–22.

Mugglestone, L. C. "Cobbett's Grammar: William, James Paul, and the Politics of Prescriptivism." *Review of English Studies*, n.s., 48, no. 192 (November 1997): 471–88.

Nagenda, John. "Conference Notebook." *Transition*, no. 5 (July 30–August 29, 1962): 8–9.

Naifeh, Steven. "The Myth of Oshogbo." *African Arts* 14, no. 2 (February 1981): 25–27, 85–86, 88.

Neethling, S. J. "On Translating A.C. Jordan's *Ingqumbo Yeminyanya* into Afrikaans." *South African Journal of African Languages* 17, no. 1 (1997): 18.

Neogy, Rajat. "Do Magazines Culture?" *Transition*, no. 24 (1966): 30–32.

Newell, Stephanie. *Readings in African Popular Fiction*. London: International African Institute, in association with Indiana University Press, 2002.

Ngũgĩ, Mũkoma Wa. "The Language Question." E-mail interview, 4 April 2015.

Ngũgĩ, Mũkoma Wa. *Nairobi Heat*. Brooklyn, NY: Melville House, 2010.

Ngugi, Tee. "Anthills of the Aberdares: How Achebe Lost His Lunch." *East African*, 30 March 2013. http://www.theeastafrican.co.ke/OpEd/comment/How-Achebe-lost-his-lunch/434750-1734572-a9ibxd/index.html. Accessed 20 March 2017.

Nigerian Correspondent. "Portrait: A Life in the Bush of Ghosts." In *Critical Perspectives on Amos Tutuola*, edited by Bernth Lindfors, 35–38. Washington, DC: Three Continents Press, 1975.

Nwaubani, Adaobi Tricia. "In Africa, the Laureate's Curse." *New York Times*, 11 December 2010. http://www.nytimes.com/2010/12/12/opinion/12nwaubani.html. Accessed 11 July 2014.

Obiechina, Emmanuel N. *Language and Theme: Essays on African Literature*. Washington, DC: Howard University Press, 1990.

Okafor, Clement Abiaziem. "Joseph Conrad and Chinua Achebe: Two Antipodal Portraits of Africa." *Journal of Black Studies* 19, no. 1 (September 1988): 17–28.

Omolewa, Michael. "Educating the 'Native': A Study of the Education Adaptation Strategy in British Colonial Africa, 1910–1936." *Journal of African American History* 91, no. 3 (Summer 2006): 267–87.

Olaniyan, Tejumola. "The Paddle That Speaks English: Africa, NGOs, and the Archaeology of an Unease." *Research in African Literatures* 42, no. 2 (2011): 46–59.

Onwuemezi, Natasha. "African Publisher Cassava Republic to Launch in UK." *The Bookseller*, 24 November 2015. Accessed 15 April 2016.

Opland, Jeff. "The Publication of A. C. Jordan's Xhosa Novel, 'Ingqumbo yeminyanya' (1940)." *Research in African Literatures* 21, no. 4 (Winter 1990): 135–47.

Ormrod, W. M. "The Peasants' Revolt and the Government of England." *Journal of British Studies* 29, no. 1 (January 1990): 1–30.

Ormrod, W. M. "The Use of English: Language, Law, and Political Culture in Fourteenth-Century England." *Speculum* 78, no. 3 (July 2003): 750–87.

Owomoyela, Oyekan. *Amos Tutuola Revisited.* New York: Twayne, 1999.

Owomoyela, Oyekan. "The Literature of Empire: Africa." *Empire Online,* 2004. http://www.empire.amdigital.co.uk/Essays/OyekanOwomoyela. Accessed March 16, 2016.

Patterson, Frederick. "Education in Nigeria." *Journal of Negro Education* 24, no. 2 (Spring 1955): 93–105.

Petersen, Kirsten Holst. *Criticism and Ideology: Second African Writers' Conference, Stockholm 1986.* Uppsala: Scandinavian Institute of African Studies, 1988.

Phillips, Julie. "Petina Gappah on Zimbabwe, Language, and 'Afropolitans.'" *LitHub,* 22 February 2016. Accessed 18 March 2016.

Pilkington, Ed. "A Long Way from Home." *Guardian,* 10 July 2007. https://www.theguardian.com/books/2007/jul/10/chinuaachebe. Accessed 9 March 2012.

Pini, Robert. "Review: *The Worlds of a Maasai Warrior: An Autobiography* by Tepilit Ole Saitoti." *Africa Today* 36, no. 2 (1989): 29–30.

Plaatje, Sol T. *Mhudi.* Long Grove, IL: Waveland, 2014.

Plaatje, Sol T. *Native Life in South Africa, Before and Since the European War and the Boer Rebellion.* 1914. Available at: http://www.sahistory.org.za/sites/default/files/Native%20Life%20in%20South%20Africa_0.pdf

Povey, J. F. "How Do You Make a Course in African Literature?" *Transition,* no. 18 (1965): 39–42.

Powell, David, and Eric Robinson, eds. *John Clare.* Oxford: Oxford University Press, 1984.

Prelog, Vladimir. "Chirality in Chemistry." *Science,* n.s, 193, no. 4247 (July 2, 1976): 17–24.

Quayson, Ato. *Strategic Transformations in Nigerian Writing: Orality and History in the Work of Rev. Samuel Johnson, Amos Tutuola, Wole Soyinka and Ben Okri.* Oxford: J. Currey, 1997.

Reaver, Russell. "Fiction." *English Journal* 48, no. 5 (May 1959): 286–87.

Reckord, Barry, Ezekiel Mphahlele, Gerald Moore, Wole Soyinka, Denis Williams, and Jan Knappert. "Polemics: The Dead End of African Literature." *Transition* (1997): 335–41.

Reddick, Allen. *The Making of Johnson's Dictionary, 1746–1773.* Cambridge: Cambridge University Press, 1996.

Richey, William, and Daniel Robinson. *William Wordsworth and Samuel Taylor Coleridge: Lyrical Ballads and Related Writings.* New York: Houghton Mifflin, 2002.

Rodman, Selden. "New York Times Book Review, September 20, 1953." In *Critical Perspectives on Amos Tutuola,* edited by Bernth Lindfors, 15–16. Washington, DC: Three Continents Press, 1975.

Rogin, Michael. "Rousseau in Africa." *Transition*, no. 10 (September 1963): 23–25.

Rubadiri, David. "Why African Literature?" *Transition*, no. 15 (1964): 39–42.

Ruddell, David. "Class and Race: Neglected Determinants of Colonial 'Adapted Education' Policies." *Comparative Education* 18, no. 3 (1982): 293–303.

Ryan, W. Carson. "The Phelps-Stokes Fund and Educational Adaptation." *Journal of Social Forces* (1923): 279–81.

Sala-Molins, Louis. *Dark Side of the Light: Slavery and the French Enlightenment*. Minneapolis: University of Minnesota Press, 2006.

Saleh, Tayeb. *Season of Migration to the North*. Washington, DC: Three Continents Press, 1980.

Samatar, Sofia, Keguro Macharia, and Aaron Bady. "What Even Is African Literature Anyway." *New Inquiry*, 9 February 2015. https://thenewinquiry.com/what-even-is-african-literature-anyway/. Accessed 9 March 2015.

Sanneh, Lamin. "'They Stooped to Conquer': Vernacular Translation and the Socio-Cultural Factor." Special issue, "The Language Question." *Research in African Literatures* 23, no. 1 (Spring 1992): 95–106.

"Sarkozy's Africa Vision under Fire." *News24*, 28 July 2007. http://www.news24.com/Africa/News/Sarkozys-Africa-vision-under-fire-20070728. Accessed 25 July 2014.

Santana, Stephanie. "Exorcizing Afropolitanism: Binyavanga Wainaina Explains Why 'I Am a Pan-Africanist, not an Afropolitan' at ASAUK 2012." Africa in Words blog, 8 February 2013. https://africainwords.com/2013/02/08/exorcizing-afropolitanism-binyavanga-wainaina-explains-why-i-am-a-pan-africanist-not-an-afropolitan-at-asauk-2012/. Accessed 14 July 2017.

Saro-Wiwa, Ken. "The Language of African Literature: A Writer's Testimony." Special issue, "The Language Question." *Research in African Literatures* 23, no. 1 (Spring 1992): 153–57.

Sauer, Charles. "The Place of the Vernacular Language in Colonial Education." *Modern Language Journal* 27, no. 3 (March 1943): 180–83.

Selasi, Taiye. "African Literature Doesn't Exist." Opening Address, 13th International Literature Festival, Berlin, 2013.

Selasi, Taiye. "Bye-Bye Babar (Or What Is an Afropolitan)." *LIP Magazine*, 3 March 2005. http://thelip.robertsharp.co.uk/?p=76. Accessed 1 July 2014.

Shank, Jenny. Review of *We Need New Names*, NoViolet Bulawayo. *Dallas News*, 31 May 2013. https://www.dallasnews.com/arts/books/2013/05/31/book-review-we-need-new-names-by-noviolet-bulawayo. Accessed 14 July 2017.

Sicherman, Carol. "Ngugi's Colonial Education: 'The Subversion . . . of the African Mind.'" *African Studies Review* 38, no. 3 (December 1995): 11–41.

Sigei, Julius. "We'll Stick to Creative Works, but Text Books Bring in Cash." *Nation*, 22 August 2015. http://www.nation.co.ke/lifestyle/weekend/Well-stick-to-creative-works-but-text-books-bring-in-cash/1220-2840110-cpgdk8z/index.html. Accessed 15 June 2016.

Siskind, Mariano. "The Globalization of the Novel and the Novelization of the Global: A Critique of World Literature." *Comparative Literature* 62, no. 4 (2010): 336–60.

Skotte, Kim. "Taiye Selasi: I'm a Multi Local Afropolitan." *YouTube*, 26 February 2014. https://www.youtube.com/watch?v=4XgRINx5mj4. Accessed 9 March 2015.

S. M. "'Look-Reads' Exploit Cultural Needs of Young Africa." *Washington Post*, 5 October 1969.

Smith, Olivia. *The Politics of Language, 1791–1819*. Oxford: Clarendon, 1984.

Soyinka, Wole. *The Open Sore of a Continent: A Personal Narrative of the Nigerian Crisis*. New York: Oxford University Press, 1996.

Soyinka, Wole. "The Writer in an African State." *Transition* 31 (1967): 11–13.

Sontag, Susan. "At The Same Time . . . (The Novelist and Moral Reasoning)." *English Studies in Africa* 48, no. 1 (2005): 5–17.

Stratton, Florence. *Contemporary African Literature and the Politics of Gender*. New York: Routledge, 1994.

Thiong'o, Ngugi Wa. "The Achebe I Knew." *The Nation*, 26 March 2013. http://thenation onlineng.net/the-achebe-i-knew-by-ngugi-wa-thiongo/. Accessed 20 March 2017.

Thiong'o, Ngugi Wa. "A Kenyan at the Conference." *Transition*, no. 5 (30 July–29 August 1962): 7.

Thiong'o, Ngugi Wa. *Decolonising the Mind: The Politics of Language in African Literature*. London: J. Currey, 1986.

Thiong'o, Ngugi Wa. *Globalectics: Theory and the Politics of Knowing*. New York: Columbia University Press, 2012.

Thiong'o, Ngugi Wa. *Homecoming: Essays on African and Caribbean Literature, Culture and Politics*. Heinemann, 1972.

Thiong'o, Ngugi Wa. "I've Lost My Literary Sister, Kenya Has Lost a Literary Icon." *Daily Nation*, 22 March 2015. http://www.nation.co.ke/lifestyle/weekend/-Kenya-has-lost-a-literary-icon/1220-2660572-svkwwlz/index.html. Accessed 25 March 2017.

Thiong'o, Ngugi Wa. "The Language of African Literature." In *African Literature: An Anthology of Criticism and Theory*, edited by Tejumola Olaniyan and Ato Quayson, 285–306. Oxford: Blackwell, 2007.

Thiong'o, Ngugi Wa. "Makerere Dreams: Language and New Frontiers of Knowledge." University of East Africa 50th Anniversary Celebrations, Makerere University, Kampala, 29 June 2013. *Makerere University*. Accessed 24 June 2014.

Thiong'o, Ngugi Wa. "On the Abolition of the English Department." In *The Post-colonial Studies Reader*, edited by Bill Ashcroft, Gareth Griffiths, and Helen Tiffin. London: Routledge, 1995.

Thiong'o, Ngugi Wa. "Recovering the Original." *World Literature Today* 78, nos. 3/4 (September–December 2004): 13–15.

Thiong'o, Ngugi Wa. *Writing Against Neocolonialism*. London: Vita, 1986.

Thomas, Dylan. "Blithe Spirits." In *Critical Perspectives on Amos Tutuola*, edited by Bernth Lindfors. Washington, DC: Three Continents Press, 1975.

Tobias, Steven. "Amos Tutuola and the Colonial Carnival." *Research in African Literatures* 30, no. 2 (Summer 1999): 66–74.

Tucker, A. N. "The Scholar and His Passport." *Transition*, no. 14 (1964): 19–20.

Turley, Richard. *The Politics of Language in Romantic Literature.* New York: Palgrave Macmillan, 2002.

Tutuola, Amos. *The Palm-Wine Drinkard*; and, *My Life in the Bush of Ghosts.* 1954, reprint, Grove Press, 1994.

Tutuola, Amos. *Simbi and the Satyr of the Dark Jungle.* London: Faber & Faber, 2015.

Tutuola, Amos, Alessandra Di Maio, and Claudio Gorlier. *Tutuola at the University: The Italian Voice of a Yoruba Ancestor.* Rome: Bulzoni, 2000.

Unigwe, Chika. "The Jalada Conversations No. 3." *Jalada*, 1 September 2015. https://jaladaafrica.org/jalada-conversations/the-jalada-conversations-no-3-chika-unigwe/. Accessed 29 January 2016.

Wainaina, Binyavanga. *How to Write about Africa.* Nairobi: Kwani Trust, 2008.

Wainaina, Binyavanga. *One Day I Will Write about This Place: A Memoir.* Minneapolis, MN: Graywolf Press, 2011.

Wanner, Zukiswa. "Bibi Comes to London." *New African* No. 561 (May 2016).

Wali, Obiajunwa. "The Dead End of African Literature." *Transition*, nos. 75/76 (1997): 330–35.

Wali, Obiajunwa. "A Reply to Critics from Obi Wali." *Transition*, no. 50 (October 1975–March 1976): 46–47.

West, Anthony. "New Yorker Review." In *Critical Perspectives on Amos Tutuola*, edited by Bernth Lindfors, 17–18. Washington, DC: Three Continents Press, 1975.

Westley, David. "African-Language Literature in English Translation: An Annotated Bibliography." Special issue, "Soviet Scholarship on African Literatures." *Research in African Literatures* 18, no. 4 (Winter 1987): 499–509.

White, Tim. "The Lovedale Press during the Directorship of RHW Shepherd, 1930–1955." *English in Africa* (1992): 69–84.

Willan, Brian P. *Sol Plaatje: South African Nationalist, 1876–1932.* Berkeley: University of California Press, 1988.

Williams, Raymond. *The Country and the City.* New York: Oxford University Press, 1973.

Wolde-Giorghis, Hailou. "An African Encounters the United States." *Transition*, no. 15 (1964): 22–25.

Wordsworth, William, and Samuel Taylor Coleridge. *Lyrical Ballads and Other Poems.* Edited by Martin Scofield. Ware: Wordsworth Ed., 2003.

Yellin, Eric. "The (White) Search for (Black) Order: The Phelps-Stokes Fund's First Twenty Years, 1911–1931." *Historian* 65, no. 2 (Winter 2002): 319–52.

Young, Robert. *Colonial Desire: Hybridity in Theory, Culture and Race.* London: Routledge, 1995.

Mphahlele, Ezekiel, 130, 137, 169; arguments for English, 44–45; at Makerere Conference, 2, 11, 191n27; name change to Es'kia Mphahlele, 189n8; political exile, 2–3; on translation, 52; on writing in English, 49

Mpondomise people, 108–9, 116, 119–20, 124

Mqhayi, Samuel, 4–5; *Ityala Lamawele* (*The Lawsuit of the Twins*), 104

*Mrs. Shaw* (Ngũgĩ), 156, 181

Mufti, Aamir, 155

Mugo, Micere, 2–3, 107

*Mutiiri* (Gikuyu literary journal), 70

Mwangi, Meja, 154–55

Mzilikazi, 145–47

Naipaul, V. S., 55

Nairobi, Kenya, 160–61, 181

*Nairobi Heat* (Ngũgĩ), 66, 153–62, 181–82

Nakasa, Nat, 136

naming, 146–47

Napoleon, 167

National Association for the Advancement of Colored People (NAACP), 6

nationalism, 85, 108, 113–14; black, 6, 114, 124; linguistic, 22

national language, English as, 43–47. *See also* English language

native languages, 30–31, 134. *See also* African languages

*Native Life in South Africa* (Plaatje), 6

Ndebele, Njabulo, 133

Ndebele people, 174

Ndibe, Okey, 175

Negritude, 58, 138, 196

neocolonial states. *See* African states, neocolonial

Neogy, Rajat, 3

*New Yorker*, 197n19

*New York Times*, 87, 175

Ngugi, James. *See* Thiong'o, Ngugi Wa

Ngugi, Tee, 46

Nigeria: Biafra, 2, 149; decolonization, 61,

86, 120, 129; folktales, 85; neocolonialism, 106, 194n21; publishers in, 151–53. *See also* Igbo culture; Yoruba culture

Njau, Rebecca, 2

Nkosi, Lewis, 136

"Nkosi Sikelel' iAfrika" (ANC), 5

Nkrumah, Kwame, 184

Nobel Prize for Literature, 59, 134

noble savage myth, 142, 146, 165, 167

*No Longer at Ease* (Achebe), 9, 103–4, 106–7, 111–15, 117, 120–22, 199n4 (chap. 3); intertextuality, 127–28; linearity, 129; representation of language, 60, 63; translation strategies, 128; women in, 124–26

novels. *See* African literary tradition; African literature; decolonization novels; political novels, African; popular fiction; synthesis novels

Nwaubani, Adaobi Tricia, 59

Obonyo, Amoko Apollo, 140

Odour, Okwiri, 67

Ogoni people, 50, 194n21

Ogot, Grace, 2, 107

Ogude, S. E., 131

Okafor, Clement Abiaziem, 165, 200n1

Okigbo, Christopher, 2, 149

Okorafor, Nnedi, *Who Fears Death*, 136

Olaniyan, Tejumola, 8, 128

Oliver, Jocelyn, 73

Omolewa, Michael, 34

Omotoso, Kole, 97–98

opacity, 64

oral stories, 39–40, 95–98, 100–101, 104–5

orature, 54, 88–90, 167, 193n13; in African languages, 39–40; literature and, 98, 100, 104–5, 128, 134; study of, 140

orientalism, 155

originality, 88, 100

Ormrod, W. M, 21–22, 191n35

Orwell, George, *Animal Farm*, 23, 195n35

Owomoyela, Oyekan, 37, 78, 85, 142, 193n9

Owour-Anyumba, Henry, 139

*We Need New Names* (Bulawayo), 9–10,
  63–64, 66, 103, 106–8, 113–15, 118–19,
  131, 146, 177, 182
West, centering of, 182–84
West, Anthony, 197n19
West African publishing market, 24–25
Western attitudes toward Africa, 34–38,
  85, 87, 141, 163–70
westernization, 85, 109, 115
white gaze, 163–64
whiteness, 92, 106, 109–19, 122, 129, 131,
  166
white women, 125–26, 160
women: representations of, 124–27; violence and, 159–60. *See also* gender
women writers, African, 60–61, 106–7.
  *See also individual writers*
Wordsworth, William, 40, 105, 167, 193n15
World Congress of Negro Writers, 190n12

world languages, 16, 31, 50. *See also* English metaphysical empire
world literature, 155–57, 177–78, 182
*The Wrath of the Ancestors* (Jordan), 4–5,
  9, 106–17, 119–21, 124–26, 128–29, 142
Wright, Richard, 3
Writivism Festival, 25

Yoruba culture, 55, 78–80, 101
Yoruba language, 20, 39, 55, 83, 193n11;
  transliteration of, 93–95
Young, Robert, 179–80

Zimbabwe, 10, 106, 108, 113–14, 118–19,
  129, 146, 172–74; Shona language, 48,
  64–66
Zimbabwe International Book Fair
  (ZIBF), 135
Zirimu, Pio, 40